Ethical Relativity

Ethical Relativity

BY

EDWARD WESTERMARCK

PH.D., HON. LL.D. (GLASGOW AND ABERDEEN)
PROFESSOR OF PHILOSOPHY AT THE ACADEMY OF ÅBO (FINLAND)
LATE PROFESSOR OF SOCIOLOGY IN THE UNIVERSITY OF LONDON

GREENWOOD PRESS, PUBLISHERS
WESTPORT, CONNECTICUT

Originally published in 1932
by Kegan Paul, Trench, Trubner & Co., Ltd., London

First Greenwood Reprinting 1970

Library of Congress Catalogue Card Number 76-109875

SBN 8371-4366-7

Printed in the United States of America

CONTENTS

CONTENTS

III. The Moral Emotions   62

IV. The Moral Emotions (concluded)   89

IX. The Emotional Background of Normative Theories (concluded)

CONTENTS

PREFACE

IN AN earlier book, *The Origin and Development of the Moral Ideas,* it was my object to study the moral consciousness as it displays itself among mankind at large. In spite of its numerous references to customs, laws, and institutions, my inquiry was essentially concerned not with behaviour, but with opinions. I arrived at the conclusion that moral judgments are ultimately based on emotions, the moral concepts being generalizations of emotional tendencies; although I recognized at the same time the enormous influence that intellectual considerations exercise upon those judgments, in the first place through the cognitions by which the moral emotions are determined. In a short introductory chapter I indicated that the emotional origin of moral judgments consistently leads to a denial of the objective validity ascribed to them both by common sense and by normative theories of ethics. This idea will be further developed in the present treatise.

I shall examine the main arguments adduced in support of the notion of moral objectivity, and try to show that they are incompatible with facts on which ethical subjectivism establishes its claims, nay, that the normative theories themselves have an emotional foundation. In my analyses of the moral emotions, the principal moral concepts, and the subjects of moral judgments, I shall have to repeat much that I have said in my earlier book (which I may do by kind permission of its publishers, Messrs. Macmillan & Co.); but while my views on these topics have remained substantially the same, they have undergone various modifications in detail. For other reasons also I am glad to have an opportunity to deal with those subjects afresh. I shall be able to discuss objections raised to my former treatment of them by other writers in the course of the many years—about a quarter of a century— which have elapsed since the first publication of my *Moral Ideas;* to give a more precise formulation of my views by corrections and additions; and to make them stand out more clearly by detaching them from the mass of anthropological and historical particulars, which seem to have disabled some of my earlier readers from seeing the wood for the trees.

It appears to me that the present publication of a book in defence of ethical subjectivism and relativity is the more timely, as the large bulk of ethical literature which has been produced in this country since the beginning of the century has championed the opposite cause.

I beg to express my best thanks to Miss Agnes Dawson for valuable suggestions of a formal character.

E. W.

Villa Tusculum,
outside Tangier,
19th August, 1931.

Ethical Relativity

CHAPTER I

THE SUPPOSED OBJECTIVITY OF MORAL JUDGMENTS

ETHICS is generally looked upon as a "normative" science, the object of which is to find and formulate moral principles and rules possessing objective validity. The supposed objectivity of moral values, as understood in this treatise, implies that they have a real existence apart from any reference to a human mind, that what is said to be good or bad, right or wrong, cannot be reduced merely to what people think to be good or bad, right or wrong. It makes morality a matter of truth and falsity, and to say that a judgment is true obviously means something different from the statement that it is thought to be true. The objectivity of moral judgments does not presuppose the infallibility of the individual who pronounces such a judgment, nor even the accuracy of a general consensus of opinion; but if a certain course of conduct is objectively right, it must be thought to be right by all rational beings who judge truly of the matter and cannot, without error, be judged to be wrong.

In spite of the fervour with which the objectivity of moral judgments has been advocated by the exponents of normative ethics there is much diversity of opinion with regard to the principles underlying the various systems. This discord is as old as ethics itself. But while the evolution of other sciences has shown a tendency to increasing agreement on points of fundamental importance, the same can hardly be said to have been the case in the history of

3

ethics, where the spirit of controversy has been much more conspicuous than the endeavour to add new truths to results already reached. Of course, if moral values are objective, only one of the conflicting theories can possibly be true. Each founder of a new theory hopes that it is he who has discovered the unique jewel of moral truth, and is naturally anxious to show that other theories are only false stones. But he must also by positive reasons make good his claim to the precious find.

These reasons are of great importance in a discussion of the question whether moral judgments really are objective or merely are supposed to be so; for if any one of the theories of normative ethics has been actually proved to be true, the objectivity of those judgments has *eo ipso* been established as an indisputable fact. I shall therefore proceed to an examination of the main evidence that has been produced in favour of the most typical of these theories.

I shall begin with hedonism, according to which actions are right in proportion as they tend to promote happiness, and wrong in proportion as they tend to produce the reverse of happiness. And by happiness is then meant "pleasure, and the absence of pain; by unhappiness, pain, and the privation of pleasure." [1] What is the evidence?

It has been said that the hedonistic principle requires no proof, because it is simply an analytic proposition, a mere definition. Because acts that are called right generally produce pleasure and acts that are called wrong generally produce pain, rightness and wrongness have been actually identified with the tendencies of acts to produce pleasure or pain. The following statement of Sir James Stephen is a clearly expressed instance of such an iden-

[1] J. S. Mill, *Utilitarianism* (London, 1895), p. 10.

tification:—"Speaking generally, the acts which are called right do promote, or are supposed to promote general happiness, and the acts which are called wrong do diminish, or are supposed to diminish it. I say, therefore, that this is what the words 'right' and 'wrong' mean, just as the words 'up' and 'down' mean that which points from or towards the earth's centre of gravity, though they are used by millions who have not the least notion of the fact that such is their meaning, and though they were used for centuries and millenniums before any one was or even could be aware of it." [2] A similar view is expressed by Bentham when he says that words like "ought," "right," and "wrong," have no meaning unless interpreted in accordance with the principle of utility.[3] Now the statement that a certain act has a tendency to promote happiness, or to cause unhappiness, is either true or false; and if rightness and wrongness are only other words for these tendencies, it is therefore obvious that the moral judgments also have objective validity. But it is impossible to doubt that anybody who sees sufficiently carefully into the matter must admit that the identification in question is due to a confusion between the meaning of terms and the use made of them when applied to acts on account of their tendencies to produce certain effects. Bentham himself seems to have felt something of the kind. For although he asserts that the rectitude of the principle of utility has been contested only by those who have not known what they have been meaning, he raises the question whether it is susceptible of any direct proof. And his answer is as follows:—"It should seem not: for that which is used to prove everything else, cannot itself be

[2] J. F. Stephen, *Liberty, Equality, Fraternity* (London, 1873), p. 338.
[3] J. Bentham, *An Introduction to the Principles of Morals and Legislation* (Oxford, 1879), p. 4.

proved: a chain of proofs must have their commencement somewhere." [4] The question and the answer suggest that Bentham, after all, hardly looked upon the principle of utility or, as he also calls it, the greatest happiness principle, as strictly speaking a mere definition of rightness.

Stuart Mill, also, admits that this principle, like all questions of ultimate ends, is not amenable to direct proof, "in the ordinary and popular meaning of the term." But he says that there is a larger meaning of the word proof: considerations may be presented capable of determining the intellect either to give or withhold its assent to the doctrine, and this is equivalent to proof. [5] Questions about ends are questions as to what things are desirable. "The utilitarian doctrine is, that happiness is desirable, and the only thing desirable, as an end; all other things being only desirable as means to that end. What ought to be required of this doctrine—what conditions is it requisite that the doctrine should fulfil—to make good its claim to be believed? The only proof capable of being given that an object is visible, is that people actually see it. The only proof that a sound is audible, is that people hear it; and so of the other sources of our experience. In like manner, I apprehend, the sole evidence it is possible to produce that anything is desirable, is that people do actually desire it." [6] The fallacy of this argument has often been exposed, and is indeed too obvious to be disputed. While the visible means what can be seen and the audible what can be heard, the desirable does not mean what can be desired; and Mill even understands by it what ought to be desired, which gives to the word a more specified meaning than is justified by the ordinary use of it,

[4] Bentham, *op. cit.*, p. 4.
[5] Mill, *op. cit.*, p. 6 *sq.*
[6] *Ibid.*, p. 52 *sq.*

since something may be held desirable on other than moral grounds. And yet he thinks the mere fact that a thing is desired is a sufficient proof that it is desirable, just as if people never could desire to do anything else than what they ought to desire to do.

Now the utilitarian standard is not the agent's own greatest happiness, but the greatest amount of happiness altogether. It may be defined as the rules and precepts for human conduct by the observance of which happiness might be, to the greatest extent possible, secured to all mankind; "and not to them only, but, so far as the nature of things admits, to the whole sentient creation." [7] How can this be proved? Mill argues that "no reason can be given why the general happiness is desirable, except that each person, so far as he believes it to be attainable, desires his own happiness. This, however, being a fact, we have not only all the proof which the case admits of, but all which it is possible to require, that happiness is a good: that each person's happiness is a good to that person, and the general happiness, therefore, a good to the aggregate of all persons." [8] But if a person desires his own happiness, and if what he desires is desirable in the sense that he ought to desire it, the standard of general happiness can only mean that each person ought to desire his own happiness. In other words, the premises in Mill's argument would lead to egoistic hedonism, not to utilitarianism or universalistic hedonism.

But Mill also produces another argument in favour of the utilitarian doctrine: it has the support of the social feelings of mankind. Men have a desire to be in unity with their fellow-creatures, and this desire, which is already a powerful principle in human nature, tends to become stronger from the influences of advancing civiliza-

[7] *Ibid.*, p. 16 *sq.*   [8] *Ibid.*, p. 53.

tion. The strengthening of social ties gives to each individual a stronger personal interest in consulting the welfare of others; and it also leads him to identify his *feelings* more and more with their good. In the comparatively early state of human advancement in which we now live, a person cannot indeed feel that entireness of sympathy with all others, which would make any real discordance in the general direction of their conduct in life impossible; this feeling is in most individuals much inferior in strength to their selfish feelings, and is often wanting altogether. But the deeply rooted conception which every individual even now has of himself as a social being, tends to make him feel it one of his natural wants that there should be harmony between his feeling and aims and those of his fellow-creatures. And "this conviction is the ultimate sanction of the greatest-happiness morality." [9] In this argument Mill has undoubtedly stated facts which go a long way to explain the origin and wide acceptance of the utilitarian theory, but he has by no means proved its objective validity. Nor has he even, by far, been able to claim for it the support of a consensus of moral opinion.

Another attempt to vindicate the validity of utilitarianism was made by Sidgwick. When examining the evidence presented by Mill, "the most persuasive and probably the most influential among English expositors of utilitarianism," he found it unsatisfactory. Even if it were granted that what is actually desired may be legitimately inferred to be desirable, in the sense that it ought to be desired, the proposition that the general happiness is desirable would not be established by Mill's reasoning because, so far as this reasoning goes, there is no actual desire for the general happiness. There is thus a gap in the argument, and

---

[9] Mill, *op. cit.,* p. 46 *sqq.*

this gap, according to Sidgwick, can only be filled by an intuition: an axiom or principle of "rational benevolence" is required as a basis for the utilitarian system.[10] This principle is the maxim, "that each one is morally bound to regard the good of any other individual as much as his own, except in so far as he judges it to be less, when impartially viewed, or less certainly knowable or attainable by him." The proposition, "I ought not to prefer my own lesser good to the greater good of another," presents itself to Sidgwick as no less self-evident than the mathematical axiom that "if equals be added· to equals the wholes are equal."[11] He also says, "I find that I undoubtedly seem to perceive, as clearly and certainly as I see any axiom in Arithmetic or Geometry, that it is 'right' and 'reasonable' for me to . . . do what I believe to be ultimately conducive to universal Good or Happiness."[12] Thus the utilitarian rule of aiming at the general happiness is seen to "rest on a fundamental moral intuition."

Can this claim be justified? Sidgwick observes that "there seem to be four conditions, the complete fulfilment of which would establish a significant proposition, apparently self-evident, in the highest degree of certainty attainable: and which must be approximately realized by the premises of our reasoning in any inquiry, if that reasoning is to lead us cogently to trustworthy conclusions." These four conditions are:—1. "The terms of the proposition must be clear and precise." 2. "The self-evidence of the proposition must be ascertained by careful reflection." 3. "The propositions accepted as self-evident must be mutually consistent." 4. There must be an adequate consensus of opinion in their favour.[13]—Let us see whether Sidg-

10 H. Sidgwick, *The Methods of Ethics* (London, 1913), p. 387 *sq.*
11 *Ibid.*, p. 382 *sq.*
12 *Ibid.*, p. 507.
13 *Ibid.*, p. 338 *sqq.*

wick's principle of rational benevolence fulfils these conditions.

The terms in which it is stated cannot be said to be "clear and precise." Who is that other individual whose good I am morally bound to regard as much as my own? I presume that Sidgwick means every human individual, whether he be a relative or friend or not, a compatriot or a foreigner, a civilized man or a savage. He says it may be fairly urged that practically each man ought chiefly to concern himself with promoting the good of a limited number of human beings, and that generally in proportion to the closeness of their connection with him; but he maintains that this may be done "even with a view to universal Good." [14] But what about animals? When examining the utilitarian principle, Sidgwick considers who the "all" are whose happiness is to be taken into account. He writes:—"Are we to extend our concern to all the beings capable of pleasure and pain whose feelings are affected by our conduct? or are we to confine our view to human happiness? The former view is the one adopted by Bentham and Mill, and (I believe) by the Utilitarian school generally: and is obviously most in accordance with the universality that is characteristic of their principle. It is the good *Universal,* interpreted and defined as 'happiness' or 'pleasure,' at which a Utilitarian considers it his duty to aim: and it seems arbitrary and unreasonable to exclude from the end, as so conceived, any pleasure of any sentient being." [15] Yet, in spite of this definite statement, I cannot conceive that Sidgwick would have regarded it as a self-evident proposition that I ought not to prefer my own lesser good to the greater good of a beast or bird or fish or insect, however "unreasonable" it might be to exclude them from the principle of rational benevolence. I venture

[14] Sidgwick, *op. cit.,* p. 382.   [15] *Ibid.,* p. 414.

to believe that when he formulated this principle he did not bestow on the question of animal happiness that "careful reflection" which is the second condition he requires of a self-evident proposition. And, as will be shown presently, it does not seem to be the only instance in which he has failed to fulfil this condition.

As to the third criterion, according to which the propositions accepted as self-evident must be mutually consistent, we have to consider the relations between the principle of rational benevolence and the two other principles, likewise regarded as self-evident, which are stated in connection with it. One is the axiom of prudence, or the maxim that "one ought to aim at one's own good on the whole." [16] Whatever else may be said of this principle, it is obvious that it cannot be consistent with that of rational benevolence without an important qualification, namely, that one ought to aim at one's own good on the whole only where it does not collide with the greater good of somebody else.[17] The other principle, called the principle of justice, is the proposition that "it cannot be right for A to treat B in a manner in which it would be wrong for B to treat A, merely on the ground that they are two different individuals, and without there being any difference between the natures or circumstances of the two which can be stated as a reasonable ground for difference of treatment." [18] This proposition is true, but for the simple reason that it is tautological; and the truth expressed by it applies not only to the rightness of acts, but to all moral concepts. When I pronounce an act to be right or wrong, good or bad, I mean that it is so quite independently of any reference it may have to me per-

16 *Ibid.*, p. 381.
17 *Cf.* H. Rashdall, *The Theory of Good and Evil*, i. (Oxford, 1924), p. 185.
18 Sidgwick, *op. cit.*, p. 380.

sonally or to the particular relationship in which I stand to him who is immediately affected by the act and to him who performs it. This is implied in the very meaning of those and all other moral predicates on account of the disinterestedness and apparent impartiality that characterize the moral emotions, from which all moral concepts are derived.[19] The principle of rational benevolence is certainly not inconsistent with the so-called principle of justice, but it derives absolutely no support from it. According to the latter principle it might very well be right for each person to prefer his own lesser good to the greater good of another, although it could not be right for me and wrong for another similar person in similar circumstances to do so.

The fourth criterion is stated in much less definite terms than the previous ones. Sidgwick writes:—"Since it is implied in the very notion of Truth that it is essentially the same for all minds, the denial by another of a proposition that I have affirmed has a tendency to impair my confidence in its validity. And in fact 'universal' or 'general' consent has often been held to constitute by itself a sufficient evidence of the truth of the most important beliefs; and is practically the only evidence upon which the greater part of mankind can rely. A proposition accepted as true upon this ground alone has, of course, neither self-evidence nor demonstrative evidence for the mind that so accepts it; still, the secure acceptance that we commonly give to the generalizations of the empirical sciences rests—even in the case of experts—largely on the belief that other experts have seen for themselves the evidence for these generalizations, and do not materially disagree as to its adequacy. And it will be easily seen that

[19] See *infra*, p. 90 *sqq*.

the absence of such disagreement must remain an indispensable negative condition of the certainty of our beliefs." [20]

When examining the moral notions that present themselves with a *prima facie* claim to furnish independent and self-evident rules of morality, Sidgwick has in each case found that from such regulation of conduct as the common sense of mankind really supports, "no proposition can be elicited which, when fairly contemplated, even appears to have the characteristic of a scientific axiom." [21] He expressly points out that the duty of benevolence as recognized by common sense seems to fall somewhat short of the principle of rational benevolence. Yet he thinks "that a 'plain man' in a modern civilized society, if his conscience were fairly brought to consider the hypothetical question, whether it would be morally right for him to seek his own happiness on any occasion if it involved a certain sacrifice of the greater happiness of some other human being,—without any counterbalancing gain to any one else,—would answer unhesitatingly in the negative." [22] Well, in many cases he undoubtedly would, but in other cases he most decidedly would not. Suppose that I endeavour to obtain a good which another person also tries to obtain, and that I do so in spite of my belief that it will be a lesser good to me than it would be to him if he succeeded in achieving it; would common sense condemn my action, even though I could claim no counterbalancing gain to any one else as an excuse for my behaviour? For example, would it require that I, being a merchant, should abstain from some business if it is likely that another competing merchant would make a larger profit than I

[20] Sidgwick, *op. cit.*, p. 341 *sq.*
[21] *Ibid.*, p. 360.
[22] *Ibid.*, p. 382.

could by engaging in the business?[23] Or, again, would common sense agree that he who possesses some good is morally bound to share it with others if their gain thereby outweighs his own loss? Or if I, by sacrificing my own life, could save another person's life, which is a greater good to him or to others, than my life is to me or others, would it be my duty to make such a sacrifice? Can anybody doubt that common sense, without hesitation, would answer these questions in the negative? It seems fairly obvious that Sidgwick has considerably exaggerated even that limited support his principle of rational benevolence could receive from the "plain man."[24] Hutcheson, in whose system benevolence is the very essence of virtue and who was apparently the author of the utilitarian formula that "that action is best which procures the greatest happiness for the greatest numbers,"[25] goes so far as to say that "we do not positively condemn those as evil, who will not sacrifice their private interest to the advancement of the positive good of others, unless the private interest be very small, and the public good very great."[26]

As to the question of experts, on whose consensus we are to rely, Sidgwick does not discuss how we are to ascertain them.[27] In an early letter he writes, "My difficulty is that I cannot give to principles of conduct either the formal certainty that comes from exact science or the practical certainty that comes from a real Consensus

[23] Cf. G. Cohn, Etik og sociologi (Kjöbenhavn & Kristiania, 1913), p. 62 sqq.

[24] See also infra, pp. 208, 209, 227.

[25] F. Hutcheson, An Inquiry into the Original of our Ideas of Beauty and Virtue (London, 1753), p. 185.

[26] Idem, An Essay on the Nature and Conduct of the Passions and Affections. With Illustrations on the Moral Sense (London, 1756), p. 318.

[27] Cf. Sidgwick, op. cit., p. 343 n. 1.

of Experts";[28] and he never succeeded in solving this difficulty. Yet his principle of rational benevolence seemed to him to be in substantial agreement with the doctrines of "those moralists who have been most in earnest in seeking among commonly received rules for genuine intuitions of the Practical Reason," particularly Clarke and Kant.[29] In a subsequent chapter I shall show that he was hardly justified in claiming the authority of Kant in support of it.[30] Among more recent writers on ethics Sidgwick's principle of rational benevolence has been accepted by some, but rejected by others.

Altogether, then, it must be admitted that this supposed axiom does not fulfil the conditions which in Sidgwick's own opinion have to be approximately realized for the establishment of a self-evident proposition. And thus the final attempt to vindicate the objective validity of utilitarianism has proved to be a failure. By itself alone that principle would in no case have afforded a sufficient intuitional basis for utilitarianism, since the "good" mentioned in it has been left undefined. But in Sidgwick's eyes it did so when combined with the proposition that "happiness (a term which he used as convertible with pleasure [31]) is the only rational ultimate end of action," which also appeared to him as an object of intuition.[32]

In its earlier days utilitarianism was frequently supported by theological considerations. It was widely held that the moral agent could ultimately will only his own happiness, and the question arose how this could lead him to act for the common good. In the natural course

[28] *Henry Sidgwick.* A Memoir by A. S. and E. M. S. (London, 1906), p. 259.
[29] Sidgwick, *op. cit.,* p. 384 *sqq.*
[30] *Infra,* p. 281 *sq.*
[31] Sidgwick, *op. cit.,* p. 92.
[32] *Ibid.,* p. 201.

of things private and public happiness by no means always coincide; hence a coincidence can be brought about only by "the lively and active belief in an all-seeing and all-powerful God," who will hereafter make men happy or miserable, "according as they designedly promote or violate the happiness of their fellow-creatures." [33] "The will of God is the immediate criterion of virtue, and the happiness of mankind the criterion of the will of God." [34] "God Almighty wills and wishes the happiness of his creatures; and, consequently, . . . those actions which promote that will and wish, must be agreeable to him; and the contrary." [35] And the rewards he bestows on those who obey his will and the punishments he inflicts on the disobedient, will naturally suffice to make it always every one's interest to promote universal happiness to the best of his knowledge; indeed, the penalties and rewards became so tremendous that selfishness was inevitable. These opinions, which were advocated by a section of eighteenth century utilitarians, subsequently lost their influence. Sidgwick admits that the existence of divine sanctions to the code of social duty as constructed on a utilitarian basis would secure the much needed reconciliation of duty and self-interest and settle the relation of rational self-love to rational benevolence, which he regards as "the profoundest problem of Ethics." [36] But he cannot find, attainable by mere reflective intuition, any cognition that there actually is a Supreme Being who will adequately reward

[33] J. Brown, *Essays on the Characteristics of the Earl of Shaftesbury* (London, 1751), p. 210.

[34] J. Gay, *Preliminary Dissertation. Concerning the Fundamental Principle of Virtue or Morality*, prefixed to E. Law's translation of W. King's *Essay on the Origin of Evil* (London, 1732), p. xxxxix.

[35] W. Paley, *The Principles of Moral and Political Philosophy*, ii. 4 (*Works* [Edinburgh, 1834], p. 14).

[36] Sidgwick, *op. cit.*, pp. 387 n. 1, 506.

men for obeying the rules of duty or punish them for violating them.[37]

It may be asked if the so-called "theological utilitarianism" really is utilitarianism, or if it belongs to the doctrine of egoistic hedonism. The answer, of course, depends on the meanings given to these terms, and these meanings are by no means free from ambiguities. Sidgwick uses the term egoistic hedonism to denote "a system which prescribes actions as means to the end of the individual's happiness or pleasure," [38] and by utilitarianism he means "the ethical theory, that the conduct which, under any given circumstances, is objectively right, is that which will produce the greatest amount of happiness on the whole; that is, taking into account all whose happiness is affected by the conduct." [39] Dr. Albee raises the question whether egoistic hedonism is a method of ethics at all, even according to Sidgwick's "carefully formulated definitions." There is indeed, he says, no question that many English moralists, from the time of Hobbes down at least to the time of J. S. Mill, held that the motive of the moral agent was necessarily egoistic; and "if, then, all were to be classed as Egoists who held this theory of the moral motive, we should plainly have to include all the English Utilitarians before Mill, with the exception of Cumberland, Hartley, and Hume (*i.e.*, as represented by the second form of his theory)." But he argues that the egoistic theory of the moral motive cannot be what Sidgwick means, when he speaks of egoistic hedonism as constituting a separate method of ethics, that is, as one of "the different methods of obtaining reasoned convictions as to what ought to be done." [40] For "it may confidently be maintained that not one of the many moral-

[37] *Ibid.*, p. 507.
[38] *Ibid.*, p. 89.
[39] *Ibid.*, p. 411.
[40] *Ibid.*, p. v.

ists referred to above, as holding or seeming to hold the egoistic theory of the moral motive, ever so much as suggested that one could obtain 'reasoned convictions as to what ought to be done' by merely computing what would bring the most pleasure to one's self." [41] This statement I cannot accept.

The "theological utilitarians" looked upon self-love as the ground for accepting the will of God as our rule. Gay says:—"Obligation is the necessity of doing or omitting any action in order to be happy. . . . So that obligation is evidently founded upon the prospect of happiness, and arises from the necessary influence which any action has upon present or future happiness or misery. . . . How can the good of mankind be any obligation to *me,* when perhaps in particular cases, such as laying down my life, or the like, it is contrary to my happiness?" [42] Paley defines virtue as "the doing good to mankind, in obedience to the will of God, and for the sake of everlasting happiness." [43] Are not these "reasoned convictions as to what ought to be done," which fall within the scope of Sidgwick's definition of egoistic hedonism? Indeed, he speaks himself of Paley's egoistic hedonism as something which seems to the latter self-evident as a fundamental principle of rational conduct.[44] And what may be said of Dr. Albee's indictment that Sidgwick "has unconsciously developed, in what he terms Egoism, the conception of a form of hedonistic theory which in reality has never existed in modern Ethics," [45] when we read the following reasoned argument in Waterland's "Sermon on Self-

---

[41] E. Albee, *A History of English Utilitarianism* (London, 1902), p. 382 *sq.*
[42] Gay, in *op. cit.,* pp. xxxvii., lxi.
[43] Paley, *op. cit.,* i. 7 (Works, p. 9).
[44] Sidgwick, *op. cit.,* p. 121 *sq.*
[45] Albee, *op. cit.,* p. 384.

Love"? "The wisest course for any man to take is to secure an interest in the life to come. . . . There can be no excess of fondness, or self-indulgence, in respect of eternal happiness. This is loving himself in the best manner, and to the best purposes. All virtue and piety are thus resolvable into a principle of self-love. . . . It is with reference to ourselves, and for our own sakes, that we love even God himself." [46]

At the same time, while the so-called "theological utilitarianism" perfectly agrees with the definition of egoistic hedonism, it also agrees with the definition of utilitarianism, in which no reference is made to motives or the ultimate end of acts. Sidgwick expressly mentions Bentham's psychological doctrine, that every human being always does aim at his own greatest apparent happiness, and yet classifies him as a utilitarian. [47] He speaks of the "obvious and glaring" difference between the egoistic proposition that "each ought to seek his own happiness," and the utilitarian proposition that "each ought to seek the happiness of all"; [48] but then he does not take account of the fact that a person may aim at his own happiness as his ultimate end and at the same time aim at the happiness of all as a means to that end. If utilitarianism required the happiness of all as the ultimate end, not only Bentham, but Mill and others would have to be excluded from its followers. Mill observes that "utilitarian moralists have gone beyond almost all others in affirming that the motive has nothing to do with the morality of the action, though much with the worth of the agent." [49] A utilitarian may consequently very well seek the general happiness as a

---

[46] D. Waterland, "Sermon on Self-Love," in *The English Preacher,* i. (London, 1773), p. 101 *sq.*

[47] Sidgwick, *op. cit.,* pp. 84, 87 *sq.*

[48] *Ibid.,* p. 411 *sq.*

[49] Mill, *op. cit.,* p. 26.

means of securing his own happiness. He may be an egoistic hedonist, and an egoistic hedonist may be a utilitarian. Egoistic and universalistic hedonism, as defined
by the author of these terms, are different, but not *eo ipso*
conflicting doctrines.

If egoistic hedonism is taken to imply that each *ought*
to seek his own happiness as the end of his actions, I
doubt whether it is really found in its genuineness anywhere outside the scope of theological hedonism,[50] and
there, of course, only on the understanding that by happiness is meant everlasting happiness. As to its objective
validity I have therefore nothing more to say than what
will be found in the discussion of the claim to validity
made by theological ethics in general.

Nearly related to utilitarianism is the evolutionary
theory of Herbert Spencer. In a well-known letter to
Stuart Mill he repudiated the title anti-utilitarian, which
had been applied to him, and endeavoured to make clear
their difference of opinion. He wrote:—"The view for
which I contend is, that Morality properly so-called—the
science of right conduct—has for its object to determine
how and *why* certain modes of conduct are detrimental,
and certain other modes beneficial. These good and bad
results cannot be accidental, but must be necessary consequences of the constitution of things; and I conceive it
to be the business of Moral Science to deduce, from the
laws of life and the conditions of existence, what kinds
of action necessarily tend to produce happiness, and what
kinds to produce unhappiness. Having done this, its deductions are to be recognized as laws of conduct; and are
to be conformed to irrespective of a direct estimation of

[50] See *infra*, p. 221 *sqq.*

happiness or misery." [51] Hence "the utilitarianism which recognizes only the principles of conduct reached by induction, is but preparatory to the utilitarianism which deduces these principles from the processes of life as carried on under established conditions of existence." [52] Acts are called good or bad, according as they are well or ill adjusted to ends, and as conduct evolves there is a greater adjustment of acts to ends. "Ethics has for its subject-matter that form which universal conduct assumes during the last stages of its evolution"; and under its ethical aspects conduct is considered good or right if its acts are conducive to life in self or others, and bad or wrong if they directly or indirectly tend towards death, special or general. But an extremely important assumption underlies all such moral estimates, namely, the belief that life brings more happiness than misery. Our ideas of the moral goodness and badness of acts really originate from our consciousness of the certainty or probability that their aggregate results will be pleasurable or painful to self or others or both; [53] and the reason for this is that "there exists a primordial connection between pleasure-giving acts and continuance or increase of life, and, by implication, between pain-giving acts and decrease or loss of life." It thus lies in the very nature of sentient existence that it is "no more possible to frame ethical conceptions from which the consciousness of pleasure, of some kind, at some time, to some being, is absent, than it is possible to frame the conception of an object from which the consciousness of space is absent." [54]

It is obvious that Spencer, like the utilitarians, attributes to the moral concept objective validity. When he

[51] H. Spencer, *The Principles of Ethics,* i. (London, 1897), p. 57.
[52] *Ibid.,* i. 61.
[53] *Ibid.,* i. ch. ii. *sq.*
[54] *Ibid.,* i. 82 *sq.*

regards that conduct as good which "conduces to life in each and all" he maintains that he has the support of "the true moral consciousness," or "moral consciousness proper," which, whether in harmony or in conflict with the "pro-ethical" sentiment, is vaguely or distinctly recognized as the rightful ruler.[55] He started as a believer in a moral sense, but subsequently changed his view. He writes, "Though, as shown in my first work, *Social Statics*, I once espoused the doctrine of the intuitive moralists (at the outset in full, and in later chapters with some implied qualifications), yet it has gradually become clear to me that the qualifications required practically obliterate the doctrine as enunciated by them." [56] He still, however, speaks of moral intuitions. Thus, when saying that pleasure is an inexpugnable element of the conception of the ultimate moral aim, he adds, "It is as much a necessary form of moral intuition as space is a necessary form of intellectual intuition." [57] While rejecting the doctrine that "moral perceptions are innate in the original sense," he believes in the existence of "moral intuitions" acquired by racial experience. He quotes the following passage from the previously mentioned letter to Mill:— "Corresponding to the fundamental propositions of a developed Moral Science, there have been, and still are, developing in the race, certain fundamental moral intuitions; and . . . , though these moral intuitions are the results of accumulated experiences of Utility, gradually organized and inherited, they have come to be quite independent of conscious experience. Just in the same way

[55] Spencer, *op. cit.*, i. 337 *sq.*
[56] *Ibid.*, i. 470.
[57] *Ibid.*, i. 46. In a footnote he remarks that he ought to have said "that happiness is *more* truly a form of moral intuition than space is a form of intellectual intuition: being, as we see, a universal form of it."

that I believe the intuition of space, possessed by any living individual, to have arisen from organized and consolidated experiences of all antecedent individuals who bequeathed to him their slowly-developed nervous organizations—just as I believe that this intuition, requiring only to be made definite and complete by personal experiences, has practically become a form of thought, apparently quite independent of experience; so do I believe that the experiences of utility organized and consolidated through all past generations of the human race, have been producing corresponding nervous modifications, which, by continued transmission and accumulation, have become in us certain faculties of moral intuition—certain emotions responding to right and wrong conduct, which have no apparent basis in the individual experiences of utility. I also hold that just as the space-intuition responds to the exact demonstrations of Geometry, and has its rough conclusions interpreted and verified by them; so will moral intuitions respond to the demonstrations of Moral Science, and will have their rough conclusions interpreted and verified by them." [58]

This theory of the development of "moral intuitions" through the inheritance of the effects of the accumulated experiences of the race is based upon a huge assumption, which Spencer regarded as a scientifically demonstrated truth, namely, the belief that acquired characters may be transmitted from parent to offspring. But the heredity of "acquired characters" is nowadays emphatically disputed by a large school of biologists, and can certainly not be taken for granted. Yet even if Spencer's theory were correct, it would only explain the origin of certain instincts through earlier generations' continued experience. What he calls "moral intuitions" is, to use his own

[58] *Ibid.*, i. 123.

words, simply "certain emotions responding to right and wrong conduct," or "preferences and aversions . . . rendered organic by inheritance of the effects of pleasurable and painful experiences in progenitors."[59] And an emotion "corresponding to," or caused by, a certain course of conduct cannot possibly make that course of conduct objectively right or wrong. Spencer's theory might at most be a contribution to the history of the growth of moral ideas, but could have no bearing whatever on the question of their validity.

Another representative of what has been called evolutionary hedonism or utilitarianism is Leslie Stephen. He criticizes the utilitarian conception of society as a mere aggregate of individuals. The true unit is not the individual but society, which may be regarded as an aggregate organism; and morality is "the sum of the preservative instincts of a society."[60] "The moral law is a statement of certain essential conditions of the vitality of the society";[61] healthy development implies an efficient moral code and social degeneration implies the reverse.[62] There is this difference between the utilitarian and the evolutionist criterion of morality—that the former is happiness and the latter the health of the society.[63] But at the same time the two criteria "are not really divergent; on the contrary, they necessarily tend to coincide." There is a correlation between the pernicious and the painful on the one hand, and on the other between the beneficial and the agreeable; the "useful," in the sense of pleasure-giving, must approximately coincide with the "useful" in the sense of life-preserving.[64]

[59] Spencer, *op. cit.*, i. 123 *sq.*
[60] L. Stephen, *The Science of Ethics* (London, 1882), p. 217.
[61] *Ibid.*, p. 219.
[62] *Ibid.*, p. 397.
[63] *Ibid.*, p. 366.
[64] *Ibid.*, p. 353 *sqq.*

But why is the health of the society the criterion of morality? Stephen writes, "Our moral judgment must condemn instincts and modes of conduct which are pernicious to the social vitality, and must approve the opposite; but it does not necessarily follow that it must condemn or approve them because they are perceived to be pernicious or beneficial." [65] And in another place:—
"Moral approval is the name of the sentiment developed through the social medium which modifies a man's character in such a way as to fit him to be an efficient member of the social 'tissue.' It is the spiritual pressure which generates and maintains morality." [66] These statements, however, can only be answers to the question why we have moral sentiments and pronounce moral judgments, but tell us nothing about that objective validity which Stephen evidently attributes to his criterion of morality. He says that it is "a simple 'objective' fact that a man acts rightly or wrongly in a given case, and a fact which may be proved to him. . . . If I can prove drunkenness to be socially mischievous, I shall certainly prove it to be wicked." [67] But surely he cannot prove it to be wicked simply by proving that it is socially mischievous. Of the validity of his fundamental proposition Stephen has given us no proof at all.

Many ethical writers agree with the hedonists in regarding pleasure as a good, but disagree with the contention that pleasure alone is good as an end. It has often been argued that Mill himself was not a consistent exponent of utilitarianism owing to his admission that "some *kinds* of pleasure are more desirable and more valuable than others," and his reference to the "sense of dignity" as the ground of the preference that is given to

[65] *Ibid.*, p. 148.   [66] *Ibid.*, p. 271 *sq.*   [67] *Ibid.*, pp. 443, 453.

some pleasures over others.[68] Moreover, in Mill's famous formula that "it is better to be a human being dissatisfied than a pig satisfied," Paulsen finds the implication that the moral value lies, not in pleasure as such, but in pleasurable functions; and he consequently observes that there is no radical difference between Mill's utilitarianism and the doctrine of "energism,"[69] according to which the highest good is not the feeling of pleasure, but an "objective content of life," namely, the perfect development and exercise of life,[70] or, as he also calls it, "welfare."[71]

As hedonism is based on the proposition that each person desires his own happiness, so energism is based on the proposition that each person desires to live a human life and all that is implied in it, the goal at which the will of every living creature aims being the normal exercise of the vital functions that constitute its nature.[72] And as hedonism has been divided into egoistic and universalistic hedonism, so energism has been divided into egoistic and universalistic energism. According to the former kind of energism, the highest good, or principle of morality, is the welfare of individual life; according to the latter, it is the welfare of the race.[73] Paulsen's energism is universalistic. Every man desires to live, but he also desires to help others to live; all human beings are both egoistic and altruistic, although in very different degrees. Indeed, in the motives of actions it is impossible to draw any sharp limit between the interests of self and the interests

[68] Mill, *op. cit.*, pp. 11, 13.
[69] F. Paulsen, *System der Ethik*, i. (Stuttgart & Berlin, 1913), p. 275. In my account of Paulsen's theory I have availed myself of some expressions used in F. Thilly's English edition of his work (London, 1899).
[70] *Ibid.*, i. 223.
[71] *Ibid.*, i. 224.
[72] *Ibid.*, i. 270.
[73] F. Thilly, *Introduction to Ethics* (New York, 1905), p. 127.

of others. It is a mistake to suppose that every act has but one motive: many motives combine to influence the will to action.[74] And just as the motives of an act, so also the effects of it tend to be both egoistic and altruistic. "There is no act that does not influence the life of the individual as well as that of his surroundings, and therefore cannot and must not be viewed and judged from the standpoint of both individual and general welfare. The traditional classification, which distinguishes between duties towards self and duties towards others, cannot be recognized as a legitimate division. There is no duty towards individual life that cannot be construed as a duty towards others, and no duty towards others that cannot be proved to be a duty towards self." [75] But then, Paulsen asks, can there never be a conflict between egoism and altruism? His answer is: there are, no doubt, cases of such a conflict, but "the opposition between individual and general welfare, selfish and altruistic motives, forms not the rule, but the exception. As a rule, there is harmony in the effects as well as in the motives." [76]

So far we have only considered the prevalence of desires to promote welfare, not the moral valuation of such desires. But there is, according to Paulsen, a close connection between the morality of acts and their tendency to gratify the desire for welfare. Good is that which gratifies a desire, and morally good is an act if it tends to promote the welfare of the individual and the society and at the same time is performed from a sense of duty. But the goodness of the motive depends upon its tendency to express itself outwardly in good acts. Morality is not an end in itself but a means to an end, namely, the realiza-

[74] Paulsen, *op. cit.*, i. 246, 247, 390 *sqq.*
[75] *Ibid.*, i. 387 *sqq.*
[76] *Ibid.*, i. 394.

tion of the highest good, that which human beings strive after, individual and racial welfare.[77]

It seems, then, that Paulsen repeats the hedonistic fallacy of regarding the prevalence of a desire as evidence of the morality of its realization: the moral goodness of a particular motive depends upon the effect which it tends to produce in action, and the effect itself is good because man wills it. Now it may possibly be argued that Paulsen has not definitely attributed objective validity to his ethical principle, that his ways of expressing himself often are so vague that when he speaks of moral goodness or badness, duty or virtue, he may ultimately mean what he and others *consider* to be good or bad, obligatory or virtuous. But if Paulsen had looked upon moral values as merely subjective, he could not have represented his theory of the goodness of the will as a development of the Kantian doctrine of the moral law, supplying it with a teleological ground for "the validity of the moral norms . . . , the obedience to which gives moral value to the will." [78] Paulsen admits that the moral nihilism which denies the validity of all moral norms and values cannot be logically disproved. But he argues that it is also impossible to convince a delirious person or a madman of the unreality of his hallucinations or delusions [79]—an argument which seems to imply that the existence of moral insensibility, or "moral insanity," is no more inconsistent with the objectivity of moral values than the existence of madness is with the objectivity of truth.

According to Bradley, pleasure is *a* good, but not *the* good, because "happiness is the end," [80] and "happiness,

[77] Paulsen, *op. cit.,* i. 227 *sqq.,* 342.
[78] *Ibid.,* i. 222.
[79] *Ibid.,* i. 376 *sqq.*
[80] F. H. Bradley, *Ethical Studies* (Oxford, 1927), p. 125.

for the ordinary man, neither means a pleasure nor a number of pleasures. It means in general the finding of himself, or the satisfaction of himself as a whole, and in particular it means the realization of his concrete ideal of life." [81] "Morality is co-extensive with self-realization, as the affirmation of the self which is one with the ideal." [82] The good self is the self whose end and pleasure is the realization of the ideal self; "which is interested in and bound up with pursuits, activities, in a word, with ends that realize the good will. The good will is the will to realize the ideal self." [83] Now "man is a social being; he is real only because he is social, and can realize himself only because it is as social that he realizes himself." "Leaving out of sight the question of a society wider than the state, we must say that a man's life with its moral duties is in the main filled up by his station in that system of wholes which the state is, and that this, partly by its laws and institutions, and still more by its spirit, gives him the life which he does live and ought to live." [84] "What is moral *in any particular given case* is seldom doubtful. Society pronounces beforehand; or, after some one course has been taken, it can say whether it was right or not." [85] As Hegel pointed out, "the wisest men of antiquity have given judgment that wisdom and virtue consist in living agreeably to the Ethos of one's people." [86] What interests us in this connection is not the theory as such, but its foundation. Why is self-realization, conceived in the sense indicated, a moral obligation? I can find no other answer to this question in Bradley's *Ethical Studies* than the view that it is an object of desire,

[81] *Ibid.*, p. 96.
[82] *Ibid.*, p. 224.
[83] *Ibid.*, p. 279.

[84] *Ibid.*, p. 174.
[85] *Ibid.*, p. 198.
[86] *Ibid.*, p. 187.

in other words, that we ought because we will.[87] "The good self satisfies us because it answers to our real being. . . . In taking its content into our wills and realizing that, we feel that we realize ourselves as the true infinite, as one permanent harmonious whole." On the other hand, "the bad self not only does not realize our true being, but is never, for its own sake and as such, desired at all." [88]

Other moralists, whose theories are teleological without being hedonistic, base their validity on intuitions. According to Dr. Rashdall, the true criterion of morality is the tendency of an act to promote a well-being or good, which besides pleasure includes many other elements possessing different values. The right action is always that which, so far as the agent has the means of knowing, will produce the greatest amount of good upon the whole. The values of the elements included in the good are intuitively discerned and compared with one another by the moral or practical reason. A paramount position among these intuitions is occupied by the three axioms of prudence, rational benevolence, and equity, which we have already discussed in connection with utilitarianism. "It does on reflection strike us as self-evident that I ought to promote my own good on the whole (where no one else's good is affected), that I ought to regard a larger good for society in general as of more intrinsic value than a smaller good, and that one man's good is (other things being equal) of as much intrinsic value as any other man's." Among the many good things included in well-being virtue is the greatest. Even those virtues which are most obviously altruistic in their tendency are also ends

[87] Bradley, *op. cit.,* pp. 71, 73, 95, 279, etc. This has also been pointed out by Dr. W. O. Stapledon in his book *A Modern Theory of Ethics* (London, 1929), pp. 33, 34, 41 *sq.*
[88] Bradley, *op. cit.,* p. 303.

in themselves—having a value independent of, and in some cases much greater than, the mere pleasure which they cause in others; hence it becomes rational to encourage the cultivation and exercise of these virtues even in ways which cannot always be shown to produce a net gain in pleasure on the whole. Again, as to the less obviously utilitarian virtues and duties it is said that through all of them there seems to run the general principle that a higher value should be attributed to the exercise and cultivation of the higher—that is to say, of the intellectual, aesthetic, and emotional—faculties than to the indulgence of the merely animal and sensual part of our nature.[89] Rashdall says, "The view that we have arrived at is that the morality of our actions is to be determined ultimately by its tendency to promote a universal end, which end itself consists of many ends, and in particular two—Morality and pleasure." [90] I should have thought that no particular intuition was needed to tell us that the morality of our actions is to be determined by its tendency to promote—morality.

Another moralist whose theory is closely related to the utilitarian principle as developed by Stuart Mill is Professor Hobhouse. He accepts Mill's admission that one kind of pleasure is intrinsically superior to another but, like many others, he regards it as fatal to the maintenance of simple pleasurableness as the standard of action, and asks what sort of experience it is that will yield pleasure of the most desirable quality. He replies that "it is the harmonious fulfilment of human powers. The end, as thus conceived, does not separate happiness from the kind of life in which it is sought, but treats them as two elements in the same whole, as the experience and the feeling-tone

[89] Rashdall, op. cit., i. 90, 91, 93, 184 sqq.
[90] Ibid., i. 219.

which qualifies the experience. The rational object of human action is a type of life, not merely a type of feeling."[91] And the rational good is the mode of life sustained by a harmony of feeling, "a harmonious fulfilment of vital capacity, or the fulfilment of vital capacity as a whole. Feeling in harmony with its object is what we call Pleasure. The body of feeling in harmony with itself and the body of its objects is what we call happiness. Viewed as feeling, then, Rational Good is happiness, viewed as the object of this feeling it is the fulfilment of vital capacity as a consistent whole. Viewed in both aspects together it is happiness found in such fulfilment."[92] By happiness is then meant happiness of all beings capable thereof, and by fulfilment of vital capacity is meant fulfilment in all living beings so far as it can attain harmonious expression. "It is this universal harmony of feeling and vital activity which is the good, and the end which each individual is required to serve, not his own happiness or the fulfilment of his own power."[93] The principle of harmony involves, or rather is conditioned by, the axiom that "what is unambiguously good is good universally"; "one feeling is not to be preferred to another because it is the feeling of this man rather than that, except in so far as the preference is required on universal principles which are integral parts of the general system of harmony."[94] And the fundamental principles in which the system of feeling at the basis of our social action expresses itself, "e.g., that I must consider my neighbour as myself, are justified in reason, and the

[91] L. T. Hobhouse, *The Rational Good* (London, 1921), p. 139.
[92] *Ibid.*, p. 114.
[93] *Ibid.*, p. 117.
[94] L. T. Hobhouse, *The Elements of Social Justice* (London, 1922), p. 106. *Idem, The Rational Good*, p. 80.

judgments of right and wrong founded upon them are true." [95]

So far as I can see, this essentially coincides with Sidgwick's principle that "I ought not to prefer my own lesser good to the greater good of another," which, as I have tried to show, is not a self-evident proposition. Professor Hobhouse supports his theory by an attempt to prove that the contrary principle of self-preference, whether of an individual or a group, involves inconsistencies and is by definition irrational. He maintains that if I adopt the system of self-preference, "the principle of universals" will compel me to admit that "you will form a similar system for yourself and that these systems may clash. If, then, both systems are rational, rational systems may be inconsistent, which is contrary to definition." [96] But why should the two systems clash and, therefore, be inconsistent? As I have said before, when I pronounce an act to be good or bad, right or wrong, I mean that it is so not only for myself but for all similar persons in similar circumstances; hence it would be self-contradictory to say that it is right for me to be an egoist though not for another similar person in similar circumstances. But I can find nothing irrational or inconsistent in the proposition that it is right for everybody to be an egoist, myself as well as others. The common sense opinion that, in certain circumstances, we have a right to prefer our own lesser good to the greater good of another, cannot be refuted by any arguments of reason.

While the teleological theories imply that such acts are good or right as tend to produce certain results or

---

[95] *Idem, The Elements of Social Justice,* p. 24.
[96] *Idem, The Rational Good,* p. 82. *Cf. Idem, The Elements of Social Justice,* p. 23.

effects, or to realize a certain end, there is another doctrine according to which certain kinds of action are unconditionally prescribed without regard to ulterior consequences, or at most with a very partial consideration of consequences. It is held that duty is not usually a difficult thing for an ordinary man to know, that we have the power of seeing clearly that certain courses of conduct are right in themselves, that, for example, "duty should be performed 'advienne qui pourra,' that truth should be spoken without regard to consequences, that justice should be done 'though the sky should fall.' " [97] This has been called intuitionism, in the narrow sense of the term, and has also been called unphilosophical intuitionism, in distinction from philosophical intuitionism, which intuitively judges some general rule of conduct to be true or evident and from this rule deduces the morality or immorality of this or that particular course of conduct, as we have seen to be the case with various teleological theories of ethics. Intuitionism of the former kind is practically the morality of common sense, the opinions of ordinary men. These opinions are not only loose and shifting, but in many points mutually contradictory, and cannot therefore possibly be regarded as self-evident truths. In his classical review of common sense Sidgwick observes that from such regulation of conduct as the common sense of mankind supports no proposition can be elicited which, when fairly contemplated, even appears to have the characteristic of a scientific axiom. [98]

[97] Sidgwick, *op. cit.*, p. 200.   [98] *Ibid.*, p. 360.

CHAPTER II

THE SUPPOSED OBJECTIVITY OF
MORAL JUDGMENTS (*concluded*)

IT WILL perhaps be argued that even though this or that
moral principle, or even all moral principles hitherto laid
down, fail to be objectively valid or express a moral
truth, there may nevertheless be in the human mind some
"faculty" which makes the pronouncement of objectively valid moral judgments possible. There are so many
"theoretical" truths which have never been discovered,
and yet we have in our intellect a "faculty" enabling us
to pronounce judgments that are true. So also moralists
of different normative schools of ethics maintain that we
possess a faculty which can pronounce true moral judgments. This faculty has been called by names like "moral
sense," "conscience," or "practical" or "moral reason,"
or been simply included under the general terms "reason"
or "understanding."

According to the moral sense school, the morality or
immorality of conduct is discriminated by a special sense
"implanted" in us for this purpose. It perceives virtue and
vice as the eye perceives light and darkness. Shaftesbury
observes that man possesses "natural affections, which
lead to the good of the publick"; "self-affections, which
lead only to the good of the private"; and "unnatural affections," which lead neither to public nor private good.
Virtue consists in a harmony or proper balance between
the two first kinds of affections; and it is by means of the
moral sense that we can tell whether these affections are

35

properly balanced or not.[1] Its verdict is final: neither the
applause of custom nor the sanction of religion can ever
alter "the eternal measures, and immutable independent
nature of worth and virtue." [2] According to Hutcheson,
again, our moral sense proves that the essence of virtue
consists in benevolence: "that action is best, which procures the greatest happiness for the greatest numbers; and
that worst, which, in like manner, occasions misery." [3]
It has often been remarked that the term "moral sense" is
a misnomer: this supposed "faculty" not only lacks a
bodily organ, but its perceptions lack the uniformity which
characterizes our sensations under similar physiological
conditions.[4] It is essentially an emotional faculty. Shaftesbury says that a natural affection, which is "an original
one of earliest rise in the soul or affectionate part," makes
the sense of right and wrong [5]—that is, the moral sense;
and that this sense "must consist in a real antipathy or
aversion to injustice or wrong, and a real affection or love
towards equity and right, for its own sake, and on account of its own natural beauty and worth." [6] Hutcheson
writes in his work, the *Inquiry*:—"Some actions have to
men an immediate goodness; . . . by a superior sense,
which I call a moral one, we approve the actions of others,
and perceive them to be their perfection and dignity, and
are determin'd to love the agent; a like perception we
have in reflecting on such actions of our own, without any

---

[1] Shaftesbury, *Characteristicks*, ii. (London, 1733), p. 86 *sqq.* The
expression "moral sense"—which is rarely used by him—is found in
the marginal notes *ibid.* pp. 41, 42, 44-46, 53 *sq.*, and in the text p. 46.
[2] *Ibid.*, ii. 35 *sq.*
[3] F. Hutcheson, *An Inquiry into the Original of our Ideas of
Beauty and Virtue* (London, 1753), p. 185.
[4] *Cf.* S. Spalding, *The Philosophy of Christian Morals* (London,
1843), p. 315 *sq.*
[5] Shaftesbury, *op. cit.*, ii. 44 *sq.*
[6] *Ibid.*, ii. 42.

view of natural advantage from them."[7] In his later works he also assigns some importance to reason in the process attending moral decisions;[8] yet the understanding "judges about the means or the subordinate ends: but about the ultimate ends there is no reasoning."[9] Rationalistic moralists have justly made the objection to this moral sense theory that it is totally unable to give any objective validity to the moral perceptions.[10] In his criticism of it Kant observes that "feelings which naturally differ infinitely in degree cannot furnish a uniform standard of good and evil, nor has any one a right to form judgments for others by his own feelings."[11] Hutcheson himself frankly admits that "every one judges the affections of others by his own sense; so that it seems not impossible that in these senses men might differ as they do in taste."[12]

Butler calls "the moral faculty" conscience, but as a synonym for it he frequently uses the term "principle of reflection." It has two aspects, a purely cognitive and an authoritative, and on its cognitive side it "pronounces determinately some actions to be in themselves just, right, good; others to be in themselves evil, wrong, unjust."[13]

[7] Hutcheson, *An Inquiry into the Original of our Ideas of Beauty and Virtue* (London, 1753), p. 109 *sq.*

[8] *Cf.* W. R. Scott, *Francis Hutcheson* (Cambridge, 1900), p. 204 *sqq.*

[9] Hutcheson, *A System of Moral Philosophy,* i. (London, 1755), p. 38.

[10] *E.g.,* H. Rashdall, *The Theory of Good and Evil,* i. (London, 1924), p. 144 *sqq.*

[11] I. Kant, *Grundlegung zur Metaphysik der Sitten,* sec. ii. (*Gesammelte Schriften,* iv. [Berlin, 1911], p. 442; T. K. Abbott's translation in *Kant's Critique of Practical Reason and other Works on the Theory of Ethics* [London, 1898], p. 61).

[12] Hutcheson, *An Essay on the Nature and Conduct of the Passions. With Illustrations on the Moral Sense* (London, 1756), p. 237.

[13] J. Butler, *Sermon II.—Upon Human Nature,* § 8 (*Works,* i. [London, 1900], p. 45).

Sometimes he even calls it reason. But his dominant view seems to be that which lays stress on the instinctive intuition rather than the reflection.[14] He says :—"In all common ordinary cases we see intuitively at first view what is our duty. . . . This is the ground of the observation, that the first thought is often the best. In these cases doubt and deliberation is itself dishonesty. . . . That which is called considering what is our duty in a particular case, is very often nothing but endeavouring to explain it away." [15] But how, then, is it that different consciences so often issue conflicting orders? This question is never raised by Butler. He gives us no criterion of rightness and wrongness apart from the voice of conscience.[16] It has been said that when Butler and other intuitionist writers refer to the conscience as the supreme principle of morals, they do not mean by it a "private conscience" but rather what may be called "the universal conscience"—that ultimate recognition of the rightness and wrongness of actions which is latent in all men, but which in some men is more fully developed than in others.[17] Whewell wrote :—

[14] Cf. J. Bonar, Moral Sense (London, 1930), p. 64.
[15] Butler, Sermon VII.—Upon the Character of Balaam, § 14 (Works, i. 100).
[16] Cf. J. M. Wilson and T. Fowler, The Principles of Morals (Introductory Chapters) (Oxford, 1886), p. 56; C. D. Broad, Five Types of Ethical Theory (London, 1930), p. 82 sq. Professor A. E. Taylor ("Some Features of Butler's Ethics," in Mind, N. S. xxxv. [London, 1926], p. 276 sq.) says that it is no fault of the Sermons, in which Butler's ethical doctrine is chiefly conveyed to us, that they did not consider the possibility of conflicting moral codes and the grounds on which a choice could be made between them, because the object of the preacher was to impress on his audience the necessity of conducting their lives virtuously, and they would be agreed, in all essentials, on the question what sort of conduct is right and wrong. But his disregard of the apparent or real variations in the deliverance of "conscience" certainly obscures his ethical theory in its most essential point.
[17] J. S. Mackenzie, A Manual of Ethics (London, 1929), p. 150. See also Taylor, loc. cit., p. 291.

"As each man has his reason, in virtue of his participation in the common reason of mankind, so each man has his conscience, in virtue of his participation in the common conscience of mankind. . . . As the object of reason is to determine what is true, so the object of conscience is to determine what is right. As each man's reason may err, and thus lead him to a false opinion, so each man's conscience may err, and lead him to a false moral standard. As false opinion does not disprove the reality of truth, so the false moral standards of men do not disprove the reality of a supreme rule of human action." [18] This appeal to a mysterious universal conscience as an infallible judge of right and wrong merely assumes the existence of an objectively valid standard in morals instead of proving it. For Butler conscience really represented the will of God.

Cudworth, Clarke, Price, and Reid are names that recall to our mind a theory according to which the morality of actions is perceived by the intellect, just as are number, diversity, causation, proportion. "Morality is eternal and immutable," says Richard Price. "Right and wrong, it appears, denote what actions are. Now whatever anything is, that it is, not by will, or decree, or power, but by nature and necessity. Whatever a triangle or circle is, that it is unchangeably and eternally. . . . The same is to be said of right and wrong, of moral good and evil, as far as they express real characters of actions. They must immutably and necessarily belong to those actions of which they are truly affirmed." [19] And as having a real existence

[18] W. Whewell, *The Elements of Morality including Polity* (Cambridge, 1864), p. 151. In the same sense Th. Lipps (*Die ethischen Grundfragen* [Leipzig & Hamburg, 1912], p. 181) speaks of the "absolute" conscience.

[19] R. Price, *A Review of the Principal Questions in Morals* (London, 1787), pp. 63, 74 *sq.*

outside the mind, they can only be discerned by the understanding. It is true that this discernment is accompanied with an emotion:—"Some impressions of pleasure or pain, satisfaction or disgust, generally attend our perceptions of virtue and vice. But these are merely their effects and concomitants, and not the perceptions themselves." [20] Samuel Clarke is of opinion that if a man endowed with reason denies the eternal and necessary moral differences of things, it is the very same "as if a man that has the use of his sight, should at the same time that he beholds the sun, deny that there is any such thing as light in the world; or as if a man that understands Geometry or Arithmetick, should deny the most obvious and known propositions of lines or numbers." [21]

Since the days of Kant moral judgments have been referred to a special faculty or a part of the general faculty of reason, called "practical" or "moral" reason, as the source of the objective validity assigned to them; according to Kant the speculative and the practical reason "can ultimately be only one and the same reason which has to be distinguished merely in its application." [22] The very existence of this mysterious faculty presupposes that there really are self-evident or axiomatic moral propositions; hence if no such proposition can be shown to exist we have no right whatever to postulate that there is a faculty which ever could give us any. It is perfectly clear that Kant *assumed* the objectivity of duty, and that this assumption led him to the idea of a pure practical reason,

[20] Price, *op. cit.*, p. 63.
[21] S. Clarke, *A Discourse concerning the Being and Attributes of God, the Obligations of Natural Religion, and the Truth and Certainty of the Christian Revelation* (London, 1732), p. 179.
[22] Kant, *op. cit.*, Vorrede (*Gesammelte Schriften*, iv. 391; Abbott's translation, p. 7). See also *Idem, Kritik der praktischen Vernunft,* i. 1. 3 (*Gesammelte Schriften*, v. [Berlin, 1913], p. 89 *sqq.*; Abbott, p. 182 *sqq.*).

not *vice versa*.[23] He needed a faculty to explain the moral law, which he regarded as a fact of pure reason, "of which we are *a priori* conscious, and which is apodictically certain," and the objective reality of which "cannot be proved by any deduction by any efforts of theoretical reason." [24] The same is the case with Sidgwick. In referring moral judgments to reason he simply means to imply their objectivity, *i.e.*, that "what I judge ought to be must, unless I am in error, be similarly judged by all rational beings who judge truly of the matter"; he does not mean "to prejudice the question whether valid moral judgments are normally attained by a process of reasoning from universal principles or axioms, or by direct intuition of the particular duties of individuals." [25] Dr. Rashdall writes:—"We may if we like call Practical Reason a separate faculty from speculative Reason—that is only a question of words. We really mean simply that they are distinguishable aspects of one and the same rational self. The important thing is that we should recognize that moral judgments possess an absolute truth or falsity, which is equally valid for all rational beings; and, if that is recognized, it seems most natural to ascribe them to Reason." [26]

The question to be answered, then, is whether any of the moral principles that have been regarded as self-evident really is so. If ethics is to be taken as the term for a normative science, I agree with Professor Moore's statement that "the fundamental principles of Ethics must be self-evident." I also agree with him when he says:—"The expression 'self-evident' means properly that the proposition

[23] *Cf.* A. Hägerström, *Kants Ethik* (Uppsala, 1902), p. 594.
[24] Kant, *Kritik der praktischen Vernunft*, i. 1. 1. 8 (v. 47; Abbott, p. 136).
[25] H. Sidgwick, *The Methods of Ethics* (London, 1913), p. 33.
[26] Rashdall, *op. cit.*, i. 166.

so called is evident or true, *by itself* alone; that it is not an inference from some proposition other than *itself*. The expression does *not* mean that the proposition is true, because it is evident to you or me or all mankind, because in other words it appears to us to be true. That a proposition appears to be true can never be a valid argument that true it really is." [27] Just as the statement "this proposition is true" does not mean the same as to say, "I consider this proposition to be true," so also the statement "this moral principle is self-evident" does not mean the same as to say, "this moral principle appears self-evident to me." But how, then, can I know if a proposition is really self-evident or only supposed to be so? In the case of theoretical truths no truth is considered to have a claim to self-evidence which is not generally accepted as self-evident or axiomatic by all those whose intellect is sufficiently developed to have an opinion on the matter worthy of any consideration at all. It is true, as Kant said, that universal assent does not prove the objective validity of a judgment [28]—indeed, there are mathematical axioms that have been called in question although they have passed current for centuries; but, to speak with Sidgwick, the absence of disagreement between experts must be an indispensable negative condition of the certainty of our beliefs.[29] In the case of moral principles enunciated as self-evident truths disagreement is rampant.

The great variability of moral judgments does not of course *eo ipso* disprove the possibility of self-evident moral intuitions. It is incompatible with that cruder kind

[27] G. E. Moore, *Principia Ethica* (Cambridge, 1922), p. 143.
[28] Kant, *Kritik der praktischen Vernunft,* Vorrede (v. *12 sq.;* Abbott, p. 98).
[29] *Supra,* p. *12 sq.*

of intuitionism which maintains that some moral faculty directly passes true moral judgments on particular courses of conduct at the moment of action. But what about the differences of opinion as regards the great moral principles that are supposed to be self-evident? Dr. Rashdall writes:—"Neither the slow development of the moral faculty nor its unequal development in different individuals at the same level of social culture forms any objection to the *a priori* character of moral judgments. We do not doubt either the axioms of Mathematics or the rules of reasoning, because some savages cannot count more than five, or because some highly educated classical scholars are incapable of understanding the fifth proposition of Euclid's first book. . . . Self-evident truths are not truths which are evident to everybody. There are degrees of moral illumination just as there are degrees of musical sensibility or of mathematical acuteness." [30] But is it really possible to assume that defective "moral illumination" could sufficiently explain the existence of so many different ethical theories, each of which is based on one or more principles regarded as self-evident intuitions, and as to some of which there is the same disagreement now as there was two thousand years ago? How can there be such a great diversity of opinion among "moral specialists" with regard to propositions that are assumed to be axioms? Some of these specialists say it is an axiom that I ought not to prefer my own lesser good to the greater good of another; whilst others not only deny the self-evidence, but thoroughly disagree with the contents, of this proposition. According to Sidgwick the proposition that pleasure is the only rational ultimate end of action is an object of intuition; [31] according to Dr. Moore, also a professor of moral philosophy, the untruth of this pro-

[30] Rashdall, *op. cit.,* i. 84 *sq.*   [31] *Supra,* p. 15.

position is self-evident.[32] The latter finds it self-evident that good cannot be defined;[33] but others, who have no smaller claim to the epithet "moral specialists," are of the very contrary opinion. What should we say if two professors of mathematics quarrelled about the axiom that "if equals be added to equals the wholes are equal," to which Sidgwick compares one of his moral axioms?[34]

There are no doubt moral propositions which really are certain and self-evident, for the simple reason that they are tautological, that the predicate is but a repetition of the subject; and moral philosophy contains a great number of such tautologies, from the days of Plato and Aristotle to the present times. But apart from such cases, which of course tell us nothing, I am not aware of any moral principle that could be said to be truly self-evident. The presumed self-evidence is only a matter of opinion; and in some cases one might even be inclined to quote Mr. Bertrand Russell's statement that "if self-evidence is alleged as a ground of belief, that implies that doubt has crept in, and that our self-evident proposition has not wholly resisted the assaults of scepticism."[35] None of the various theories of normative science can be said to have proved its case; none of them has proved that moral judgments possess objective validity, that there is anything truly good or bad, right or wrong, that moral principles express anything more than the opinions of those who believe in them.

But what, then, has made moralists believe that moral judgments possess an objective validity which none of

[32] Moore, op. cit., pp. 75, 144.
[33] Ibid., pp. 6, 8, 148.
[34] Supra, p. 9.
[35] B. Russell, The Analysis of Mind (London, 1922), p. 263. See also H. H. Joachim, The Nature of Truth (Oxford, 1906), p. 55.

them has been able to prove? What has induced them to construct their theories of normative ethics? What has allured them to invent a science the subject-matter of which—the objectively good or right—is not even known to exist? The answer is not difficult to find. It has often been remarked that there is much greater agreement among moralists on the question of moral practice than on the question of theory. When they are trying to define the ultimate end of right conduct or to find the essence of right and wrong, they give us the most contradictory definitions or explanations—as Leslie Stephen said, we find ourselves in a "region of perpetual antinomies, where controversy is everlasting, and opposite theories seem to be equally self-evident to different minds." [36] But when they pass to a discussion of what is right and wrong in concrete cases, in the various circumstances of life, the disagreement is reduced to a surprising extent. They all tell us that we should be kind to our neighbour, that we should respect his life and property, that we should speak the truth, that we should live in monogamy and be faithful husbands or wives, that we should be sober and temperate, and so forth. This is what makes books on ethics, when they come to the particular rules of life, so exceedingly monotonous and dull; for even the most controversial and pugnacious theorist becomes then quite tame and commonplace. And the reason for this is that all ethical theories are as a matter of fact based on the morality of common sense. Professor Carveth Read rightly observes :—"We cannot be so deceived as to imagine that the moral rules that may seem to be conclusions in any system, are really inferences from its characteristic

[36] L. Stephen, *The Science of Ethics* (London, 1882), p. 2. *Cf.* H. Sidgwick, "My Station and Its Duties," in *International Journal of Ethics,* iv. (Philadelphia, etc., 1893), p. 13 *sq.*

conceptions. With some slight qualifications, the rules are rules of Common Sense, and are the premises, the true *principia*, from which the theory is inferred. To agree with them on the whole is a test that no theory can ever evade." [37] So also normative ethics has adopted the common sense idea that there *is* something right and wrong independently of what is thought to be right or wrong. People are not willing to admit that their moral convictions are a mere matter of opinion, and look upon convictions differing from their own as errors. If asked why there is so much diversity of opinion on moral questions, and consequently so many errors, they would probably argue that there *would* be unanimity as regards the rightness or wrongness of a given course of conduct *if* everybody possessed a sufficient knowledge of the case and all the attendant circumstances and *if,* at the same time, everybody had a sufficiently developed moral consciousness—which practically would mean a moral consciousness as enlightened and developed as their own. This characteristic of the moral judgments of common sense is shared by the judgments of philosophers, and is at the bottom of their reasoned arguments in favour of the objectivity of moral values.

The common sense idea that moral judgments possess objective validity is itself regarded as a proof of their really possessing such validity. It is argued that the moral judgment "claims objectivity," that it asserts a value which is found in that on which it is pronounced. "This is the meaning of the judgment," says Professor Sorley. "It is not about a feeling or attitude of, or any relation to, the subject who makes the judgment." [38] Dr. Rashdall

[37] Carveth Read, *Natural and Social Morals* (London, 1909), p. 9.
[38] W. R. Sorley, *Moral Values and the Idea of God* (Cambridge, 1924), p. 150.

writes:—"Is not this idea of objectivity just the most fundamental of our moral convictions? . . . If there is in the human mind this consciousness of an objective 'ought,' it must be derived from the intellectual part of our nature . . . If the notion of duty is as inexpugnable a notion of the human mind as the notion of quantity or cause or substance or the like, we have every reason that we can possibly have for believing in its objective validity." [39] Yet in another place he implicitly admits that, after all, there is in point of universality some difference between these notions. He admits that most, and possibly the whole, of the savage's actual morality and of his intellectual beliefs about morality can be satisfactorily explained upon the emotional view; and he says that it would not matter, for the purpose of his argument, if we had to ascend to a comparatively advanced stage in the development of morality before we reached any ideas about human conduct that could be described as a sense of duty. [40] The whole argument is really reduced to the assumption that an idea—in this case the idea of the validity of moral judgments—which is generally held, or held by more or less advanced minds, must be true: people claim objective validity for the moral judgment, therefore it must possess such validity. The only thing that may be said in favour of such an argument is, that if the definition of a moral proposition implies the claim to objectivity, a judgment that does not express this quality cannot be a moral judgment; but this by no means proves that moral propositions so defined are true—the predicated objectivity may be a sheer illusion.

Well then, it might be argued, if you do not admit that

[39] H. Rashdall, *Is Conscience an Emotion?* (London, 1914), pp. 34, 36, 39.
[40] *Ibid.*, p. 70 *sq.*

there is anything objectively right or wrong, you must not use these or any other moral predicates, because if you do, you assign to them a meaning that they do not possess. But what about other predicates which are also formally objective and yet, when we more carefully consider the matter are admitted to be merely subjective estimates? The aesthetic judgment makes claim to objectivity: when people say that something is beautiful, they generally mean something more than that it gives, or has a tendency to give, them aesthetic enjoyment; and there are also many philosophers who uphold the objectivity of beauty and maintain that the beauties of nature exist apart from a beholding eye or a hearing ear. But even those who agree with Hume that beauty is no quality in things themselves, but exists merely in the mind which contemplates them,[41] do not hesitate to speak of "beauty," and would consider it absurd to be taken to task for doing so. Sidgwick admits that if I say "the air is sweet" or "the food is disagreeable," it would not be exactly true that I mean no more than that I like the one or dislike the other, although, if my statement is challenged, I shall probably content myself with affirming the existence of such feelings in my own mind.[42] So also, if anybody calls a certain wine or cigar good, there is some objectivity implied in the judgment, and however willing he is to recognize that the so-called goodness is a mere matter of taste, he will certainly, even if he is a philosopher, continue to call the wine or cigar good, just as before. Or, to take an instance from the sphere of knowledge: Hume, in expounding his own view, still speaks with the man in the street of objects and processes in nature, although his very aim is to convince

[41] D. Hume, "Essay xxiii.—Of the Standard of Taste," in *Philosophical Works,* iii. (London, 1875), p. 268.
[42] Sidgwick, *op. cit.,* p. 27.

us that what we know is really limited to impressions and ideas. And every one of us makes use of the words sunrise and sunset, which are expressions from a time when people thought that the sun rose and set, though nobody now holds this view. Why, then, should not the ethical subjectivist be allowed to use the old terms for moral qualities, although he maintains that the objective validity generally implied in them is a mere illusion? Dr. Rashdall himself, as we just saw, speaks of an emotional "morality" among savages, that is, a morality without validity.

There is thus a very general tendency to assign objectivity to our subjective experience, and this tendency is particularly strong and persistent with regard to our moral experience. Why we attribute validity to it is of course a matter that does not trouble the moral intuitionist any more than the mathematician looks for a ground for his axioms. He is not concerned with the question of origins. Professor Moore says that the questions as to the origin of people's moral feelings and ideas are of course "not without interest, and are subjects of legitimate curiosity," but "only form one special branch of Psychology or Anthropology." [43] And Professor Sorley remarks that when we ask, "Why do we assign validity to our moral approval and to moral ideas generally?" the history of their genesis gives us no answer.[44] For my own part I maintain, on the contrary, that an examination into the history of the moral consciousness of mankind gives us a clue to its supposed objectivity, as well as to its other characteristics.

People are generally inclined to assume that what makes a certain impression upon their minds also makes a similar impression upon the minds of others. This assump-

[43] G. E. Moore, *Ethics* (London, *s.d.*), p. 130 *sq.*
[44] Sorley, *op. cit.*, p. 64.

tion is very largely confirmed by facts; and, generally speaking, people's inclination to generalize their judgments is greater in proportion as the impressions are found to be similar in each particular case. If "there is no disputing of tastes," that is because taste is so very variable; and yet even in this instance we recognize a certain standard by speaking of a "good" and a "bad" taste. On the other hand, if the appearance of objectivity in the moral judgments is so illusive as to make it seem necessary to refer them to reason, that is partly on account of the comparatively uniform nature of the moral consciousness. Society is the school in which we learn to distinguish between right and wrong. The headmaster is Custom, and the lessons are the same for all the members of the community. The first moral judgments were pronounced by public opinion; public indignation and public approval are the prototypes of the moral emotions. As regards questions of morality there was in early society no difference of opinion; hence a character of universality was from the very beginning attached to the moral judgments. And when, with advancing civilization, this unanimity was to some extent disturbed by individuals who ventured to dissent from the opinions of the majority, the disagreement largely arose from circumstances which did not affect the moral principle itself, but had reference only to its application, that is, from circumstances of a purely intellectual character, from the knowledge of, or attention paid to, positive facts.

But besides the relative uniformity of moral opinions and the possibility of considerably harmonizing conflicting opinions by a demonstration of facts, there are other circumstances which have in a large measure contributed to the strong belief in moral truths. From our earliest childhood we are taught that certain acts *are* right and that others *are* wrong. The leading-string in the child's ethical growth is, all the time, the presence of other persons, whose "word of command" is authoritative and not to be trifled with.[45] There is further the authority of public opinion, custom, and law, with disagreeable consequences for those who act contrary to their decrees. There is the influence of some great teacher whose mind was ruled by the ideal of moral perfection, and whose words became sacred on account of his supreme wisdom, like Confucius or Buddha, or on religious grounds, like Jesus. There is the belief in an all-wise and all-powerful God, whose will is the supreme law and who inflicts punishment on the transgressor. And besides the external authority of the rules of conduct there is the internal authority assigned to the moral law, the sense of obligatoriness, which has much impressed moralists of different schools. It filled Kant with the same awe as the star-spangled firmament. According to Butler, conscience is "a faculty in kind and in nature supreme over all others, and which bears its own authority of being so."[46] Its supremacy is said to be "felt and tacitly acknowledged by the worst no less than by the best of men."[47] Adam Smith calls the moral faculties the "vicegerents of God within us," who "never fail to punish the violation of them by the torments of inward shame and self-condemnation; and, on the contrary, always reward obedience with tranquillity of mind, with contentment, and self-satisfaction."[48] Even Hutcheson, who raises the question why the

[45] *Cf.* J. M. Baldwin, *Social and Ethical Interpretations in Mental Development* (New York, 1897), p. 298.

[46] Butler, *Sermon II.—Upon Human Nature*, § 8 (*Works*, i. 45).

[47] Dugald Stewart, *The Philosophy of the Active and Moral Powers of Man*, i. (Edinburgh, 1828), p. 302.

[48] Adam Smith, *The Theory of Moral Sentiments* (London, 1887), p. 235.

moral sense should not vary in different men as the palate does, considers it from its very nature "to be designed for regulating and controlling all our powers." [49]

The authority of the moral law has been taken as a clear manifestation of the objectivity of duty and as a testimony of the subjectivistic fallacy. "If moral approbation is a mere feeling," says Dr. Rashdall, "how can it claim any superiority over other feelings?" [50] But if all external motives of a social and religious character be put aside, it may be fairly asked if the influence of the moral law upon the conduct of men is really so great as well-meaning moralists try to make us believe. It does not seem to command obedience in any exceptional degree, the regard for it can hardly be called the mainspring of action. It is only one spring out of many, and variable like all others. In some instances it may be a dominant power in a man's life, in others it is a voice calling in the wilderness; and the majority of people seem to be more afraid of the blame or ridicule of their fellowmen, or of the penalties with which the law of the country threatens them, than of "the vicegerents of God" in their own hearts. Kant speaks of "the peace of conscience of so many (in their own opinion conscientious) men, when . . . they have merely had the good fortune to escape bad consequences." [51] It has been said that mankind prefer the possession of virtue to all other enjoyments, and look upon vice as worse than any other misery; [52] that the pleasures and pains of conscience are in the normally constituted mind far more intense

[49] Hutcheson, *A System of Moral Philosophy*, i. 61.
[50] Rashdall, *The Theory of Good and Evil*, i. 143.
[51] Kant, *Von der Einwohnung des bösen Princips neben dem guten*, 3 (*Gesammelte Schriften*, vi. [Berlin, 1914], p. 38; Abbott's translation, p. 345).
[52] Hutcheson, *An Inquiry into the Original of Beauty and Virtue*, p. 252.

and durable than any other pleasures or pains.[53] But as a matter of fact, the obedience to the moral law, as to any ordinary law, is seldom accompanied with any distinct feeling of pleasure at all: the "good" conscience chiefly means the absence of a bad one.[54] And as for the bad conscience, I think we may agree with Leslie Stephen that "most men find nothing easier than to suppress its stings, when some immediately bad consequence, or the contempt and abhorrence of their neighbours, does not constantly instil the venom." [55] It is said that virtue bears in itself its own reward, and vice its own punishment. But what an unjust retributor conscience is. The more a person habituates himself to virtue the more he sharpens its sting, the deeper he sinks in vice the more he blunts it. While the best men have the most sensitive consciences, the worst have hardly any conscience at all. We are reminded that men are rewarded for good and punished for bad acts by the moral approval or disapproval of their neighbours. But public opinion and law judge of detected acts only; their judgment is seldom based upon an exhaustive examination of the case; all that they require is formal compliance with the more elementary rules of duty. Moreover,

[53] T. Fowler, *Progressive Morality* (London, 1895), p. 39.
[54] *Cf.* L. Feuerbach, *Sämmtliche Werke*, x. (Stuttgart, 1911), p. 283; N. H. Bang, *Begrebet Moral* (Köbenhavn, 1897), p. 168; M. Scheler, *Der Formalismus in der Ethik* (Halle a. d. S., 1927), p. 334. Kant (*Kritik der praktischen Vernunft*, 1, 2. 2. 2 [v. 117; Abbott, p. 214]) says that the consciousness of virtue is accompanied, not with enjoyment, but with self-contentment, which in its proper signification always designates only a negative satisfaction in one's existence, in which one is conscious of needing nothing." Yet in his discussion of duties of "indeterminate obligation" (*Einleitung zur Tugendlehre*, § 7 [*Gesammelte Schriften*, vi. [Berlin, 1914], p. 391; Abbott, p. 301] he speaks of "a moral pleasure which goes beyond mere satisfaction with one's self (which may be merely negative), and of which it is proudly said that in this consciousness virtue is its own reward."
[55] Stephen, *op. cit.*, p. 319.

a person is respected or praised, blamed or despised, on other grounds than his moral qualities; indeed, the admiration which men feel for intellectual superiority, artistic genius, courage, strength, or even accidental success, is often more intense than the admiration they feel for virtue. Thus the supposed supremacy of the moral law receives but scanty recognition in the practice and actual feelings of men. And to say that, whether its dictates are obeyed or not, they ought to be obeyed—or, as Butler put it, that conscience, "had it strength, as it has right; had it power, as it has manifest authority, . . . would absolutely govern the world"[56]—is simply to say that what ought to be ought to be. There are even philosophers who have actually denied that the moral values are the highest of all values.[57]

The authority assigned to conscience is really only an echo of the social or religious sanctions of conduct: it belongs to the "public" or the religious conscience, *vox populi* or *vox dei*. In theory it may be admitted that every man ought to act in accordance with his conscience. But this phrase is easily forgotten when, in any matter of importance, the individual's conscience comes into conflict with the common sense of his community; or doubt may be thrown upon the sincerity of his professed convictions, or he may be blamed for having such a conscience as he has. There are philosophers, like Hobbes and Hegel, who

[56] Butler, *Sermon II.—Upon Human Nature*, § 14 (*Works*, i. 48).
[57] *Cf.* H. Münsterberg, *Der Ursprung der Sittlichkeit* (Freiburg i. B., 1889), p. 115: "Man muss klar und unbeirrt erkennen, dass . . . sittlich wertlose Handlungen für die Entwickelung und Vervollkommmnung der Menschheit unendlich wertvoller sein können, als es sittliche Leistungen sind"; G. Freudenberg, *Grenzen der Ethik* (Leipzig, 1927), p. 129 *sq.*: "Es ist ein grundsätzliches Missverständnis, der Ethik die Frage zu stellen, ob die ethischen Werte 'höher' oder 'niedriger' als andere Werte seien. Offenbar wird ja auch über das Wesen der Musik gar nichts ausgesagt, wenn man sie als die höchste der Künste bezeichnet."

have denied the citizen the right of having a private conscience. The other external source from which authority has been instilled into the moral law is the alliance between morality and religion. In spite of all his efforts to base his own moral theory on a non-theological basis, Dr. Rashdall feels compelled to admit that, in his opinion, the belief in God is the logical presupposition of an "objective" or absolute morality. "A moral ideal," he says, "can exist nowhere and nohow but in a mind; an absolute moral ideal can exist only in a Mind from which all Reality is derived. Our moral ideal can only claim objective validity in so far as it can rationally be regarded as the revelation of a moral ideal externally existing in the mind of God." [58] So also Professor Bohlin, after a penetrating review of the claim to objective validity made by normative moralists, arrives at the conclusion that only a divine revelation can give morality such a validity.[59] But the belief in the authoritativeness of moral obligation may survive the religious source from which it sprang and last after the alliance between morality and religion has been broken. It has been pointed out by Schopenhauer and others [60] that Kant's categorical imperative, with its mysteriousness and awfulness, is really an echo of the old religious formula "Thou shalt," though it is heard, not as the command of an external legislator, but as a voice coming from within. Schiller wrote to Goethe, "There still remains something

[58] Rashdall, The Theory of Good and Evil, ii. 212.
[59] T. Bohlin, Das Grundproblem der Ethik (Uppsala & Leipzig, 1923), p. 428 sqq.
[60] A. Schopenhauer, Die Grundlage der Moral, §§ 4, 6 (Sämmtliche Werke, iv.[2] [Leipzig, 1916], pp. 124-126, 133 sqq.). F. Paulsen, Immanuel Kant (Stuttgart, 1899), p. 345 sq. J. Rehmke, Grundlegung der Ethik als Wissenschaft (Leipzig, 1925), p. 58. Cf. Kant, Von der Einwohnung des bösen Princips neben dem guten, Anmerkung (vi. 23 n.†; Abbott, p. 330 n.1), where he speaks of the majesty of the law "like that on Sinai."

in Kant, as in Luther, that makes one think of a monk who has left his monastery, but been unable to efface all traces of it." [61]

The theological argument in favour of the objective validity of moral judgments, which is based on belief in an all-good God who has revealed his will to mankind, contains, of course, an assumption that cannot be scientifically proved. But even if it could be proved, would that justify the conclusion drawn from it? Those who maintain that they in such a revelation possess an absolute moral standard and that, consequently, any mode of conduct which is in accordance with it must be objectively right, may be asked what they mean by an all-good God. If God were not supposed to be all-good, we might certainly be induced by prudence to obey his decrees, but they could not lay claim to *moral* validity; suppose the devil were to take over the government of the world, what influence would that have on the moral values—would it make the right wrong and the wrong right? It is only the all-goodness of God that can give his commandments absolute moral validity. But to say that something is good because it is in accordance with the will of an all-good God is to reason in a circle; if goodness means anything, it must have a meaning which is independent of his will. God is called good or righteous because he is supposed to possess certain qualities that we are used to call so: he is benevolent, he rewards virtue and punishes vice, and so forth. For such reasons we add the attributes goodness and righteousness to his other attributes, which express qualities of an objective character, and by calling him all-good we attribute to him perfect goodness.[62] As a matter of

[61] *Briefwechsel zwischen Schiller und Goethe in den Jahren 1794 bis 1805*, ii. (Stuttgart & Augsburg, 1856), p. 167.
[62] *Cf.* Shaftesbury, *op. cit.*, ii. 49 *sq.:* "Whoever thinks there is a God, and pretends formally to believe that he is just and good, must

fact, there are also many theologians who consider moral distinctions to be antecedent to the divine commands. Thomas Aquinas and his school maintain that the right is not right because God wills it, but that God wills it because it is right.

Before leaving this subject I must still mention a fact that has made moralists so anxious to prove the objectivity of our moral judgments, namely, the belief that ethical subjectivism is an extremely dangerous doctrine. In a little book called *Is Conscience an Emotion?*, largely written to oppose views held either by Professor McDougall or myself, Dr. Rashdall remarks that "the scientific spirit does not require us to blind ourselves to the practical consequences which hang upon the solution of not a few scientific problems," and that "assuredly there is no scientific problem upon which so much depends as upon the answer we give to the question whether the distinction which we are accustomed to draw between right and wrong belongs to the region of objective truth like the laws of mathematics and of physical science, or whether it is based upon an actual emotional constitution of individual human beings." [63] He maintains that the emotionalist theory of ethics, which leads to a denial of the objective validity of moral judgments, "is fatal to the deepest spiritual convictions and to the highest spiritual aspirations of the human race," and that it therefore is "a matter of great practical as well as intellectual importance" that it should be rejected. "To deny the validity of the idea

suppose that there is independently such a thing as justice and injustice, truth and falsehood, right and wrong; according to which he pronounces that God is just, righteous, and true." A similar remark has been made by C. Stumpf (*Vom ethischen Skeptizismus* [Leipzig, 1909], p. 22) and G. Heymans (*Einführung in die Ethik auf Grundlage der Erfahrung* [Leipzig, 1914], p. 8).

[63] Rashdall, *Is Conscience an Emotion?*, p. 199 sq.

of duty," he says, "has a strong tendency to impair its practical influence on the individual's life"; and "the belief in the objectivity of our moral judgments is a necessary premiss for any valid argument for the belief either in God, if by that be understood a morally good or perfect Being, or in Immortality." [64] The last statement is astounding. In another place Dean Rashdall argues that objective morality presupposes the belief in God,[65] and now we are told that any valid argument for the belief in God presupposes objective morality. These two statements combined lead to the logical conclusion that there is no valid evidence *either* for the existence of God *or* for the objectivity of moral judgments.

It is needless to say that a scientific theory is not invalidated by the mere fact that it is likely to cause mischief. The unfortunate circumstance that there do exist dangerous things in the world, proves that something may be dangerous and yet true. Another question is whether the ethical subjectivism I am here advocating really is a danger to morality. It cannot be depreciated by the same inference as was drawn from the teaching of the ancient Sophists, namely, that if that which appears to each man as right or good stands for that which is right or good, then everybody has the natural right to follow his caprice and inclinations and to hinder him doing so is an infringement on his rights. My moral judgments spring from my own moral consciousness; they judge of the conduct of other men not from their point of view but from mine, not in accordance with their feelings and opinions about right and wrong but according to my own. And these are not arbitrary. We approve and disapprove because we cannot do otherwise; our moral consciousness belongs to our mental constitution, which we cannot

[64] Rashdall, *op. cit.*, pp. 126, 127, 194.   [65] *Supra*, p. 55.

change as we please. Can we help feeling pain when the fire burns us? Can we help sympathizing with our friends? Are these facts less necessary or less powerful in their consequences, because they fall within the subjective sphere of our experience? So also, why should the moral law command less obedience because it forms a part of ourselves?

I think that ethical writers are often inclined to overrate the influence of moral theory upon moral practice, but if there is any such influence at all, it seems to me that ethical subjectivism, instead of being a danger, is more likely to be an advantage to morality. Could it be brought home to people that there is no absolute standard in morality, they would perhaps be on the one hand more tolerant and on the other hand more critical in their judgments. Emotions depend on cognitions and are apt to vary according as the cognitions vary; hence a theory which leads to an examination of the psychological and historical origin of people's moral opinions should be more useful than a theory which postulates moral truths enunciated by self-evident intuitions that are unchangeable. In every society the traditional notions as to what is good or bad, obligatory or indifferent, are commonly accepted by the majority of people without further reflection. By tracing them to their source it will be found that not a few of these notions have their origin in ignorance and superstition or in sentimental likes or dislikes, to which a scrutinizing judge can attach little importance;[66] and, on the other hand, he must condemn many an act or omission which public opinion, out of thoughtlessness, treats with indifference. It will, moreover, appear that moral estimates often survive the causes from which they sprang.

[66] See *infra,* pp. 107, 108, 258.

And what unprejudiced person can help changing his views if he be persuaded that they have no foundation in existing facts?

I have thus arrived at the conclusion that neither the attempts of moral philosophers or theologians to prove the objective validity of moral judgments, nor the common sense assumption to the same effect, give us any right at all to accept such a validity as a fact. So far, however, I have only tried to show that it has not been proved; now I am prepared to take a step further and assert that it cannot exist. The reason for this is that in my opinion the predicates of all moral judgments, all moral concepts, are ultimately based on emotions, and that, as is very commonly admitted,[67] no objectivity can come from an emotion. It is of course true or not that we in a given moment have a certain emotion; but in no other sense can the antithesis of true and false be applied to it. The belief that gives rise to an emotion, the cognitive basis of it, is either true or false; in the latter case the emotion may be said to be felt "by mistake"—as when a person is frightened by some object in the dark which he takes for a ghost, or is indignant with a person to whom he imputes a wrong that has been committed by somebody else; but this does not alter the nature of the emotion itself. We may call the emotion of another individual

[67] See, e.g., Rashdall, *The Theory of Good and Evil*, i. 145 sq., ii. 195; *Idem, Is Conscience an Emotion?*, pp. 30, 36; Sorley, *op. cit.*, p. 54; C. Hebler, *Philosophische Aufsätze* (Leipzig, 1869), p. 48; J. Watson, *Hedonistic Theories from Aristippus to Spencer* (Glasgow, 1895), p. 135; H. Maier, *Psychologie des emotionalen Denkens* (Tübingen, 1908), pp. 789, 790, 800; H. Münsterberg, *Philosophie der Werte* (Leipzig, 1908), p. 28; H. Höffding, *Etik* (Köbenhavn & Kristiania, 1913), p. 51; L. T. Hobhouse, *The Rational Good* (London, 1921), p. 16; R. Müller-Freienfels, *Irrationalismus* (Leipzig, 1922), p. 226; *Idem, Metaphysik des Irrationalen* (Leipzig, 1927), p. 400; J. Laird, *The Idea of Value* (Cambridge, 1929), pp. 247, 315.

"unjustified," if we feel that we ourselves should not have experienced the same emotion had we been in his place, or, as in the case of moral approval or disapproval, if we cannot share his emotion. But to speak, as Brentano does,[68] of "right" and "wrong" emotions, springing from self-evident intuitions and having the same validity as truth and error, is only another futile attempt to objectivize our moral judgments. Heymans regards it as self-evident that a good man deserves to be happy and a bad man unhappy;[69] but what is this "axiom" if not a mere expression of the retributive character of the moral emotions? So also other instances of the so-called *Gefühlsevidenz* are nothing but psychological facts put into propositions.[70]

If there are no moral truths it cannot be the object of a science of ethics to lay down rules for human conduct, since the aim of all science is the discovery of some truth. Professor Höffding argues that the subjectivity of our moral valuations does not prevent ethics from being a science any more than the subjectivity of our sensations renders a science of physics impossible, because both are concerned with finding the external facts that correspond to the subjective processes.[71] It may, of course, be a subject for scientific inquiry to investigate the means which are conducive to human happiness or welfare, and the results of such a study may also be usefully applied by moralists, but it forms no more a part of ethics than physics is a part of psychology. If the word "ethics" is to be used as the name for a science, the object of that science can only be to study the moral consciousness as a fact.

[68] F. Brentano, *Vom Ursprung sittlicher Erkenntnis* (Leipzig, 1921), p. 18 *sqq.*
[69] Heymans, *op. cit.*, p. 203.
[70] *Cf. infra*, p. 263.   [71] Höffding, *op. cit.*, p. 68.

CHAPTER III

THE MORAL EMOTIONS

THE contention that all moral concepts, which are used as predicates in moral judgments, are ultimately based on emotions, is of course a claim that has to be substantiated. First, what is the nature of those emotions?

Professor McDougall, though agreeing with me that original moral judgments proceed directly from emotions, denies that there are any specific emotions from which they spring. "Judgment of approval," he says, "may be prompted by admiration, gratitude, positive self-feeling, or by any one of the emotions when induced by way of the primitive sympathetic reaction; judgment of disapproval springs most frequently from anger, either in its primary uncomplicated form, or as an element in one of its secondary combinations, such as shame, reproach, scorn, but also from fear and disgust." [1] But the question to be answered is not what emotions may prompt people to pronounce moral judgments—there are certainly many different emotions that may do that—but whether there are any specific emotions that have led to the formation of the concepts of right and wrong, good and bad, and all other moral concepts, and therefore may be appropriately named moral emotions. I maintain that there are two such emotions, both complex by nature, for which I have used the traditional terms moral approval and moral

[1] W. McDougall, *An Introduction to Social Psychology* (London, 1926), p. 187 *sq. Cf.* J. Laird, *The Idea of Value* (Cambridge, 1929), p. 238.

disapproval or indignation. They have, of course, in common certain characteristics that make them moral emotions in distinction from other emotions of a non-moral character, but at the same time both of them belong to a wider class of emotions, which I have called retributive emotions. Again, they differ from each other in points that make each of them allied to certain non-moral retributive emotions, disapproval to anger and revenge, and approval to what I have called non-moral retributive kindly emotion, which in its most developed form is gratitude. They may thus, on the one hand, be regarded as two distinct divisions of the moral emotions, whilst, on the other hand, moral disapproval, like anger and revenge, forms a subspecies of resentment, and approval, like gratitude, forms a subspecies of retributive kindly emotion.

Professor McDougall has criticized this scheme both in point of terminology and classification. He has raised the objection that approval and disapproval are not emotions but judgments, and that to describe them as emotions is to perpetuate the chaos of psychological terminology.[2] My reply to this objection is that moral approval or approbation and moral disapproval or disapprobation have been used as terms for emotions by moralists and psychologists at least from the eighteenth century and continue to be so used, even after and in spite of Professor McDougall's criticism;[3] that their application both to judgments and emotions is parallel to the varied meanings given to many other terms—he speaks himself of revenge as an emotion, although it also means an act; and that he has escaped the necessity of finding another name for moral approval only by ignoring the emotion itself. He further

---

[2] McDougall, *op. cit.*, p. 124.

[3] *E.g.*, by L. T. Hobhouse, *The Rational Good* (London, 1921), p. 74 n.; R. H. Thouless, *Social Psychology* (London, 1925), p. 252.

reproaches me for co-ordinating anger—including, of course, disinterested anger, which he seems to identify with moral indignation—and revenge as subspecies of resentment, which he describes as "the fusion of anger and positive self-feeling immediately evoked by an act of aggression." [4] But here again, in my use of the term resentment, I may appeal to the traditional meaning of the term, for which I may refer, *e.g.*, to Shaftesbury,[5] Butler,[6] Bain,[7] and the *Oxford Dictionary;* and I doubt whether it helps to bring order into the chaos of psychological terminology to invent a new meaning for it.

Professor McDougall also says that I have failed to see the difference between anger and revenge. I have written:—"Resentment may be described as an aggressive attitude of mind towards a cause of pain. Anger is sudden resentment, in which the hostile reaction against the cause of pain is unrestrained by deliberation. Revenge, on the other hand, is a more deliberate form of non-moral resentment, in which the hostile reaction is more or less restrained by reason and calculation." [8] My view that the emotion of revenge is, generally speaking, more deliberate than ordinary anger is, I believe, in agreement with the common use of the terms;[9] but I have added that it is impossible to draw any distinct limit between these two types of resentment. Professor McDougall's criticism is provoked by the fact that, in his view, anger is a "pri-

---

[4] McDougall, *op. cit.,* p. 123. See also *ibid.,* p. 120.
[5] Shaftesbury, *Characteristicks,* ii. (London, 1733), 144 *sqq.,* 420.
[6] J. Butler, *Sermon VIII.—Upon Resentment.*
[7] A. Bain, *The Emotions and the Will* (London, 1880), pp. 181, 182, 291.
[8] *The Origin and Development of the Moral Ideas,* i. (London, 1906), p. 22.
[9] See, *e.g.,* Shaftesbury, *op. cit.,* ii. 145; Butler, *Sermon VIII.— Upon Resentment;* Bain, *op. cit.,* p. 181 *sq.;* Th. Ribot, *The Psychology of the Emotions* (London, 1897), p. 222; A. F. Shand, *The Foundations of Character* (London, 1920), p. 229.

mary" emotion, whereas revenge is a "binary compound of anger and positive self-feeling." [10] He says I maintain "against Steinmetz that self-feeling is not an essential element in vengeful emotion"; [11] but this brief statement is a very defective summary of the views expressed by me.

According to Steinmetz, revenge is essentially rooted in the feeling of power and superiority. It arises consequent on the experience of injury, and its aim is to enhance the self-feeling, which has been lowered or degraded by the injury suffered. It answers this purpose best if it is directed against the aggressor himself, but it is not essential to it that it should take any determinate direction: *per se* and originally it is "undirected." [12] In examining in detail all the facts adduced by Dr. Steinmetz as evidence for his hypothesis of an original stage of undirected revenge I found that they were no evidence at all. They only show that in certain circumstances, either in a fit of passion or when the actual offender is unknown or out of reach, some innocent person, who is in no way connected with the inflictor of the injury, may become an object of retaliation. There is such an intimate connection between the suffering of an injury and the hostile reaction by which the injured individual gives vent to his passion, that the reaction does not fail to appear even when it misses its aim. In the institution of the blood-feud some sort of collective responsibility is usually involved, but here the guilt extends itself, as it were, in the eyes of the offended party to the kinsmen of the man-slayer; and besides, the strong tendency to discrimination that characterizes resentment is not wholly lost even behind the veil of common responsibility. We are often

10 McDougall, *op. cit.*, p. 122 *sq.*
11 *Ibid.*, p. 122.
12 S. R. Steinmetz, *Ethnologische Studien zur ersten Entwicklung der Strafe* (Leiden & Leipzig, 1894), *passim.*

told that the blood-feud is in the first place directed against the malefactor, and against some relative of his only if he cannot be found; this is stated even of so low savages as Australian natives.[18] After this criticism I made some remarks, unnoticed by Professor McDougall, which bring my view of revenge much nearer to his than his readers are made to believe. I wrote:[14]

"I certainly do not mean to deny that violation of the 'self-feeling' is an extremely common and powerful incentive to resentment. It is so among savage and civilized men alike; even dogs and monkeys get angry when laughed at. Nothing more easily arouses in us anger and a desire for retaliation, nothing is more difficult to forgive, than an act which indicates contempt, or disregard of our feelings. Long after the bodily pain of a blow has ceased, the mental suffering caused by the insult remains and calls for vengeance. This is an old truth often told. According to Seneca, 'the greater part of the things which enrage us are insults, not injuries.' Plutarch observes that, though different persons fall into anger for different reasons, yet in nearly all of them is to be found the idea of their being despised or neglected. 'Contempt,' says Bacon, 'is that which putteth an edge upon anger, as much, or more, than the hurt itself.' But . . . in all cases revenge implies, primordially and essentially, a desire to cause pain or destruction in return for hurt suffered, whether the hurt be bodily or mental; and if to this impulse is added a desire to enhance the wounded 'self-feeling,' that does not interfere with the true nature of the primary feeling of revenge. There are genuine specimens of resentment without the co-operation of self-regarding pride; and, on the other hand, the reaction of the wounded 'self-feeling' is not necessarily, in the first place, concerned with the

18 *Moral Ideas,* i. 35 *sq.*   14 *Ibid.,* i. 38 *sqq.*

infliction of pain. If a person has written a bad book which is severely criticized, he may desire to repair his reputation by writing a better book, not by humiliating his critics; and if he attempts the latter rather than the former, he does so not merely in order to enhance his 'self-feeling,' but because he is driven on by revenge." [15]

If I, instead of saying that violation of the self-feeling is an extremely common incentive to resentment (by which I did not mean merely revenge), had said that it is a regular incentive to revenge, which I have not denied and which is most probably true, there would, so far as I can see, be no real disagreement between Professor McDougall and myself as to the nature of revenge. He says himself that his account of revenge is nearer to that of Steinmetz than to mine; but I doubt the accuracy of this statement, as he recognizes anger as one element in revenge and regards anger not as undirected, but as essentially directed against the object or person provoking it.[16] Both of us agree that a violent assertion of one's power is not an adequate characteristic of the act in which revenge

[15] It must be due to careless reading of this sentence that Prof. McDougall (*op. cit.*, p. 122 *sq.*) makes the following confused remark:—"Westermarck seeks to support his view (I suppose the view that 'self-feeling is not an essential element in vengeful emotion') by saying that, if one has written a book and it has been adversely criticized, though our self-feeling receives a painful check we do not seek vengeance on the critic but rather set out to write a better book. Now, it is dangerous to trust to the consideration of the emotions of the most cultivated and intellectual class of men in seeking light on the origin of the emotions, but I think that most authors would avenge themselves on the unjust and damaging critic, if they could find an easy opportunity; and our literary disputes frequently are but the most refined expression of this emotion." Surely Prof. McDougall could no more than myself consider the writing of a better book to be an act of revenge if no anger be connected with it, since he regards anger as an essential element in revenge.

[16] McDougall, *op. cit.*, p. 51. *Idem, An Outline of Psychology* (London, 1926), p. 321: "When we are angry, we feel the impulse to attack the object that angers us."

seeks its satisfaction. And I find no reason to dispute Professor McDougall's view that revenge is a "fusion of anger and positive self-feeling . . . developed within the system of the self-regarding sentiment—to which circumstance it owes its persistent character—with the addition of painful feeling arising from the continued thwarting of the two impulses." [17] But I maintain that thwarting of the self-feeling is also a very frequent, though of course not a necessary, incentive to anger, and cannot, therefore, be regarded as a characteristic by which revenge is distinguished from anger. As Dr. Shand observes, anger "may be aroused by the sharp and sudden pain of a blow, or by being insulted, scorned, mocked at, or even neglected." [18] Indeed, Professor McDougall seems himself to have been unable to uphold his distinction between anger and revenge. He says, "If a man strikes me a sudden and unprovoked blow, . . . the impulse, the thwarting of which in this case provokes my anger, is the impulse of self-assertion." [19]

In classifying certain emotions under the common heading "resentment" I have done so because they may all be described as a hostile attitude of mind towards a living being, or something taken for a living being, as a cause of pain, whatever the circumstances may be that have aroused it in each particular case. This common characteristic seems to me a most legitimate ground of classification on account of the uniformity of its function and its extreme importance in the life of the species. Resentment, like protective reflex action, from which it has gradually developed, is a means of protection for the animal owing to its tendency to remove a cause of danger.

[17] *Idem, An Introduction to Social Psychology,* p. 123.
[18] Shand, *op. cit.,* p. 227. *Cf.* Bain, *op. cit.,* p. 177.
[19] McDougall, *An Introduction to Social Psychology,* p. 51 n.1.

The disposition to experience it may consequently be regarded as an element in the animal's mental constitution which has been acquired through the influence of natural selection in the struggle for existence. In comparison with these facts it is a matter of minor importance whether the hostile reaction is connected with a thwarting of the self-feeling or not. Indeed, as this may be the case not only in revenge but also in anger, it is, for this reason also, impossible to draw any distinct limit between these two types of resentment. Nor is it possible to discern where an actual desire to inflict pain comes in. We may assume that in its primitive form anger, even when directed against a living being, could not have been connected with a representation of the enemy as suffering. But as a successful attack is necessarily accompanied with such suffering, the desire to produce it naturally became, with the increase of intelligence, an important factor in resentment. And when pain was distinguished as a normal effect of resentment, the infliction of it could also be aimed at as an end in itself. Resentment is particularly apt to assume this character under the influence of the self-feeling of the injured party, as a means of humiliating the offender.[20]

That moral disapproval is closely connected with non-moral resentment is indicated by language: we may feel indignant on other than moral grounds, and we may feel "righteous anger." The relationship between these emotions is also conspicuous in their outward expressions, which, when the emotion is strong enough, present similar characteristics. When possessed with deep moral indignation, a person looks as if he were angry, and so he really is, in the wider sense of the term. This relationship has been ignored by those who have described moral approval and disapproval merely as feelings of pleasure or pain.

[20] *Cf.* Ribot, *op. cit.,* p. 221; Shand, *op. cit.,* p. 243 *sq.*

Yet it was recognized already some two thousand years ago in a remarkable passage of the Greek historian Polybius, who wrote :—"If a man has been rescued or helped in an hour of danger, and, instead of showing gratitude to his preserver, seeks to do him harm, it is clearly probable that the rest will be displeased and offended with him when they know it, sympathizing with their neighbour and imagining themselves in his case. Hence arises a notion in every breast of the meaning and theory of duty, which is in fact the beginning and end of justice." [21] Hartley regarded resentment and gratitude as "intimately connected with the moral sense"; [22] and Adam Smith made the resentment and gratitude of the "impartial spectator" a corner stone of his theory of the moral sentiments. The elaborate and acute arguments with which he supported his moral theory could not fail to exercise some influence on subsequent moral philosophy, but though his book on the subject rapidly won popularity when it first appeared, it was afterwards largely forgotten, save by historians of philosophy, whose remarks on it, in England, were generally frigid and sometimes almost contemptuous. [23]

[21] Polybius, *Historiæ*, vi. 6.

[22] D. Hartley, *Observations on Man*, i. (London, 1810), p. 520.

[23] Leslie Stephen writes (*History of English Thought in the Eighteenth Century*, ii. [London, 1927], p. 77) :—"It is impossible to resist the impression . . . that we are not listening to a thinker really grappling with a difficult problem, so much as to an ambitious professor who has found an excellent opportunity for displaying his command of language, and making brilliant lectures. . . . Smith's main proposition was hardly original." In the historical survey of moral theories in J. M. Wilson's and T. Fowler's *Principles of Morals* (Oxford, 1886), it is said to be unnecessary to speak of his ethical philosophy at any length (*Introductory Chapters*, p. 61). Dr. J. Bonar (*Moral Sense* [London, 1930], p. 168) asserts that it has needed all the fame of Adam Smith's second book, *The Wealth of Nations*, "to keep alive the memory of his first, which founded no school, and is usually passed over with the faint praise due to the author's reputation." In striking contrast with this is the regard which German historians of philosophy have shown for Adam

For my own part I maintain that Adam Smith's *Theory of Moral Sentiments* is the most important contribution to moral psychology made by any British thinker, and that it is so in the first place on account of the emphasis it lays on the retributive character of the moral emotions.

As there are varieties of non-moral resentment so there are also varieties of moral disapproval. Under the influence of the altruistic sentiment its aggressiveness has been subject to modifications. At its earlier stages the desire to cause suffering or destruction to the offender is a very marked characteristic of it. To take revenge on an enemy is regarded as a duty, or, in other words, the omission to do so calls forth moral disapproval. This is the case not only in the savage world. In the Old Testament the spirit of vindictiveness pervades both the men and their God; it is the duty of a man to avenge the murder of his relative,[24] and the enemies of Yahveh can expect no mercy from him, but utter destruction is their lot. To do good to a friend and to do harm to an enemy was a maxim of the ancient Scandinavians.[25] It was taken as a matter of course by popular opinion in Greece [26] and Rome. According to Aristotle, "it belongs to the courageous man never to be worsted"; to take revenge on a foe rather than to be reconciled is just, and therefore honourable.[27] Cicero defines a good man as a person "who serves whom he can, and injures none save when provoked by injury." [28]

Smith's book on the *Moral Sentiments*. A new German edition of it appeared only a few years ago.

[24] *Numbers*, xxxv. 19.

[25] K. Maurer, *Die Bekehrung des Norwegischen Stammes zum Christenthume*, ii. (München, 1856), p. 154 *sq.*

[26] L. Schmidt, *Die Ethik der alten Griechen*, ii. (Berlin, 1882), p. 309 *sqq.*

[27] Aristotle, *Rhetorica*, i. 9. 24. *Cf.* Aeschylus, *Choeophori*, 309 *sqq.*; Plato, *Meno*, p. 71; Xenophon, *Memorabilia*, ii. 6. 35.

[28] Cicero, *De Officiis*, iii. 19. *Cf. ibid.*, ii. 14.

That revenge is considered a duty implies, of course, that the person on whom it is incumbent is an object of moral blame if he does not perform that duty; but behind this censure there is obviously a desire to see the injurer suffer. Yet the moral disapproval may in these cases differ from the revenge of the offended party as to the intensity of suffering required by it. Sometimes his feeling of revenge may seem to outsiders to be too weak or too much checked by other impulses, but in other cases it appears unduly great. In early society we often find that the practice of revenge is regulated by a rule that requires equivalence between the injury and the suffering inflicted in return for it. Sometimes this rule demands that only one life shall be taken for one, sometimes that a man-slayer shall die in the same manner as his victim, sometimes that other injuries also shall be retaliated by the infliction of similar injuries on the offenders.[29] This strict equivalence is not characteristic of resentment as such. There is undoubtedly a certain proportion between the injury inflicted and the resentful reaction; other things being equal, the resentment increases in intensity along with the pain arousing it. The more a person feels offended, the greater is his desire to retaliate by inflicting counter-pain, and the greater is the pain he desires to inflict. Moreover, the desire to pull down the humiliating arrogance of the aggressor is naturally influenced by the idea of paying him back in his own coin; and it is probable that the disposition to imitate, especially in cases of sudden anger, acts in the same direction. But resentment involves no accurate balancing of suffering against suffering, hence there may be a crying disproportion between the act of revenge and the injury that provoked it.[30] As Sir Thomas Browne observes, a revengeful mind "holds no

[29] *Moral Ideas,* i. 178.　　　　[30] *Ibid.,* i. 178.

rule in retaliation, requiring too often a head for a tooth, and the supreme revenge for trespasses, which a night's rest should obliterate." [31] The *lex talionis*, which requires equivalence between suffering and suffering, has undoubtedly a social origin. If the offender is a person with whose feelings men are ready to sympathize, their sympathy will keep the desire to see him suffer within certain limits; and if, in ordinary circumstances, they tend to sympathize equally with both parties, the injurer and the person injured, and in consequence confer upon these equal rights, they will demand a retaliation that is only equal in degree to the offence. If this explanation is correct, the rule of equivalence must originally have been restricted to offences within the social group; for according to early custom and law only members of the same society have equal rights. In speaking of the tit-for-tat system prevalent among the Guiana Indians, Sir E. F. Im Thurn expressly says, "Of course all this refers chiefly to the mutual relations of members of the same tribe." [32] And when we find savages acting according to the same principle in their relations to other tribes, the reason for this may be sought partly in the strong hold which that principle has taken of their minds, and partly in the dangers accompanying intertribal revenge, which make it desirable to restrict it within reasonable limits. The desire that the offender shall suffer and the desire that his suffering shall correspond to his guilt have also contributed to the substitution of punishment for revenge and to the rise of a judicial organization. For as long as retaliation is in the hands of private individuals, there is no guarantee, on the one hand, that the offender will have to suffer, on the other

[31] T. Browne, *Christian Morals* (Cambridge, 1716), iii. 12, p. 94.
[32] E. F. Im Thurn, *Among the Indians of Guiana* (London, 1883), p. 214.

hand, that the act of retaliation will be sufficiently discriminating.[33]

The more the moral consciousness is influenced by the altruistic sentiment, the more severely it condemns any retributive infliction of pain that it regards as undeserved; and it seems to be in the first place with a view to preventing such injustice that teachers of morality have enjoined upon men to forgive their enemies. Side by side with the doctrine of resentment we find among peoples of culture the doctrine of forgiveness. In Leviticus there is the rule, "Thou shalt not avenge, nor bear any grudge against the children of thy people." [34] Sirach, who counts among the nine causes of a man's happiness to see the fall of his enemy, says in another passage, "Forgive thy neighbour the hurt that he has done unto thee, so shall thy sins also be forgiven when thou prayest." [35] According to the Talmud he who does not persecute those who persecute him, and he who takes an offence in silence, are the friends of God.[36] The Koran, while repeating the old rule, "An eye for an eye and a tooth for a tooth," at the same time teaches that paradise is "for those who repress their rage, and those who pardon men"; [37] and according to Mohammedan tradition the Prophet laid down the rule, "Resolve that if people do good to you, you will do good to them, and if they oppress you, oppress them not again." [38] The principle of forgiveness had also

[33] *Moral Ideas,* i. 180 *sqq.*
[34] *Leviticus,* xix. 18.
[35] *Ecclesiasticus,* xxv. 7; xxviii. 2.
[36] E. Deutsch, *Literary Remains* (London, 1874), p. 58.
[37] *Koran,* ii. 190; iii. 125.
[38] S. Lane-Poole, *The Speeches and Table-Talk of the Prophet Mohammad* (London, 1882), p. 147. In Moorish proverbs we also find the doctrine of forgiveness side by side with that of resentment (E. Westermarck, *Wit and Wisdom in Morocco* [London, 1930], p. 50 *sq.*).

advocates in Greece and Rome. In one of the Platonic
dialogues Socrates says, "We ought not to retaliate or
render evil for evil to any one, whatever evil we may have
suffered from him"; though he adds that "this opinion
has never been held, and never will be held, by any considerable number of persons." [39] The Stoics condemned
anger as unnatural and unreasonable. According to Seneca, "it is the part of a great mind to despise wrongs done
to it"; but he also shrewdly remarks that "the most contemptuous form of revenge is not to deem one's adversary
worth taking vengeance upon." [40] The Chinese philosopher
Lao-Tsze said, "Recompense injury with kindness." [41] In
the Laws of Manu, the mythical Hindu legislator, the
rule is laid down that a twice-born man should not show
anger against one who is angry, but bless any one who
curses him. [42] In the Buddhist Dhammapada it is said,
"Let a man overcome anger by love; let him overcome
evil by good; let him overcome the greedy by liberality,
the liar by truth." [43] Forgiveness of enemies is thus by
no means an exclusively Christian tenet.

The rule of retaliation and the rule of forgiveness are
not so radically opposed to each other as they may appear
to be. What the latter condemns is really not every kind
of resentment, but non-moral resentment, not impartial
indignation but personal hatred. It prohibits revenge but
not punishment. According to the Laws of Manu crime
was so indispensably to be followed by punishment, that

[39] Plato, *Crito*, p. 49.
[40] Seneca, *De ira*, ii. 32.
[41] *Tâo Teh King*, ii. 63. 1 (in *The Sacred Books of the East*,
xxxix. [Oxford, 1891]).
[42] *The Laws of Manu*, vi. 48 (in *The Sacred Books of the East*,
xxv. [Oxford, 1886]).
[43] *Dhammapada*, xvii. 223 (in *The Sacred Books of the East*, x.
[Oxford, 1898]). For other instances of the doctrine of forgiveness
see *Moral Ideas*, i. 74 *sqq.*

if the king pardoned a thief or a perpetrator of violence, instead of slaying or striking him, the guilt fell on the king.[44] Jesus was certainly not free from righteous indignation. It does not appear that he ever forgave the legalists who sinned against the kingdom of God, and he told his disciples that if a brother who had trespassed against his brother neglected to hear the church, he should be looked upon as a heathen and a publican.[45] Christian writers have laid much stress upon the circumstance that Jesus enjoined men to forgive their own enemies, but not to abstain from resenting injuries done to others. According to Thomas Aquinas, "the good bear with the wicked to this extent, that, so far as it is proper to do so, they patiently endure at their hands the injuries done to themselves; but they do not bear with them to the extent of enduring the injuries done to God and their neighbours." [46] Yet it would be absurd to blame a person for expressing moral indignation at an act simply because he himself happens to be the offended party; practically we allow him to be even more indignant than the impartial spectator would be, whereas excessive placability often meets with censure. We agree with Aristotle that anger admits not only of an excess but of a defect,[47] and that "to submit to insult, or to overlook an insult offered to our friends, shows a slavish spirit." [48]

The aggressive character of moral disapproval has become modified not only by a more scrutinizing attitude towards resentment and retaliation, but also by a condemnation of causing suffering merely for the sake of retribution. For ages it was looked upon as a matter of

[44] *The Laws of Manu,* viii. 316, 346 *sq.*
[45] *St. Matthew,* xviii. 15 *sqq.*
[46] Thomas Aquinas, *Summa Theologica,* ii.-ii. 108. 1. 2.
[47] Aristotle, *Ethica Nicomachea,* ii. 7. 10; iii. 1. 24; iv. 5. 3 *sqq.*
[48] *Ibid.,* iv. 5. 6.

course that if a person had committed a crime he should have to suffer for it. This is still the notion of the multitude, as also of a host of theorizers, who by calling punishment an expiation, or a reparation, or a restoration of the disturbed equilibrium of justice, or some similar term, only endeavour to give a philosophical sanction to a social institution rooted in an emotion. The infliction of pain, however, is not an act which the moral consciousness regards with indifference even in the case of a criminal; and to many enlightened minds with keen sympathy for human suffering it has appeared both unreasonable and cruel that the State should wilfully torment him to no purpose. Retributive punishment is condemned; but punishment itself is defended. It is only looked upon in a different light, not as an end in itself, but as a means of attaining an end. It is to be inflicted not because wrong has been done, but in order that wrong be not done. Its object is held to be either to deter from crime, or to reform the criminal, or by means of elimination or seclusion to make it physically impossible for him to commit fresh crimes. These views were expressed already in Greek and Roman antiquity. In a later age the view taken by Hobbes, that "the aym of Punishment is not a revenge, but terrour," [49] remained for a long time the leading doctrine on the subject among philosophers as well as legislators. During the nineteenth century the principle of determent was largely superseded by the principle of reformation; and a new school of criminologists advocated the opinion that punishment should aim at repressing crime by an "absolute" or "relative" elimination of the criminal, that is, in extreme cases by killing him, but generally by incarcerating him in a criminal lunatic asylum, or by banishing him for ever or for a certain period,

[49] T. Hobbes, *Leviathan,* ii. 28 (Oxford, 1881), p. 243.

or by interdicting him from a particular neighbourhood.

For my own part I maintain that those theorists who think it possible to make punishment independent of moral resentment are victims of an illusion.[50] Let us consider some consequences to which the principles of determent and reformation might lead if each of them were carried out consistently. The principle of elimination may at once be put aside, because it has no reference to the *punishment* of criminals, although it contains a suggestion—and a most excellent one—as to the proper mode of treating them. Their exclusion from the company of their fellow-men—not to speak of their elimination by death—certainly entails suffering, but according to the principle in question this suffering is not directly *intended*. On the other hand, punishment, in the ordinary sense of the word, always involves an express intention to inflict pain, whatever be the object in inflicting it. We do not punish an ill-natured dog when we tie him up in order to prevent him from doing harm, nor do we punish a lunatic by confining him in a madhouse.

According to the principle of determent the infliction of suffering in consequence of an offence is justified only as a means of increasing public safety: the offender is sacrificed for the common weal. But why should the punishment necessarily be restricted to the offender? It might be a more effective way of deterring from crime to punish his children as well or, if he cannot be caught, to punish them only; and if the notions of desert and justice derived all their import from the socially useful result achieved by the punishment, there would be nothing unjust in doing

[50] The arguments adduced by Dr. Ewing in his recent book, *The Morality of Punishment* (London, 1929), coincide in many respects with mine, which I have previously stated in my *Moral Ideas*, vol. ii. p. 82 *sqq.*

so. The only objection which from this point of view could ever be raised against the practice of visiting the wrongdoings of the fathers upon the children, is that it is needlessly severe; the innocence of the children could count for nothing. Professor Carveth Read has argued against me that we are then "supposed to entirely disregard the feelings, or the rights, of the innocent." [51] But why should we have to regard their feelings more than those of the offender, if the infliction of suffering in both cases serves the same useful end, the deterring from crime? Moreover, if the object of punishment is merely preventive, the heaviest punishment should be threatened where the strongest motive is needed to restrain, and an injury committed under great temptation, or in a passion, should consequently be punished with particular severity. To this Professor Read remarks that "great temptation and passion exclude the consideration of other motives; so that threats are useless." [52] But if they are useless, why should there in such cases be any punishment at all?

Again, if punishment were to be regulated by the principle of reforming the criminal, the result would in some cases be very astonishing. There is no set of offenders more difficult to reform than habitual vagrants and drunkards, whereas experience has shown that the most easily reformed of all offenders is often some person who has committed a serious crime. If reformation is the only end of punishment, the latter should soon be set free, while the petty offender might have to be shut up for all his life. Nay more, if the criminal proves absolutely incorrigible and not the slightest hope of his reformation is left, there would no longer be any reason for punishing

[51] Carveth Read, *Natural and Social Morals* (London, 1909), p. 200.
[52] *Ibid.*, p. 201.

him at all.[53] Professor Read makes the remark, "As if determent and repression should count for nothing";[54] but I am here speaking of the principle of reformation alone, not of a combination of different principles. The reformationist may also be asked why he does not try some more humane method of improving people's characters than the infliction of suffering.

It may seem strange that theories which are open to such objections should have been able to attract so many intelligent partisans. These theories must at least possess a certain plausibility. If punishment on the one hand springs from moral indignation and on the other hand is frequently interpreted as a means either of deterring from crime or of reforming the criminal, there must obviously be some connection between these ends and the retributive aim of moral resentment. There must be certain facts that to some extent lessen the gap between the theory of retribution and the other theories of punishment.

The doctrine of determent regards punishment as a means of preventing crime. A crime implies that a person's behaviour is a cause of pain. The one thing which men try to prevent for its own sake is pain, and the one thing which causes resentment is likewise pain. There must consequently be a general coincidence between the courses of behaviour that people resent and those which the law would punish if it were framed on the principle of determent. But the resemblance between the desire to deter and resentment is greater still. Resentment is not only aroused by pain, but is a hostile attitude towards its cause, and its tendency is to remove this cause, that

[53] Cf. W. D. Morrison, *Crime and its Causes* (London, 1891), p. 203; E. Durkheim, *De la division du travail social* (Paris, 1893), p. 94.
[54] Read, *op. cit.*, p. 201.

is, to prevent pain. An act of moral resentment is therefore apt to resemble a punishment inflicted with a view to deterring from crime, provided that the punishment is directed against the cause of crime—the criminal himself—and its severity is proportioned to his guilt.

The doctrine of reformation aims at the removal of a criminal disposition of mind by improving the offender. Moral resentment likewise aims at the removal of a volitional cause of pain, by bringing about repentance in the offender. That repentance ought to be followed by forgiveness, partial or total, is a widely recognized moral claim. But it does not only blunt the edge of moral indignation and recommend the offender to the mercy of men and gods: it is the sole ground on which pardon can be given by a scrupulous judge. When sufficiently guided by deliberation and left to itself, without being unduly checked by other feelings, moral resentment is apt to be felt as long as its cause remains unaltered, that is, until the will of the offender has ceased to be offensive; and it ceases to be offensive only when he acknowledges his guilt and repents. He who commanded his followers to forgive a brother for his trespass at the same time pronounced the qualification: "If he repent." [55] It is worth noticing that when moral indignation is appeased by repentance, and repentance alone, it is so, not on account of its specifically moral character, but because it is a form of resentment. The angry or revengeful man is also apt to be in a similar way influenced by the sincere apologies of the offender. As Aristotle said, men are placable in regard to those who acknowledge and repent their guilt: "there is proof of this in the case of chastising servants; for we chastize more violently those who contradict us,

[55] St. Luke, xvii. 3 sq.

and deny their guilt; but towards such as acknowledge themselves to be justly punished we cease from our wrath." [56] No doubt, in the case of revenge external satisfaction or material compensation is often allowed to take the place of genuine repentance, and the humiliation of the adversary may be sufficient to quiet the angry passion. But the revenge felt by a reflecting mind is not so readily satisfied: it wants effectively to remove the cause that aroused it. The object which resentment is chiefly intent upon, Adam Smith observes, "is not so much to make our enemy feel pain in his turn, as to make him conscious that he feels it upon account of his past conduct, to make him repent of that conduct, and to make him sensible, that the person whom he injured did not deserve to be treated in that manner." [57] The delight of revenge, says Bacon, "seemeth to be not so much in doing the hurt, as in making the party repent." [58]

We can now see the origin of the notion that the end of punishment should be the reformation of the criminal. This principle emphasizes the most humane element in resentment, the demand that the offender's will shall cease to be offensive; hence the doctrine of reformation has itself a retributive origin. This explains the fact, otherwise inexplicable, that the amendment which it has in view is to be effected by the infliction of pain. It also accounts for the inconsistent attitude of the reformationist towards incorrigible offenders. Resentment gives way to forgiveness only in the case of repentance, not in the case of incorrigibility. Hence if the reformationist does not regard incorrigibility as a legitimate ground for exempting a person from punishment, he has to admit that

[56] Aristotle, *Rhetorica,* ii. 3. 5.
[57] Adam Smith, *op. cit.,* p. 138 *sq.*
[58] Bacon, "Essay IV. Of Revenge," in *Essays* (London, 1864), p. 59.

punishment is justified also on some other ground than the reformation of the criminal.

Thus the theories both of determent and of reformation are ultimately offspring of the same emotion that first induced men to inflict punishment on their fellow-creatures. It escaped the advocates of these theories that they themselves were under the influence of the very principle they fought against, because they failed to grasp its true import. Rightly understood, resentment is preventive in its nature, and when sufficiently deliberate, regards the infliction of suffering as a means rather than as an end. It not only gives rise to punishment, but readily suggests as its proper end either determent or amendment or both. But first of all, moral resentment raises a protest against wrong. And whatever theorists may say on the matter, its immediate aim has always been to give expression to the righteous indignation of the society which inflicts it.

Now it may be thought that men have no right to give vent to their moral resentment in a way which hurts their neighbours unless some benefit may be expected from it. In the case of many other emotions we hold that the conative element in the emotion ought not to be allowed to develop into a distinct volition or act; and it would seem that a similar view might be taken with reference to the aggressiveness of moral disapproval. It is a notion of this kind that is at the bottom of the utilitarian theories of punishment. They are protests against purposeless infliction of suffering, against crude ideas of retributive justice, against theories hardly in advance of the feelings of the popular mir . if they are open to objections which seem incontestable, that is certainly due to other circumstances than their demand that punishment shall serve a useful end. Punishment must be kept within the limits recognized as legitimate by the moral consciousness, and, as I have tried to show, the consequences to which the purely utilitarian theories might lead transgress these limits. On the other hand, it may be said that while those theories seem to exaggerate the deterring or reforming influence which punishment exercises upon criminals, they in other respects take too narrow a view of its social usefulness. Whether its voice inspire fear or not, whether it awaken a sleeping conscience or not, punishment at all events tells people in plain terms what, in the opinion of the society, they must not do. It gives the multitude a severe lesson in public morality; and it is difficult to see how quite the same effect could be attained by any other method. Retaliation is such a spontaneous expression of indignation that people would hardly realize the offensiveness of an act that evoked no signs of resentment. Of course, punishment in the legal sense of the term is only one form—the most concrete form—of public retaliation; it is, indeed, probable that public opinion exercises a greater influence than punishment would do without its aid.[59] But punishment in combination with public opinion has no doubt in some measure an educating, and not merely a deterring, influence on the members of a society. As Sir James Stephen observes, "the sentence of the law is to the moral sentiment of the public in relation to any offence what a seal is to hot wax. It converts into a permanent final judgment what might otherwise be a transient sentiment."[60] Moreover, it must not be overlooked that the infliction of punishment upon the perpetrator of a grave offence gratifies a strong general desire, and even if the dissatisfaction that accompanies

[59] Cf. J. Locke, *An Essay concerning Human Understanding*, ii. 28. 12 (vol. i. [Oxford, 1894], p. 479 *sq.*) ; Shaftesbury, *op. cit.*, ii. 64.

[60] J. F. Stephen, *A History of the Criminal Law of England*, ii. (London, 1883), p. 81.

an ungratified desire does not by itself afford a sufficient justification for subjecting the offender to suffering, other more serious consequences would undoubtedly in many cases result from leaving him unpunished. Public indignation might find a vent in some less regular and less discriminating mode of retaliation, like lynching; or private retaliation would take the place of punishment.

A modification of the aggressive element in moral disapproval is, finally, apparent in the attempt to narrow the channel of its activity by the rule that we should hate not the sinner but only the sin. This may be a beautiful maxim, but can it be realized? To hate a certain act implies hatred of its volitional element, the intention of him who performs the act; but to separate a volition from the will that wills it is of course impossible. Hence the hostile reaction against the sin must turn against the sinner. We have seen that while deliberate and discriminating resentment aims at influencing the offender's will, its immediate desire is nevertheless to inflict suffering; and it may be questioned whether the hatred of the sin without any such desire would be anything more than a strong dislike similar to that which we feel for a nasty animal or a heap of dirt. It is the instinctive desire to inflict counter-pain—not necessarily physical—that gives to moral indignation its most important characteristic. Without it, moral condemnation and the ideas of right and wrong would never have come into existence. Without it, we should no more condemn a bad man than a poisonous plant. The reason why moral judgments are passed on volitional beings, or their behaviour, is not merely that they are volitional, but that they are sensitive as well; and however much we try to concentrate our indignation on the act, it derives its distinctive character from being directed against a sensitive agent. I have heard persons assert that a wrong act awakens in them only sorrow or compassion; but then I strongly suspect that they do not understand their own minds. I do not think there is any man who does not in some measure resent a gross injury of which he himself is the victim; and I refuse to believe that there is any one who is so utterly incapable of feeling sympathetic resentment on behalf of an injured fellow-creature, that he, even in a case of the greatest atrocity, could be merely sorry for the offender. And in any case, could even the most ardent anti-retributionist imagine that he, quite apart from any utilitarian considerations, would feel the same sympathy with a person who suffers on account of some wrong he has committed, as with one who suffers innocently? It is one of the most interesting facts relating to the moral consciousness of the most humane type, that it in vain condemns the gratification of the very desire from which it sprang. It reminds one of a man of low extraction who, in spite of all acquired refinement, still bears his origin stamped on his face.

While resentment is a hostile attitude of mind towards a living being (or something taken for a living being) as a cause of pain, retributive kindly emotion is a friendly attitude of mind towards such a being as a cause of pleasure. Just as in the lower forms of anger there can be no definite desire to produce suffering, so in the lower forms of retributive kindliness there can be no definite desire to produce pleasure. When an emotion of a non-moral kind contains such a desire to give pleasure in return for pleasure received, it is called gratitude. Intermingled with gratitude there is often a feeling of indebtedness: he upon whom a benefit has been conferred feels himself a debtor and regards the benefactor in a way as his creditor. This feeling has even been represented as essential to, or as a condition of, gratitude;[61] but it is one thing to be grateful and another thing to feel that it is one's duty to requite a benefit. A depression of the self-feeling, a feeling of humiliation, also frequently accompanies gratitude as a motive for such a requital; but I cannot consider it a necessary element in gratitude itself.[62] We may be grateful without experiencing such a feeling,[63] and we may be anxious to repay a benefit without feeling gratitude.

Retributive kindly emotion is of much less frequent occurrence in the animal kingdom than the emotion of resentment. In a large number of species not even the germ of it is found, and where it occurs it is generally restricted within narrow limits. Anybody may provoke an animal's anger, but only towards certain individuals is it apt to feel retributive kindliness. The limits for this emotion are marked off by the conditions under which altruistic sentiments tend to arise. In its primitive form it is found among animals living in groups, including the small group consisting of mother, or parents, and offspring. The associated animals take pleasure in each other's company, and with this pleasure is intimately connected kindliness towards its cause, the companion himself, who is conceived of as a friend. The altruistic senti-

---

[61] A. Horwicz, *Psychologische Analysen auf physiologischer Grundlage* (Halle & Magdeburg, 1878), p. 333.

[62] *Cf.* E. von Hartmann, *Das sittliche Bewusstsein* (Leipzig [1886]), p. 176 *sq.*

[63] Professor McDougall (*An Introduction to Social Psychology,* p. 114) maintains that "the act that is to inspire gratitude must make us aware, not only of the kindly feeling, the tender emotion, of the other towards us; it must also make us aware of his power, we must see that he is able to do for us something that we cannot do for ourselves." But surely we may feel grateful for a token of goodwill without experiencing at all "that negative self-feeling which is evoked by the sense of the superior power of another."

ment would never have come into existence without such a reciprocity of feeling.

Retributive kindly emotion has the tendency to retain a cause of pleasure, just as resentment has the tendency to remove a cause of pain. And as natural selection accounts for the origin of the disposition to feel resentment, so also it accounts for the origin of the disposition to feel retributive kindly emotion. Both of these emotions are useful to the species: by resentment evils are averted, by retributive kindliness benefits are secured. That there is such an enormous difference in their prevalence is easily explained by the simple facts that the living in groups is an advantage only to certain species, and that even gregarious animals have many enemies but few friends.

That moral approval—by which I understand that emotion of which moral praise or reward is the outward manifestation—is a kind of retributive kindly emotion, and as such allied to gratitude, will probably be admitted without much hesitation. Its friendly character is not, like the hostile character of moral disapproval, disguised by any apparently contradictory facts. While the infliction of suffering is generally *prima facie* revolting to our moral consciousness, the very reverse is the case with the bestowal of a benefit.

CHAPTER IV

THE MORAL EMOTIONS
(concluded)

WE HAVE seen that moral disapproval is a form of resentment, and that moral approval is a form of retributive kindly emotion. It still remains for us to examine in what respects these emotions differ from kindred non-moral emotions, disapproval from anger and revenge and approval from gratitude—in other words, what characterizes them as specifically *moral* emotions.[1]

It is a common opinion, held by moralists who regard the intellect as the source of moral concepts, that moral emotions only arise after and in consequence of an intellectual process through which the moral quality of a certain course of conduct has been discerned. When I hear of a murder, for instance, I must realize the wrongness of the act before I can feel moral indignation at all; and if I delight in contemplating a virtuous action, it is because I think the action to be good, and not *vice versa*.[2] According to this theory, then, the moral judgment

[1] Professor McDougall (*An Introduction to Social Psychology* [London, 1926], p. 124) makes the truly amazing statement that I have no criterion by which to distinguish moral from non-moral resentment. I have expressly devoted two whole chapters of my *Moral Ideas* (chs. iv. and v.) to this very subject; and if he had taken any notice of them, he would have found how closely his own views on the nature and origin of moral indignation resemble mine.

[2] W. Fleming, *A Manual of Moral Philosophy* (London, 1867), p. 97 *sqq.* J. M. Wilson and T. Fowler, *The Principles of Morals,* ii. (Oxford, 1887), pp. 198, 199, 202. T. Fowler, *Progressive Morality* (London, 1895), p. 44 *sqq.* W. D. Ross, *The Right and the Good* (Oxford, 1930), p. 131.

is antecedent to, and determines the moral emotion; and if it were correct, moral emotions could be simply described as resentment or retributive kindly emotion called forth by moral judgments. But in my opinion such a definition would be absolutely meaningless. Whatever emotions may follow moral judgments, such judgments could never have been pronounced unless there had been moral emotions in somebody antecedent to them. The moral concepts, which form their predicates, are ultimately generalizations of tendencies to feel either moral approval or disapproval with reference to that of which those concepts are predicated; and if a judgment containing such a predicate evokes a moral emotion, it can only do so because its predicate is based on a similar emotion. The criterion of a moral emotion can therefore in no case depend upon its proceeding from a moral judgment. But at the same time moral judgments, being definite expressions of moral emotions, can help us to discover the true nature of these emotions.

A moral judgment always has the character of disinterestedness. When pronouncing an act good or bad, I mean that it is so quite independently of any reference it might have to me personally. If a person condemns an act which does him harm, how can he vindicate the moral nature of his judgment? Only by pointing out that his condemnation is not due to the particular circumstance that it is he himself who is the sufferer, that his judgment would be the same if anybody else in similar circumstances had been the victim, in other words, that it is disinterested. Even the egoistic hedonist, who regards acts as good or bad according as they give pleasure or pain to the agent, recognizes disinterestedness as essential to a moral judgment, in so far as he holds the judgment applicable to all similar cases, whether he himself or some one else happens to be the agent. Now, if the moral concepts are generalizations of tendencies to feel moral emotions and at the same time contain the notion of disinterestedness, we must conclude that the emotions from which they spring are felt disinterestedly. And it does not affect the real character either of the moral judgments or the moral emotions that he who pronounces such a judgment is often in practice influenced by the intrusion of a non-moral element into the emotion expressed in it. As Hume observed, "it seldom happens, that we do not think an enemy vicious, and can distinguish betwixt his opposition to our interest and real villainy or baseness." [3]

Of the disinterestedness of the moral emotions we find an echo—more or less faithful—in the maxims of ethical theorists as well as practical moralists. I have previously spoken of Sidgwick's "principle of justice," which merely states the disinterestedness involved in the very concept of "right." [4] The same notion is contained in Samuel Clarke's "rule of equity," "Whatever I judge reasonable or unreasonable for another to do for me; that, by the same judgment, I declare reasonable or unreasonable, that I in the like case should do for him"; [5] in Kant's formula, "Act only on that maxim whereby thou canst at the same time will that it should become a universal law"; [6] in the biblical saying, "Whatsoever ye would that men should do

[3] D. Hume, *A Treatise of Human Nature*, iii. 1. 2 (Oxford, 1896, p. 472).

[4] *Supra*, p. 11 *sq.*

[5] S. Clarke, *A Discourse concerning the Being and Attributes of God, the Obligations of Natural Religion, and the Truth and Certainty of the Christian Revelation* (London, 1732), p. 202.

[6] Kant, *Grundlegung zur Metaphysik der Sitten*, sec. ii. (*Gesammelte Schriften*, iv. [Berlin, 1911], p. 421; T. K. Abbott's translation in *Kant's Critique of Practical Reason and other Works on the Theory of Ethics* [London, 1898], p. 38). Cf. *infra*, p. 276.

to you, do ye even so to them"; [7] in Hobbes' "laws of nature" expressed in "this one sentence, approved by all the world, Do not that to another, which thou thinkest unreasonable to be done by another to thy selfe." [8] In the Indian Mahabharata it is said:—"Let no man do to another that which would be repugnant to himself; this is the sum of righteousness; the rest is according to inclination. In refusing, in bestowing, in regard to pleasure and to pain, to what is agreeable and disagreeable, a man obtains the proper rule by regarding the case as like his own." [9] When Confucius was asked if there is any rule that may serve as a rule of practice for all one's life, he answered, "Is not reciprocity such a word? What you do not want done to yourself, do not do to others"; and in another utterance he showed that the rule had for him not only a negative, but a positive form as well. [10] The disinterestedness of the moral emotions partly underlies the utilitarian demand that, in regard to his own happiness and that of others, an agent should be "as strictly impartial as a disinterested and benevolent spectator"; [11] and the biblical rule, "Thou shalt love thy neighbour as thyself." [12] But these maxims, as we shall see, [13] contain much more than the disinterestedness of the concept of duty.

The disinterestedness by which moral approval and disapproval are distinguished from other, non-moral, kinds

[7] *St. Matthew*, vii. 12.

[8] T. Hobbes, *Leviathan*, ii. 26. 8 (Oxford, 1881), p. 210.

[9] *Mahabharata*, xiii. 5571 *sq.* (J. Muir, *Religious and Moral Sentiments metrically rendered from Sanskrit Writers* [London, 1875], p. 107).

[10] *Lun Yü*, xv. 23; *Chung Yung*, xiii. 4 (in J. Legge, *The Chinese Classics*, vol. i. [Oxford, 1893]).

[11] J. S. Mill, *Utilitarianism* (London, 1895), p. 24.

[12] *Leviticus*, xix. 18. *St. Matthew*, xxii. 39.

[13] *Infra*, pp. 205 *sqq.*, 229.

of resentment or retributive kindly emotion is really a form of a more comprehensive quality of the moral emotions, namely, impartiality, real or apparent. If I pronounce an act done to a friend or to an enemy good or bad, that implies that I assume the act to be so independently of the fact that the person to whom it is done is my friend or my enemy. Conversely, if I pronounce an act done by a friend or by an enemy good or bad, that implies that I assume it to be so independently of my friendly or hostile feelings towards the agent. All this means that resentment and retributive kindly emotion are moral emotions if they are assumed by those who feel them to be uninfluenced by the particular relationship in which they stand both to those who are immediately affected by the acts in question and to those who perform the acts. A moral emotion, then, is tested by an imaginary change of the relationship between him who approves or disapproves of the mode of conduct by which the emotion was evoked and the parties immediately concerned, while the relationship between the parties themselves is left unaltered. At the same time it is not necessary that the moral emotion should be really impartial; it is sufficient that it is tacitly assumed to be so, or even that it is not knowingly partial. In attributing different rights to different individuals or classes of individuals, we are often in reality influenced by the relationship in which we stand to them; and yet those "rights" may be real, moral rights, not merely preferences, namely, if we assume that any impartial judge would share our views, or even if we are unaware of their partiality. Similarly, when the savage censures a homicide committed upon a member of his own tribe, but praises one committed upon a member of another tribe, his censure and praise are certainly influenced by his rela-

tions to the parties in question. He does not reason thus:
it is blamable to kill a member of one's own tribe and
praiseworthy to kill a member of another tribe, whether
the tribe be *my* own tribe or not. Nevertheless his blame
and praise can hardly be denied to be expressions of moral
emotions.

The analysis of the moral emotions that I have now
attempted applies not only to such emotions as we feel
on account of the conduct of others, but to such as we
feel on account of our own conduct as well, however
much the latter may be blended with other emotions, as
being caused by our own behaviour. Remorse is a state
of mind that contains a hostile attitude towards oneself.
It involves vaguely or distinctly some desire to suffer.
The remorseful man wants to think of the wrong he has
committed, he wants clearly to realize its wickedness; and
he wants to do this not merely because he desires to become a better man, but because it gives him some relief
to feel the sting in his heart. We may feel actual hatred
against ourselves, we may desire to inflict bodily suffering
on ourselves as a punishment for what we have done;
there are even instances of criminals guilty of capital
offences who have given themselves up to the authorities
in order to appease their consciences by suffering the
penalty of the law.[14] Yet the desire to punish ourselves
has a natural antagonist in our aversion to pain, and this
often blunts the sting of the conscience. Self-approval,
again, is not merely joy at one's own conduct, but is a
kindly emotion, a friendly attitude towards oneself, which
makes one feel that one's behaviour merits praise or reward. We more often, however, hear of a "good con-

[14] P. J. A. von Feuerbach, *Aktenmässige Darstellung merkwürdiger
Verbrechen* (Giessen, 1828-29), i. 249; ii. 473, 479 *sq.*

science," which, as has been said above, generally means little more than the absence of a bad one.

As moral emotions, remorse and self-approval, must present the same characteristics as make resentment and retributive kindliness moral emotions when felt with reference to the conduct of other people: disinterestedness and apparent impartiality. We may be angry with ourselves from purely selfish motives: he who has lost at play may be vexed with himself as well as he who has cheated at play, and the egoist may reproach himself for having yielded to a momentary impulse of benevolence. So also we may be pleased with ourselves on other than moral grounds. Almost inseparable from the moral judgment that we pass on our own conduct seems to be the image of an impartial outsider who acts as our judge.

Now we once more are faced by the question of origin. We have seen that the dispositions to feel resentment and retributive kindly emotion are easily explained by their usefulness. This explanation naturally also holds true of the moral emotions in so far as they are retributive emotions: it accounts for the hostile attitude of moral disapproval towards the cause of pain and for the friendly attitude of moral approval towards the cause of pleasure. But it still remains for us to discover the origin of those elements in the moral emotions by which they are distinguished from other, non-moral, retributive emotions. First, how shall we explain their disinterestedness?

We have to distinguish between different classes of conditions under which disinterested retributive emotions arise. In the first place, we may feel disinterested resentment, or disinterested retributive kindly emotion, on account of an injury inflicted, or a benefit conferred, upon another individual with whose pain, or pleasure, we sympathize and in whose welfare we take a kindly interest. Our retributive emotions are, of course, always reactions against pain or pleasure felt by ourselves; this holds good of the moral emotions as well as of anger, revenge, and gratitude. The question to be answered, then, is, Why should we, quite disinterestedly, feel pain calling forth disapproval because our neighbour is hurt, and pleasure calling forth approval because he is benefited?

That a certain act causes pleasure or pain to the bystander may be due to the close association that exists between these feelings and their outward expressions. The sight of a happy face tends to produce some degree of pleasure in him who sees it; the sight of the bodily signs of suffering tends to produce a feeling of pain. In either case the feeling of the spectator is due to the fact that the perception of the physical manifestations of the feeling produces the feeling itself on account of the established association between them. Moreover, sympathetic pain or pleasure may be the result of an association between cause and effect, between the cognition of a certain act or situation and the feeling generally evoked by this act or situation: a blow may cause pain to the spectator before he has witnessed its effect on the victim.

But the sympathetic feeling that results from association alone is not what is popularly called sympathy: it lacks kindliness.[15] Arising merely from the habitual connection of certain cognitions with certain feelings in the experience of the spectator, it is, strictly speaking, not at all concerned with what the other individual *feels*. On the other hand sympathy, in the popular sense of the

---

[15] *Moral Ideas,* i. 109. *Cf.* Th. Ribot, *The Psychology of the Emotions* (London, 1897), p. 233; A. F. Shand, "The Sources of Tender Emotion," in G. F. Stout's *Groundwork of Psychology* (London, 1903), p. 198 *sqq.; Idem, The Foundations of Character* (London, 1920), p. 44 *sqq.;* McDougall, *op. cit.,* p. 78 *sqq.*

word, requires the co-operation of the altruistic sentiment
or affection, a disposition of mind that is particularly apt
to display itself as kindly emotion towards other beings.
This sentiment, only, induces us to take a kindly interest
in the feelings of our neighbours. It involves a tendency,
or willingness, and, when strongly developed, gives rise
to an eager desire, to sympathize with their pains and
pleasures. Under its influence our sympathetic feeling is
no longer a mere matter of association; we take an active
part in its production, we direct our attention to any
circumstance which we believe may affect the feelings of
the person whom we love, and to any external manifestation of his emotions. We are anxious to find out his joys
and sorrows, to be able to rejoice with him and to suffer
with him, and, especially, when he stands in need of it,
to console or to help him. For the altruistic sentiment is
not merely willingness to sympathize, it is above all a
conative disposition to promote the welfare of its object.
It is true that sympathetic pain, unaided by kindliness,
may induce a person to relieve the suffering of his neighbour, instead of shutting his eyes to it; but then he does
so, not out of regard to the feelings of the sufferer, but
simply to get rid of a painful cognition. Nor must it be
supposed that the altruistic sentiment prompts to assistance only by strengthening the sympathetic feeling. The
sight of the wounded traveller may perhaps have caused
no less pain to the Pharisee than to the good Samaritan;
yet it would have been impossible for the latter to dismiss
his pain by going away, since he felt a desire to assist
the wounded man, and this desire would have been left
ungratified if he had not stopped by the wayside. To the
egoist the relief offered a sufferer is a means of suppress-
ing the sympathetic pain, to the altruist the sympathetic
pain is, so to say, a means of giving relief. The altruist

wants to know, to feel the pain of his neighbour, because he desires to help him. Why are the most kind-hearted people often the most cheerful, if not because they think of alleviating the misery of their fellow-creatures, instead of indulging in the sympathetic pain which it evokes?

The co-operation of the altruistic sentiment with sympathy also produces in us disinterested retributive emotions, when the individual towards whom we are kindly disposed is hurt or benefited. In the tendency to feel such emotions, however, there is a great difference between resentment and retributive kindliness. Resentment towards an enemy is itself, as a rule, a much stronger emotion than retributive kindly emotion towards a benefactor. And as for the sympathetic forms of these emotions, it is not surprising that the altruistic sentiment is more readily moved by the sight of pain than by the sight of pleasure, considering that it serves as a means of protection for the species. Moreover, sympathetic retributive kindliness has powerful rivals in the feelings of jealousy and envy, which tend to excite anger also towards him who bestows the benefit on the other individual. As an ancient writer observes, "many suffer with their friends when the friends are in distress, but are envious of them when they prosper." [16] Among the lower animals there seems to be no trace of retributive kindly emotion felt as a result of pleasure taken in kindness shown to another individual. On the other hand, there is sympathetic resentment in consequence of an inflicted injury. A mammalian mother is as hostile to the enemy of her young as to her own enemy. Social animals defend members of their own group, which evidently involves some degree of sympathetic anger. When a young monkey which had been

[16] L. Schmidt, *Die Ethik der alten Griechen*, i. (Berlin, 1882), p. 259.

seized by an eagle cried for assistance, "the other members of the troop, with much uproar, rushed to the rescue, surrounded the eagle, and pulled out so many feathers, that he no longer thought of his prey, but only how to escape." [17] Speaking of a group of chimpanzees, Professor Köhler says that if one of them is attacked before the eyes of the others, great excitement goes through the whole group. Even the lightest form of punishment, pulling the ear of the offender, or a playful pretence at punishment, often stirred single members of the group to much more decisive action. A little weak chimpanzee would run up excitedly, stretch out his arm to the punisher, if the ape was still being punished, try to hold the big man's arm tight, and finally, with exasperated gestures, start hitting out at him.[18] Among domesticated animals and animals in confinement sympathetic resentment may be felt even when the individual who is hurt belongs to another species. The Rev. Charles Williams mentions a dog at Liverpool who saved a cat from the hands of some young ruffians: he rushed in among the boys, barked furiously at them, terrified them into flight, and carried the cat off in his mouth to his kennel, where he nursed it.[19] Darwin speaks of a little American monkey in the Zoological Gardens of London which, when seeing a great baboon attack his friend, the keeper, rushed to the rescue and by screams and bites so distracted the

[17] Ch. Darwin, *The Descent of Man* (London, 1890), p. 101 *sq.* Various other instances of sympathetic resentment in monkeys have been stated by Brehm (see *ibid.*, p. 101; Shand, *The Foundations of Character*, p. 236).

[18] W. Köhler, *The Mentality of Apes* (London, 1927), p. 286 *sq.*

[19] Ch. Williams, *Dogs and Their Ways* (London, 1863), p. 43. For dogs resenting injuries done to other dogs see G. J. Romanes, *Animal Intelligence* (London, 1895), p. 440; and T. Medwin, *The Angler in Wales*, ii. (London, 1834), pp. 162-164, 197, 216 *sq.*

baboon, that the man was able to escape.[20] The dog who flies at any one who strikes, or even touches, his master is a very familiar instance of sympathetic resentment.

The scope of disinterested resentment naturally varies with the scope of the altruistic sentiment. For reasons which I have stated elsewhere, I think it likely that in mankind not only maternal but also paternal and conjugal affection, in some degree, existed from the very beginning, together with the family consisting of parents and offspring, which is also found among anthropoid apes.[21] In its intrinsic nature, however, parental love is not exactly what the term parental indicates. Herbert Spencer pointed out that it is not adequately defined as the instinct which attaches a creature to its young, as it is not exclusively displayed in that relation: he identified it with the love of the helpless, stimulated by the perception of "smallness joined, usually, with relative inactivity, being the chief indications of incapacity." [22] That maternal love is in some degree love of the helpless is obvious from the fact that it originally only lasts as long as the young are unable to shift for themselves. But Spencer's theory fails to explain how it is that, even in a gregarious species, mothers make a distinction between their own offspring and other young. During my stay among the mountaineers of Morocco I was often struck by the eagerness with which in the evening, when the flock of ewes and the flock of lambs were reunited, each mother sought for her own lamb and each lamb for its own mother; and

20 Darwin, *op. cit.*, p. 103.
21 E. Westermarck, *The History of Human Marriage*, i. (London, 1921), ch. i.
22 H. Spencer, *The Principles of Psychology*, ii. (London, 1890), p. 623 *sq.* See also D. Hartley, *Observations on Man*, i. (London, 1810), p. 497.

the same can be testified by every shepherd. A similar discrimination has been noticed even in cases of conscious adoption. Brehm tells us of a female baboon which had so capacious a heart that she not only adopted young monkeys of other species, but stole young dogs and cats which she continually carried about; yet her kindness did not go so far as to share food with her adopted offspring, although she divided everything quite fairly with her own young ones.[23] To account for maternal love we must therefore assume the existence of some other stimulus besides the perception of the signs of helplessness, which produces, or at least strengthens, the instinctive response in the mother. This stimulus must be rooted in the external relationship in which the offspring stand to the mother from the very beginning. She is in close proximity to her helpless young from their tenderest age; and she loves them because they are to her a cause of pleasure.[24]

The stimuli to which paternal love responds are apparently derived from the same circumstances as those which call into activity maternal love, the helplessness and proximity of the offspring; wherever it exists the father is near his young from the beginning. And here again, as in the case of maternal love, the instinctive response may be assumed to be the result of a process of natural selection, which has preserved a mental disposition necessary for the existence of the species in which it is found. Pro-

[23] Darwin, *op. cit.*, p. 70. See also F. Alverdes, *Social Life in the Animal World* (London, 1927), p. 135.

[24] Dr. Shand, who accepts my theory of maternal love, first set forth in my *Moral Ideas* (ii. 188 *sq.*), argues (*op. cit.*, p. 238) that "we shall approach closer to the facts if we substitute for this abstract term 'pleasure' the more concrete term 'joy.'" But I maintain that though the mother, as he says, feels joy and joy contains other elements besides pleasure, it is the pleasure felt at her perception of the small and weak creature in close proximity to herself that is the stimulus of her love, and the emotion she feels towards them is tender.

fessor McDougall asks how we can account for the fact that men are at all capable of this emotion and of this disinterested protective impulse; and his answer is that in its racial origin the instinct was undoubtedly primarily maternal, but, like many other characters, was transmitted to the other sex.[25] To me it seems that the origin of the paternal instinct offers no more difficult problem to solve than that of the maternal instinct. How could Professor McDougall's theory account for the parental instinct of those species in which it is found exclusively in the male, as is the rule among fishes that take any care at all of their offspring, and among certain frogs? [26] The male of certain species of *Arius* carries the ova about with him in his capacious pharynx. The male *Amia calva* guards and leads its family of young for a considerable time. The male stickleback builds a nest, in which he induces a number of females to lay their eggs, defends the nest most courageously against rival males, and guards not only the eggs but also the young for some time after they are hatched; whereas the female has no concern with her eggs after she has laid them. The male nurse-frog (*Alytes obstetricans*) carries the eggs about with him in a long string wound round his hind legs until the larvae emerge, and defends this string against marauders; and in the Chilian species of narrow-mouthed frogs (*Rhinoderma darwinii*) the male not only carries the eggs in his gular sac but the young as well, until their metamorphosis is complete. Among the birds there are a few species in

[25] McDougall, *op. cit.*, p. 59.
[26] A. C. L. G. Guenther, *An Introduction to the Study of Fishes* (Edinburgh, 1880), p. 163. A. Sutherland, *The Origin and Growth of the Moral Instinct*, i. (London, 1898), p. 32 *sqq.;* L. A. Jägerskiöld, *Några valda drag ur djurens vård om sina ungar* (Stockholm, 1902), p. 19 *sqq.;* Alverdes, *op. cit.*, p. 66 *sq.*

which both the brooding and the care of the newly-hatched young devolve exclusively on the male.[27]

We have no reason to believe that the family consisting of parents and offspring was the only social unit among primitive men, though it probably was, as among many existing savages of the lowest type,[28] the group of people who most permanently lived together. It is more probable that they at least at times, when the supply of food allowed it, lived in somewhat larger groups, or, in other words, that they were in some degree gregarious; this is the case with the gorilla and the chimpanzee, who have been found sometimes in families and sometimes in small bands.[29] Subsequently, when man gradually found out many new means of earning his living and thereby more and more emancipated himself from direct dependence on surrounding nature, the group grew in coherence and size. And thus mankind developed into the most gregarious of all animal species.

Among a gregarious species of animals the members of a herd are at ease in each other's company, suffer when they are separated, rejoice when they are reunited. And, as has been pointed out before, with the pleasure they take in each other's company is intimately connected kindliness towards its cause, the companion himself. Associated animals very frequently display affection for each other—defend each other, help each other in distress and danger, perform various other services for each other.[30] Among men the members of the same social unit are tied

---

[27] Sutherland, *op. cit.*, i. 59 *sq.* Jägerskiöld, *op. cit.*, p. 35. *Idem, Om spel och parningslekar hos djuren* (Stockholm, 1908), p. 146.

[28] *The History of Human Marriage*, i. 54 *sqq.*

[29] *Ibid.*, i. 33 *sqq.*

[30] Darwin, *op. cit.*, p. 100 *sqq.* P. Kropotkin, *Mutual Aid* (London, 1902), ch. i. *sq.* Alverdes, *op. cit.*, p. 133 *sq.*

to each other with various bonds of a distinctly human character—the same customs, laws, institutions, magic or religious ceremonies and beliefs, notions of a common descent, and so forth. As men generally are fond of that to which they are used or which is their own, they are also naturally apt to have likings for other individuals whose habits, ideas, and feelings are similar to theirs.

Thus all the various forms of the altruistic sentiment are characterized by the same tendency to feel kindliness towards an individual who is a cause of pleasure. There is no reason to regard one form of it as derived from another. The difference between its varieties lies in the difference between the individuals by the perception of whom it is stimulated, but its impulse is in all cases kindliness towards a cause of pleasure. In mankind there seems to be an innate disposition to take some pleasure in the company of a fellow-man, unless he for some special reason is a cause of fear or dislike. It may be increased by certain particular stimuli, as is the case in the parental, conjugal, and filial sentiments, and on the other hand it is checked by circumstances that restrict the size of the group.

Uncivilized peoples are as a rule described as kind towards members of their own community or tribe. Within these limits they are charitable and generous, and their customs relating to mutual aid are often much more stringent than our own; and this applies even to the very lowest among them.[31] The mutual good-will, harmony, and sense of solidarity that under normal conditions prevail in their societies lead to disinterested resentment, which is generally felt when a member of the group is hurt. Speaking of some Australian savages, Mr. Fison remarks:—"To the savage, the whole gens is the individual,

<hr />

[31] *Moral Ideas,* i. 540 *sqq.* See also Kropotkin, *op. cit.,* p. 88 *sqq.*

and he is full of regard for it. Strike the gens anywhere, and every member of it considers himself struck, and the whole body corporate rises up in arms against the striker." [32] Among certain Queensland aborigines, says Dr. Roth, a man has to reckon not only with the injured one or his relatives, but also, in some cases, with the whole camp collectively, who will take upon itself to inflict punishment upon the offender; while a woman who makes herself obnoxious in the camp, especially to the female portion of it, is liable to be set upon and "hammered" by her fellow-sisters collectively. [33] Much more frequently savage justice is administered not by the whole of the community, but by some person or persons invested with judicial authority, a council of elders or a chief. [34] But the resentment of the community also displays itself in the widespread custom which enjoins private revenge as a duty. The desire to see the offender suffer may induce the community to assist the avenger in some way or other in attaining his object, [35] or actually to compel the injured party to take revenge. Of an Australian tribe, where an offender was to receive one or more spears from the injured man when he had recovered strength or from his relatives if he was dead, we are told, "Obedience to such laws was never withheld, but would have been enforced, without doubt, if necessary, by the assembled tribe." [36]

While disinterested resentment may thus be felt in consequence of an injury inflicted upon another individual as

[32] L. Fison and A. W. Howitt, *Kamilaroi and Kurnai* (Melbourne & Sydney, 1880), p. 170.
[33] W. E. Roth, *Ethnological Studies among the North-West-Central Queensland Aborigines* (Brisbane & London, 1897), pp. 139, 141.
[34] *Moral Ideas*, i. 173 *sqq.*
[35] *Ibid.,* i. 176 *sq.*
[36] Fison and Howitt, *op. cit.,* p. 282.

a reaction against sympathetic pain, it may also be directly produced by the cognition of the signs of resentment. In the former case it is really independent of the emotion of the injured individual; we may feel resentment on his behalf though he himself feels none. In the latter case it is an emotion reflected through the medium of its outward expression and felt independently of the cause of the original emotion of which it is a reflection, which may in fact be out of sight. Professor Holmes tells us that "among bees, ants, and termites signs of anger by one individual may awaken the whole community to a high pitch of excitement." [37] So also a group of chimpanzees may be thrown into a state of blind fury by the angry cries of one of its members, "even when the majority of its members have seen nothing of what caused the first cry, and have no notion of what it is all about." [38] When the yells and shrieks of a street dog-fight are heard, dogs from all sides rush to the spot, each dog apparently ready to bite any of the others. So, too, in an infuriated crowd of men one gets angry because the other is angry, and often the question, Why? is hardly asked. This form of disinterested resentment is of considerable importance both as an originator and a communicator of moral ideas. Men are inclined to sympathize with the resentment of persons for whom they feel regard; hence an act which, though harmless by itself, is forbidden by God and man may be not only professed but actually felt to be wrong. For a similar reason the punishment inflicted by the society, which as a rule is an expression of its moral indignation, may also, by arousing sympathetic resentment, lead to the idea that the victim of it deserves to be punished.

[37] S. J. Holmes, *The Evolution of Animal Intelligence* (New York, 1911), p. 209.
[38] Köhler, *op. cit.*, p. 288.

Children, as everybody knows, grow up with their ideas
of right and wrong graduated, to a great extent, according to the temper of the father or mother; and men are
not seldom, as Hobbes said, "like little children, that have
no other rule of good and evill manners, but the correction
they receive from their Parents, and Masters." [39] Any
means of expressing resentment may serve as a communicator of the emotion. Besides punishment, language deserves special mention. Moral disapproval may be evoked
by the very sounds of words like "murder," "theft,"
"cowardice," and others, which not merely indicate a certain mode of behaviour but also express the opprobrium
attached to it. By the use of some strong word the orator
raises the indignation of a sympathetic audience to its
pitch.

There is yet a third way in which disinterested resentment may arise. In many cases people feel hostile to a
person who inflicts no injury on anybody. There are in
the human mind what Bain called "disinterested antipathies," or sentimental aversions "of which our fellow-
beings are the subjects, and on account of which we overlook our own interest quite as much as in displaying our
sympathies and affections." [40] Differences of taste, habit,
and opinion easily create similar dislikes; and these, too,
have played a prominent part in the moulding of the moral
consciousness. The antipathy which is so commonly felt
against anything unusual, new, or foreign, may lead to
the idea that it is wrong; and when a certain act, which
does no harm—apart from the painful impression it makes
on the spectator—fills people with disgust or horror, they
may feel no less inclined to inflict harm upon the agent
than if he had committed an offence against person, pro-

[39] Hobbes, *op. cit.*, i. 11, p. 76.
[40] A. Bain, *The Emotions and the Will* (London, 1880), p. 268.

perty, or good name. Such resentment may also arise from the observation of the feelings of others. As Abraham Tucker said, "we grow to love things we perceive them fond of, and contract aversions from their dislikes." [41]

We have already noticed that sympathy, in the popular sense of the word, may produce not only disinterested resentment but disinterested retributive kindliness: when taking a pleasure in the benefit bestowed upon our neighbour, we are disposed to look with kindness upon the benefactor. Moreover, as resentment may be produced by the cognition of outward signs of resentment in others, so kindly emotion may be produced by the signs of kindliness. Even a dog may be well-disposed towards a stranger when he sees a friend—whether a man or another dog— be friendly to him. Language communicates emotions by terms of praise as well as by terms of condemnation; and a reward, like a punishment, has some tendency to reproduce the emotion from which it sprang. Finally, men have disinterested likings as they have disinterested dislikes. As an instance of these may be mentioned the common admiration of courage when felt irrespectively of the object for which it is displayed—a feeling which has even elevated it to an independent virtue, and in any case tends to influence the moral verdict.

Having thus found the origin of disinterested retributive emotions, we have also partly explained the origin of the moral emotions. But, as we have seen, these emotions are not only disinterested, but impartial in a wider sense, or at least, are not knowingly partial. The possibility of such impartiality, however, is explained by the answer to the more general question, how disinterestedness and apparent impartiality have become characteristics of that

[41] A. Tucker, *The Light of Nature Pursued,* i. (London, 1840), p. 154.

particular kind of retributive emotions that we call moral emotions. The solution of this problem is not difficult to find. It lies in the fact that society is the birth-place of the moral consciousness; that the first moral judgments expressed, not the private emotions of isolated individuals, but emotions felt by the society at large; that tribal custom was the earliest rule of duty.

Customs are not merely public habits—the habits of a certain circle of men, a racial or national community, a rank or class of society—but they are at the same time rules of conduct. As Cicero observes, the customs of a people "are precepts in themselves." [42] We say that "custom commands," or "custom demands," and even when custom simply allows the commission of a certain class of actions, it implicitly lays down the rule that such actions are not to be interfered with. And the rule of custom is conceived of as a moral rule, which decides what is right and wrong.[43] "Les loix de la conscience," says Montaigne, "que nous disons naistre de nature, naissent de la coustume." [44] The Greek idea of the customary, τὸ νόμιμον, shows the close connection between morality and custom; and so do the words ἔθος, ἦθος, and ἠθικά, the Latin mos and moralis, the German Sitte and Sittlichkeit.[45] Moreover, in early society, customs are not only moral rules, but the only moral rules ever thought of. The savage strictly complies with the Hegelian command that no man must have a private conscience.

What does it mean that custom is a rule of conduct? It implies that every deviation from custom is apt to call forth public disapproval. In the lower stages of civiliza-

[42] Cicero, De Officiis, i. 41.
[43] Moral Ideas, i. 118 sq.
[44] M. de Montaigne, Essais, i. 22 (Œuvres [Paris, 1837], p. 48).
[45] For the history of these words see W. Wundt, Ethik (Stuttgart, 1912), i. 21 sqq.

tion, especially, custom is a tyrant who binds man in iron fetters, and who threatens the transgressor not only with general disgrace, but often with bodily suffering or even death. Now if custom is a moral rule, the public disapproval aroused by its transgression may be properly called a moral emotion. Moreover, where all the duties of a man are expressed in the customs of the society to which he belongs, it is obvious that the characteristics of moral disapproval are to be sought for in its connection with custom. Custom is fixed once for all, and admits of no purely personal preferences. It is equally binding for me and for you and for all the other members of the society. A breach of it is equally wrong whether I myself am immediately concerned in the act or not; this involves disinterestedness. So also the condemnation of it is independent of the relationship in which the parties concerned in it stand to me personally; this implies impartiality in a larger sense. And all this holds true whatever be the origin of any particular custom. It may have originated in selfishness or partiality: the leading men of the society may at first have prohibited certain acts because they found them disadvantageous to themselves, or to those with whom they particularly sympathized. Where custom is an oppressor of women, this oppression may, in some measure at least, be traced back to the selfishness of the men. Where custom sanctions slavery, it is certainly not impartial to the slaves. Yet in the one case as in the other custom is assumed to be in the right, irrespectively of one's own station, and the women and the slaves themselves are expected to be of the same opinion. Such an expectation is by no means a chimera. Under normal social conditions, largely owing to men's tendency to share the resentment of their superiors, the customs of a society are willingly submitted to and recognized as right by the great majority

of its members, whatever be their station. Among the Re-
jangs of Sumatra, says Marsden, "a man without property, family, or connections, never, in the partiality of
self-love, considers his own life as being of equal value
with that of a man of substance." [46] Mr. Torday observes
that in Congo the position of woman, mere chattel and
drudge as she seems to be according to our notions, is
nevertheless completely consonant with her own conception of her rights—so much so that it is precisely from
the woman's side that the European reformer is likely to
meet with the most determined opposition. However selfish, however partial a certain rule may be, it becomes a
true custom, a moral rule, as soon as the selfishness or
partiality of its makers is lost sight of.

It must not be supposed that, by deriving the characteristics of moral disapproval from its connection with
custom, I implicitly contradict my initial proposition that
moral emotions are at the bottom of all moral judgments.
Custom is a moral rule only on account of the disapproval
called forth by its transgression. In its ethical aspect it is
nothing but a generalization of emotional tendencies, applied to certain modes of conduct and transmitted from
generation to generation. In its capacity of a rule of duty
custom, *mos,* is derived from the emotion to which it gave
its name.

And as public disapproval is the prototype of moral disapproval, so public approval, expressed in public praise, is
the prototype of moral approval: it is characterized by the
same disinterestedness and apparent impartiality. But of
these two emotions public disapproval, being at the root
of custom and leading to the infliction of punishment, is
by far the more impressive. Hence it is not surprising that
the term "moral" is etymologically connected with *mos,*

[46] W. Marsden, *The History of Sumatra* (London, 1811), p. 247.

which always implies the existence of a social rule the transgression of which evokes public disapproval. Only by analogy it has come to be applied to the emotion of approval as well.

Though moral disapproval and approval have taken their place in the system of human emotions as public emotions felt by the society at large, they have not always remained inseparably connected with the feelings of any special society. The unanimity of opinion that originally characterized the members of the same social unit was disturbed by its advancement in civilization. Individuals arose who found fault with the moral ideas prevalent in the community to which they belonged, criticizing them on the basis of their own individual feelings. To deny such individuals the right of speaking in the name of morality true and proper would be to attach to this term a meaning which, in its narrowness, would be utterly different from the established usage of it. All that is required is that their retributive emotions should possess that disinterestedness and apparent impartiality which have become moral characteristics in connection with custom, but may differ from public disapproval and approval either in strength or with regard to the facts by which they are evoked. Indeed, the dissent from the orthodox views of morality often arises from the conviction that the apparent impartiality of public feelings is an illusion. In the course of progressive civilization the moral consciousness has tended towards a greater equalization of rights, towards an expansion of the circle within which the same moral rules are held applicable. And this process has been largely due to the example of influential individuals and their efforts to raise public opinion to their own standard of right.

The fact that the earliest moral emotions were public

emotions implies that the original form of the moral consciousness cannot, as is often asserted, have been the individual conscience. Martineau's observation that the inner springs of other men's actions may be read off only by inference from our own experience, by no means warrants his conclusion that the moral consciousness is at its origin engaged in self-estimation, instead of circuitously reaching this end through a prior critique upon our fellow-men.[47] The moral elements in the feelings we experience with reference to our own conduct are generally mixed up with other elements to such an extent that they can be disentangled only by a careful process of abstraction, and could never have been distinguished as specific moral emotions unless the notion of morality had been previously derived from another source.

[47] J. Martineau, *Types of Ethical Theory*, ii. (Oxford, 1891), p. 29 *sqq.*

CHAPTER V

THE MORAL CONCEPTS

THE theory of the emotional origin of moral judgments I am here advocating does not imply that such a judgment affirms the existence of a moral emotion in the mind of the person who utters it: he may do so without feeling any emotion at all. No doubt, to say that a certain act is good or bad may be the mere expression of an emotion felt with regard to it, just as to say that the sun is hot or the weather cold may be a mere expression of a sensation of heat or cold produced by the sun or the weather. But such judgments express subjective facts in terms which strictly speaking have a different meaning. To attribute a quality to something is not the same as to state the existence of a particular emotion or sensation in the mind that perceives it. This, however, does not imply that the term used to denote the quality may not have a subjective origin. I maintain, on the contrary, that the qualities assigned to the subjects of moral judgments really are generalizations derived from approval or disapproval felt with regard to certain modes of conduct, that they are tendencies to feel one or the other of these emotions interpreted as qualities, as dynamic tendencies, in the phenomena which gave rise to the emotion. A similar translation of emotional states into terms of qualities assigned to external phenomena is found in many other cases: something is "fearful" because people fear it, "admirable" because people admire it. When we call an act good or bad, we do not *state* the existence of any emotional tendencies, any

114

more than, when we call a landscape beautiful, we state any characteristics of beauty: we refer the subject of the judgment to a class of phenomena which we are used to call good or bad. But we are used to call them so because they have evoked moral approval or disapproval in ourselves or in other persons from whom we have learned the use of those words.

Most people follow a very simple method in judging of an act. Particular modes of conduct have their traditional labels, many of which are learned with language itself; and the moral judgment commonly consists simply in labelling the act according to certain obvious characteristics which it presents in common with others belonging to the same group.[1] We hear that some one has appropriated another's property, this is theft, it is wrong; some one tells an untruth, this is lying, it is wrong; some one gives money to a needy person, this is charitable, it is good; and so forth. But when we examine the nature of these acts we find that they are apt to give rise to or, as we may also put it, to become the objects of, certain emotions, either of disapproval or approval, and it is the tendency to feel one or the other of these emotions that has led people to

[1] I have copied these two sentences from my *Moral Ideas* (i. 9). They show that I was fully aware of the fact, subsequently stated by Professor McDougall (*An Introduction to Social Psychology* [London, 1926], p. 185 *sq.*), that "the emotions on which a man's moral judgments are based may be not his own emotions at the time of passing judgment, and not even his own earlier emotions, but the emotions, especially that disinterested emotion we call moral indignation, of those who in bygone ages have played their parts in the shaping of the moral tradition." His reference to my theory of the emotional origin of moral judgments suggests that I had overlooked the distinction between what he calls "original moral judgment and imitative moral judgments." As regards the latter, he says, the intellectualist doctrine, according to which the act of classing precedes and determines the moral emotion, is true; while "as regards original moral judgments, Westermarck is in the right—they proceed directly from emotions."

call them bad or good. Those who first established the use of these and all other moral concepts felt disapproval or approval and expressed in the concepts their tendency to feel such an emotion in the given circumstances. This is what may be called the intrinsic meaning of the terms. I do not say that those who use them are aware of this meaning. We are often unable to tell what is really implied in a concept that we predicate to a certain phenomenon. When any one is asked what he means by saying that something is or exists, or that something is the cause of something else, I suppose that everybody who is not a philosopher, and many a philosopher also, feels somewhat bewildered. As Mr. Bertrand Russell observes, "to say that a word has a meaning is not to say that those who use the word correctly have ever thought out what the meaning is: the use of the word comes first, and the meaning is to be distilled out of it by observation and analysis. . . . A word is used 'correctly' when the average hearer will be affected by it in the way intended." [2] When we want to find out the intrinsic meaning of a term we have to examine the circumstances in which it is used. And in analyzing the predicates of moral judgments, we are guided by the fact that if we ourselves emphatically and truly mean what we say when we pronounce such a judgment, we recognize that we are apt, or at least think we are apt, to feel a moral emotion of either approval or disapproval with regard to that on which the judgment is pronounced.

Professor Sorley, who admits that "feeling and striving" are anterior to moral ideas and moral judgment, argues that once the transition to the moral judgment is made, "we are no longer concerned with subjective emo-

[2] B. Russell, *The Analysis of Mind* (London, 1922), p. 197 *sq. Cf.* G. C. Field, *Moral Theory* (London, 1921), p. 5 *sq.*

tions but with the validity of the assertion that this or
that is good. Morality begins with judgments about good
and evil, right and wrong, and not simply with emotions—retributive, parental, sympathetic, or what not." [3]
How this transition from emotions to moral judgments
has taken place we are not told. In my opinion, as already
said, the tendency to feel moral approval or disapproval
was interpreted as a quality in the phenomenon that gave
rise to it, and, for reasons stated before, the concept expressing this quality was supposed to give objective validity to the judgment in which it was the predicate. If it
were based on an emotion it could not do so; hence the
violent opposition to the theory of the emotional origin
of moral judgments. But I feel tempted to quote Hobbes'
sagacious remarks:—"In reasoning, a man must take heed
of words; which besides the signification of what we
imagine of their nature, have a signification also of the
nature, disposition, and interest of the speaker; such as
are the names of vertues, and vices; for one man calleth
wisdome, what another calleth feare; and one cruelty,
what another justice; one prodigality, what another mag-
nanimity; and one gravity, what another stupidicy, &c.
And therefore such names can never be true grounds of
any ratiocination. No more can metaphors, and tropes of
speech: but these are less dangerous, because they profess
their inconstancy; which the other do not." [4]

In order to show that the concepts which are used as
predicates in moral judgments are ultimately based upon
emotions it is necessary to examine the relations between
the concepts and the emotions. This is a task which has
been much neglected by the moralists of the emotional

[3] W. R. Sorley, *Moral Values and the Idea of God* (Cambridge,
1924), pp. 67, 69.
[4] T. Hobbes, *Leviathan*, i. 4 (Oxford, 1881), p. 26.

school, although it is evidently a matter of paramount importance. I shall restrict my analysis to the principal terms used in English, all of which have equivalents in other European languages. To what extent they have equivalents in non-European tongues I do not take upon myself to decide. That all existing peoples, even the lowest, have moral emotions is as certain as that they have customs, and there can be no doubt that they give expression to those emotions in their speech. But it is another question how far their emotions have led to such generalizations as are implied in moral concepts. Many savages have terms more or less corresponding to our "good" and "bad," which, like our own terms, are used to express moral, as well as other, qualities.[5] It seems very probable that originally moral concepts were not clearly differentiated from other more comprehensive generalizations, and that they assumed a more definite shape only by slow degrees. At the same time we must not expect to find the beginning of this process reflected in the vocabularies of languages. There is every reason to believe that a savage distinguishes between the "badness" of a man and the "badness" of a piece of food, although he may have no clear idea of the distinction. Language is a rough generalizer: even more or less superficial resemblance between different phenomena often suffices to establish linguistic identity between them. Compare the rightness of a line with the the rightness of conduct, the wrongness of an opinion with the wrongness of an act. And notice the different significations given to the verb "ought" in the following sentences:—"They ought to be in town by this time, as the train left Paris last night"; "If you wish to be healthy

[5] See *Moral Ideas,* i. 131 *sq.;* and W. Planert, "Le développement des idées morales examiné au point de vue linguistique," in *Le Monde orientale,* xviii. (Uppsala, 1925), p. 124 *sqq.*

you ought to rise early"; "You ought always to tell the truth." But even the meaning of a term that is used in a moral sense may vary considerably. In this respect it resembles the meaning of other words, which, as Mr. Bertrand Russell puts it, "is an area, like a target: it may have a bull's eye, but the outlying parts of the target are still more or less within the meaning, in a gradually diminishing degree as we travel further from the bull's eye." [6]

In ethical treatises there are two moral concepts that compete with each other for supremacy: that of *ought* or *duty,* and that of *goodness.* According to Kant, in fact, all morality consists in the doing of duty for duty's sake, and what is good is what ought to be done. Several later writers have accepted the former of these propositions, but maintain that there are good actions which surpass acts of duty in value, though they fall outside the moral field because they are done for an end that is good and not for the sake of their intrinsic rightness. Professor de Burgh, for instance, who admits that acts done from spontaneous affection may be of higher value than acts of duty for duty's sake, argues that "it is paradoxical to confuse the two types of action and valuation by merging them, under the common rubric 'moral,' into one." [7] I think that to most people who are not swayed by the Kantian terminology it would rather seem paradoxical to deny the epithet "moral" to the conduct of a man who from pity relieves a sufferer or a mother who sacrifices health and pleasure for her child, on the ground that they act

[6] Russell, *op. cit.,* p. 197 *sq.*

[7] W. G. de Burgh, "On Right and Good: the Problem of Objective Right," in *Journal of Philosophical Studies,* v. (London, 1930), pp. 432, 254. Similar views have been expressed by H. Münsterberg (*Der Ursprung der Sittlichkeit* [Freiburg, i. B., 1889], p. 98 *sqq.*) and N. H. Bang (*Begrebet Moral* [Köbenhavn, 1897], pp. 145, 190).

thus from love without thought of moral obligation. Other writers reserve the field of morality for duty alone because they look upon social regulation as the origin of all morality. Bain says that "positive good deeds and self-sacrifice are the preserving salt of human life; but they transcend the region of morality proper, and occupy a sphere of their own." [8] Durkheim argues that it would be "contraire à toute méthode" to include under the same heading acts which are obligatory and acts which are objects of admiration, and at the same time exempt from all regulation; "si donc, pour rester fidèle à l'usage, on réserve aux premiers la qualification de moraux, on ne saurait la donner également aux seconds." [9] But does not ordinary usage sanction goodness as a moral quality as well as rightness or conformity to the rule of duty, and what would the history of ethics be if all theories of goodness were excluded from it?

At the same time it seems to me obvious that the idea of duty, being derived from custom, is prior to that of moral goodness. To say, as Green does, that the idea of an absolute and a common good "must have been at work in the minds of men before they could be capable of recognizing any kind of action as one that *ought* to be done," [10] is a philosophical construction for which there is not a whit of evidence. Professor Moore even asserts that our "duty" can only be defined "as that action, which will cause more good to exist in the Universe than any possible alternative"; [11] but then he is guilty of a confusion be-

[8] A. Bain, *The Emotions and the Will* (London, 1880), p. 292.
[9] E. Durkheim, *De la division du travail social* (Paris, 1893), p. 30. A similar view is taken by Professor R. Lagerborg ("La nature de la morale," in *Revue internationale de Sociologie*, xi. [Paris, 1903], p. 466).
[10] T. H. Green, *Prolegomena to Ethics* (Oxford, 1899), p. 239 *sq.*
[11] G. E. Moore, *Principia Ethica* (Cambridge, 1922), p. 148.

tween the concept of duty and what he thinks that people ought to do. And when he further maintains that, as we can never be sure that any action will produce the greatest value possible, "we never have any reason to suppose that an action is our duty," [12] and that if a man has adopted a given course of conduct after taking all possible care to assure himself that it is the best, and it, owing to some subsequent event, which he could not possibly have foreseen, turns out not to be the best, his action was wrong [13]—I think the aberrations of speculative ethics from the ordinary use of terms may be said to have reached their pitch; these statements make one think of the sin of unbelief attributed to the poor pagans who could never have heard of the Gospel. That any one ought to do the best he is able to do, is a proposition often heard; [14] but even if it were self-evident, as Professor Laird believes, [15] it could not affect the concept of ought, because it would only tell us what we ought to do, not what it means that we ought to do it. I venture, however, to think that those who state or accept this proposition themselves have actually two standards of duty, one by which they measure man and his doings in the abstract, with reference to an ideal which they identify with duty, and another by which they are guided in their practical moral judgments upon their own and their neighbours' conduct. It seems to me that Professor Laird himself makes an admission in this direction when he writes:—"We are reluctant to admit that *anyone* should be sacrificed deliberately in

[12] *Ibid.*, p. 149.

[13] G. E. Moore, *Ethics* (London, s.d.), p. 191 *sqq.*

[14] H. Sidgwick, *The Methods of Ethics* (London, 1913), p. 219. F. H. Bradley, *Ethical Studies* (Oxford, 1927), p. 157 n. 1. O. Stapledon, "The Bearing of Ethics on Psychology," in *Journal of Philosophical Studies,* ii. (London, 1927), p. 366. J. S. Mackenzie, *A Manual of Ethics* (London, 1929), pp. 321, 404.

[15] J. Laird, *A Study in Moral Theory* (London, 1926), p. 200.

order that others may gain, and when we are compelled to act in this fashion we do not care to think of it. On the other hand we praise, with very occasional reserve, anyone who sacrifices himself for such an end." [16] The conscientious man is apt to judge himself more severely than he judges others, and may be unwilling to admit that he ever can do more than his duty, seeing how difficult it is even to do all that he ought to do, and impressed, as he would be, with the feeling of his own shortcomings; yet I do not see how he could conscientiously deny that he has omitted to do many praiseworthy or heroic deeds without holding himself blamable for such omissions. My general conclusion, then, is that the concept of duty can no more be derived from that of goodness than the concept of goodness from that of duty. And the reason for their fundamental difference is that the concept of duty springs from the emotion of moral disapproval and that of goodness from the emotion of moral approval. Considering that disapproval has in all ages played a far more important part in the moral consciousness of mankind than approval, I am unable to subscribe to the opinion that "the conception of the Good is the central point of ethics." [17]

The notion embodied in "ought" is frequently looked upon as ultimate and unanalyzable. If this were the case we might, in our study of the moral consciousness, be able to draw up lists of duties, but we should be unable to understand or explain a single one of them, nay, the fact that there is a moral law at all would be a sheer mystery. Fortunately, however, we are not reduced to such incompetence. Far from being a simple notion, "ought" is clearly decomposable, even though it have a flavour of its

[16] Laird, *op. cit.*, p. 263.
[17] L. T. Hobhouse, *Morals in Evolution* (London, 1915), p. 19.

own which is easier to feel than to describe. First of all, it expresses a conation. When I feel that I ought to do a thing, I experience an impulse to do it, though some opposite impulse may finally determine my action; and when I say to another man, "You ought to do this or that," there is certainly implied a professed wish to influence his action in a given direction. In the notion of "duty," the ethical import of which is identical with that of "ought," the conative element is not so obvious. Closely connected with the conative nature of "ought" is the imperative character it is apt to assume; and both its conativeness and its imperativeness are determined by the cognition that the mode of conduct which ought to be performed or refrained from is not, or will possibly not be, performed or refrained from. It is also this notion of its not being so that determines the emotion which gives to "ought" the quality of a moral predicate. The doing of what ought not to be done, or the refraining from what ought not to be refrained from, is apt to call forth moral disapproval; this is the most essential fact involved in the notion of "ought."

Every "ought"-judgment contains implicitly a prohibition of that which ought *not* to be done. Nobody would ever have dreamt of laying down a moral rule if the idea of its transgression had not presented itself to his mind. We may reverse the words of the Apostle [18] and say that where no transgression is, there is no law; the law-breaker is, in a way, the law-maker. [19] When Solon was asked why he had specified no punishment for one who had murdered a father, he replied that he supposed it could not occur to any man to commit such a crime. [20] Sim-

---

[18] *Romans*, iv. 15.
[19] *Cf.* F. Thilly, *Introduction to Ethics* (New York, 1905), p. 280.
[20] Diogenes Laertius, *Solon*, 10. Cicero, *Pro S. Roscio Amerino*, 25.

ilarly, the modern Shintoist concludes that the primaeval
Japanese were pure and holy from the fact that they are
represented as a people who had no moral commandments.[21] It is this prohibitive character of "ought" that
has imparted to duty that idea of antagonism to inclination which has found its most famous expression in the
Kantian ethics, and which made Bentham look upon the
word itself as having in it "something disagreeable and
repulsive."[22] It is this intrinsic connection between
"ought" and "wrong" that has given to duty the most
prominent place in ethical speculation when moral pessi-
mism has been predominant. While the ancient Greeks,
with whom happiness was the state of nature, hardly spoke
of duty,[23] but held virtue to be the supreme good, Christianity, on the other hand, which looked upon man as a
being born and bred in sin, regarded morals pre-eminently
as a matter of duty. Then, again, in modern times, Kant's
categorical imperative came as a reaction against that
moral optimism which once more had given the preference to virtue, considering everything in the world or in
humanity as beautiful and good from the very beginning.[24]

It is not, then, in the emotion of approval that we must
seek for the origin of the concepts of "ought" and "duty."
At the same time we often applaud him who is faithful
to his duty in circumstances where the average man would
have felt a strong temptation to yield to a contrary im-

21 W. E. Griffis, *The Religions of Japan* (London, 1895), p. 72.
22 J. Bentham, *Deontology*, i. (London & Edinburgh, 1834), p. 10.
23 Professor C. C. J. Webb ("Obligation, Autonomy, and the
Common Good," in *Proceedings of the Aristotelian Society*, N. S. xx.
[London, 1920], p. 120 *sq.*) observes that Aristotle does not altogether ignore the obligatory character of morality, as appears from
his frequent use of the word δεῖ, but that he did not look upon it as
the distinctive feature of moral experience.
24 *Cf.* Th. Ziegler, *Social Ethics* (London, 1892), pp. 22, 75 *sq.*

pulse. It is to such cases that we may trace that adoration of duty, or rather of its fulfilment, which has been so common among moralists since the days of Kant, who attributed moral worth only to dutiful acts that result from a successful struggle against opposite inclinations.[25] They have a tendency to confine the words "ought" and "duty" to cases where there is generally a strong desire to do what ought not to be done.[26] Now there is no contradiction in the omission of an act being disapproved of and the performance of it being praised; and when the word "duty" is used in a derivative sense as a concrete rule of duty, it may even refer to a course of conduct the omission of which is in ordinary circumstances, but not necessarily in every instance, disapproved of.[27] Strictly speaking, however, "ought" and "duty" only express the tendency of an act's omission to call forth moral disapproval and say nothing about the consequences of its performance. "When ye shall have done all those things which are commanded you, say, We are unprofitable ser-

---

[25] See *infra*, p. 271 *sq.*

[26] *Cf.* F. Staudinger, *Das Sittengesetz* (Berlin, 1897), p. 317; C. D. Broad, *Five Types of Ethical Theory* (London, 1930), p. 164.

[27] This use of the word "duty" has made it possible to speak of "conflicting duties." Such an expression can only mean that rules of conduct which generally ought to be followed may in exceptional cases come into conflict with each other. This does not justify Bradley's phrase, "I neglect duty because of duty" (*Ethical Studies* [Oxford, 1927], p. 227); for it can never be my duty at the same time to do a thing and not to do it (*Cf.* Kant, *Einleitung in die Metaphysik der Sitten*, 4 [*Gesammelte Schriften*, vi. [Berlin, 1914], p. 224; T. K. Abbott's translation in *Kant's Critique of Practical Reason and other Works on the Theory of Ethics* [London, 1898], p. 280]). The "conflict of duties" is particularly felt by a person who in a given moment hesitates whether he ought to follow the one or the other of two conflicting general rules of duty (*Cf.* H. Y. Groenewegen, "Pflicht und Gewissen in der Ethik," in *Studier tillägnade Efraim Liljeqvist*, i. [Lund, 1930], p. 246). The subject has been discussed at considerable length by E. Laas (*Idealismus und Positivismus*, ii. [Berlin, 1882], p. 261 *sqq.*) and F. Staudinger (*op. cit.*, p. 324 *sqq.*).

vants: we have done that which was our duty to do." [28]
Duty is a stern lawgiver who threatens with punishment
but promises no reward.

The tendency in a phenomenon to arouse moral disapproval is directly expressed by the term *bad,* and closely
allied to it is the term *wrong.* But there is some difference in the use of these words. While "bad" may be applied both to a person's character and to his conduct, only
his conduct may be said to be wrong. The reason for this
is that the concept of moral wrongness is modelled on the
notion of a moral law, the breach of which is regarded
as "wrong"; and by laying down a moral law we only
enjoin a certain course of conduct, we do not command a
person to have a certain character. To say that an act
or forbearance is a duty is thus, so far as its morality
is concerned, exactly the same thing as to say that the
opposite mode of conduct is wrong.

"Wrong" is popularly regarded as the opposite of *right,*
and they really are contradictories, but only within the
sphere of positive moral valuation. We do not call the
actions of irresponsible beings, like animals and infants,
"right," although they are not wrong. Nor do we pronounce morally indifferent actions of responsible beings
"right," unless we wish thereby especially to point out
that they are not wrong; but it would be more strictly
accurate to say that people have "*a* right" to do them. A
right action, in the strict sense of the word, is on a given
occasion *the* right action, unless a choice of alternatives
is permitted by the rule of duty; right is what is in conformity to duty. Those who recognize the existence of
something super-obligatory would not say that it is not
right; they would say that it is more than right, but not
that it is more right. "Right" has no comparative; a cer-

[28] *St. Luke,* xvii. 10.

tain mode of conduct is either in conformity to the rule of duty or not. There are degrees of badness and of goodness, as the moral disapproval and the moral approval may be stronger or weaker, but there are no degrees of rightness.

The fact that the right mode of conduct is that which is in conformity to duty and not infrequently requires self-restraint, accounts for the erroneous opinion held by many ethical writers that "right" is intrinsically connected with moral approval. The choice of the right alternative, as I said in connection with the concept of duty, may give us satisfaction and call forth in us an emotion of approval, and the judgment in which we point out the rightness of the act may actually contain applause. The manner in which the judgment, "That is right," is pronounced often shows that it is meant to be an expression of praise. But this does not imply that the concept "right" by itself has reference to moral approval and involves praise. It only means that in one word is expressed a certain concept— that of conformity to duty—*plus* an emotion of approval. That "right" *per se* involves no praise is obvious from the fact that we regard it as perfectly right to pay a debt and to keep a promise, or to refrain from killing, robbing, or lying, though these acts or forbearances have no tendency whatever to evoke in us an emotion of moral approval.

The concept of "right," then, as implying that the opposite mode of conduct would have been wrong, ultimately derives its moral significance from moral disapproval. This may seem strange considering that "right" is commonly looked upon as positive and "wrong" as its negation. But we must remember that language and popular conceptions in these matters start from the notion of a moral rule or command. It is held to be of paramount importance that such modes of conduct as are apt to arouse

general moral disapproval should be avoided. People try
to prevent them by prohibitions and injunctions, often
emphasized by threats of penalties for the transgressors.
The whole moral and social discipline is based upon commands; customs are rules of conduct, and so are laws. It
is natural, then, that the notion of a command should
figure uppermost in popular conceptions of morality. Obedience to the command is right, the breach of it is wrong.
But the fact that gave birth to the command itself was
the disapproval called forth by the act which the command forbids or by the omission of that which it enjoins.

I have now spoken of "right" as an adjective. Used as
a substantive, to denote *a right,* it also, in whatever sense
it be applied, expresses a concept that is rooted in the emotion of moral disapproval. To have a right to do a thing
is to be allowed to do it, either by positive law, in the case
of a legal right, or by the moral law, in the case of a moral
right; in other words, to have a moral right to do a thing
implies that it is not wrong to do it. But generally the
concept of "a right" means something more than this.
From the fact that an act is allowable, that it is not wrong,
it follows, as a rule, that it ought not to be prevented; and
this character of inviolability is largely included in the
very concepts of rights. That a man has a right to live
does not merely mean that he commits no wrong by supporting his life, but it chiefly means that it would be
wrong of other people to prevent him from living, that it
is their duty to refrain from killing him, or even, as the
case may be, that it is their duty to help him to live.
And in order to constitute a right in him, the duty in question must be a duty *to him,* that is, a duty to be performed
for his own sake. To kill another person's slave may be
condemned as an injury done to the slave himself, in
which case it is a duty to the slave not to kill him; but it

may also be condemned on account of the loss it inflicts upon the master, and in this case it is deemed a duty to the master not to kill his slave. In the latter case we can hardly say that the duty of refraining from killing the slave constitutes a right to life in the slave: it only constitutes a right in the master to retain his slave alive and not to be deprived of him by an act causing his death.

So commonly does the conception of a right belonging to a person contain the idea of a duty which other persons owe him, that it seems necessary to point out the existence of rights in which no such idea is involved. A man's right to defend his country, for instance, does not intrinsically imply that it is wrong of the enemy to disable him from doing so. But on the other hand there are rights which are nothing else than duties towards those who have the rights. A right is not always a person's right to do, or to refrain from doing, something; it may have exclusive reference to other people's conduct. That a father has a right to be obeyed by his children only means that it is a duty incumbent on them to obey him. That a person has the right to bodily integrity only means that it is wrong to inflict on him a bodily injury. These rights may, no doubt, if violated, give rise to certain rights of activity: the father may have a right to exact from his children the obedience they owe him, the person who is attacked may have a right to defend himself. But in such cases the right of exacting obedience or of resisting wrong is certainly not identical with the right of being obeyed or of not being wronged.

It is commonly said that rights have their corresponding duties. But if this expression is to be used, it must be remembered that the duty which "corresponds" to a right is, as a matter of fact, either included in that right or simply identical with it. The identity between the right and the duty, then, consists in this, that the notion of a right belonging to a person is identical with the notion of a duty towards him. Rights and duties are not identical in the sense that it is always a duty to insist on a right, though this has been urged. If anybody prevents me from making use of my right, it may no doubt be deemed a duty on my part not to tolerate the wrong committed against me, but nothing of the kind is involved in the concept of a right. And the same may be said with reference to the assertion that a right to do a thing is always, at the same time, a duty to do it—an assertion which is a consequence of the doctrine that there is nothing morally indifferent and nothing that goes beyond duty; in other words, that all conduct of responsible beings is either wrong or obligatory. Even if this doctrine were accepted by our common moral experience—which it certainly is not—even if there were a constant coincidence between the acts which a person has a right to perform and such as it is his duty to perform, that would not constitute identity between the concepts of "right" and "duty." According to the meaning of a right, A's right may be B's duty towards A; but A's right cannot mean A's duty towards B or anybody else.

Closely connected with the notions of wrongness and rightness are the notions of *injustice* and *justice*. Injustice is a kind of wrongness. To be unjust is always to be unjust to somebody, a violation of some one's right. Justice is a kind of rightness. It involves the notion that a duty to somebody, a duty corresponding to a right in him, is fulfilled; [29] we may say that justice "demands" that it should be fulfilled. As an act is "right" if its omission is wrong, so an act is "just" in the strict sense of the word,

---

[29] According to the *Instutiones* of Justinian (i. 1. 1), "justice is the constant and perpetual will to render to each one his right."

if its omission is unjust. But like the adjective "right," the adjective "just" is also sometimes used in a wider sense, to denote that something is "not unjust." As non-obligatory acts that are not wrong can hardly be denied to be right, so non-obligatory acts that are not unjust can hardly be denied to be just, although they are not demanded by justice.

At the same time "injustice" and "justice" are not simply other names for violating or respecting rights. Whenever we style an act unjust, we emphasize that it involves partiality. We do not generally call murder and robbery unjust but wrong or criminal, because the partiality involved in their commission is quite obscured by their glaring wrongness or criminality; but we at once admit their gross injustice when we consider that the murderer and robber indulged their own inclinations with utter disregard of their neighbours' rights. On the other hand, we look upon "unjust" as an exceedingly appropriate term for a judge who condemns an innocent man with the intention to save the culprit; and we say it is just or, more emphatically, that justice demands that the innocent should not suffer in the place of the guilty. When we style an act "just," in the strict sense of the term, we point out that an undue preference would have been shown some one by its omission. It is true, as Adam Smith observes, that "we may often fulfil all the rules of justice by sitting still and doing nothing," [30] and that the man who barely refrains from violating the person or estate or reputation of his neighbours so far does justice to them; but in such cases we hardly apply the epithet "just," simply because there is no reason to emphasize the partiality of those who act in the contrary manner.

[30] Adam Smith, *The Theory of Moral Sentiments* (London, 1887), p. 117.

It is the emphasis laid on the duty of impartiality that gives justice a special prominence in connection with punishments and rewards. A man's rights depend to a great extent upon his actions. Other things being equal, the criminal has not the same rights to inviolability as regards reputation, freedom, property, or life as the innocent man; the miser and egoist have not the same rights as the benefactor and the philanthropist. On these differences in rights due to differences in conduct the terms "just" and "unjust" lay stress; for in such cases an injustice would have been committed if the rights had been equal. When we say of a criminal that he has been "justly" imprisoned, we point out that he was no victim to undue partiality, as he had forfeited the general right to freedom on account of his crime. When we say of a benefactor that he has been "justly" rewarded, we point out that no favour was partially bestowed upon him in preference to others, as he had acquired the special right of being rewarded. But the "justice" of a punishment or a reward, strictly speaking, involves something more than this; as we have seen, what is strictly just is always the discharge of a duty corresponding to a right that would have been in a partial manner disregarded by a transgression of the duty. If it is just that a person should be rewarded he ought to be rewarded, and to fulfil this duty is to do him justice. Again, if it is just that a person should be punished he ought to be punished, and his not being punished is an injustice to other persons. It is an injustice towards all those whose condemnation of the wrong act finds its recognized expression in the punishment, inasmuch as their rightful claim that the criminal should be punished, their right of resisting wrong, is thereby violated in favour of the wrong-doer. Moreover, his not being punished is an injustice towards other criminals, who have been, or who will be, punished for similar acts, in so far as they have a right to demand that no undue preference should be shown to anybody whose guilt is equal to theirs. Retributive punishment may admit of a certain latitude as to the retribution. It may be a matter of small concern from the community's point of view whether men are fined or imprisoned for the commission of a certain crime. But justice demands that in equal circumstances all of them should be punished with the same severity, since the crime has equally affected their rights.

The emphasis which "injustice" lays on the partiality of a certain mode of conduct always involves a condemnation of that partiality. Like every other kind of wrongness, "injustice" is thus a concept that is obviously based on the emotion of moral disapproval. And so is the concept of "justice," whether it involves the notion that an injustice would be committed if a certain duty is not fulfilled, or is simply used to denote that a certain course of conduct is "not unjust." But there is yet another sense in which the word "just" is applied. It may emphasize the impartiality of an act in a tone of praise. Considering how difficult it may be to be perfectly impartial and give every man his due, especially when one's own interests are concerned, it is only natural that men may be applauded for being just, and, consequently, that to call a person "just" may be to praise him. So, also, "justice" is used as the name for a virtue, "the mistress and queen of all virtues." [31] But all this does not imply that an emotion of moral approval enters into the *concept* of "justice." It only means that one word is used to express a certain concept—a concept which, as we have seen, ultimately derives its import from moral disapproval—and in addition an emotion of approval. That the concept of "justice" by

[31] Cicero, *De officiis*, iii. 6.

itself has no reference to the emotion of approval appears from the fact that it is no praise to say of an act that it is "only just."

From the concepts springing from moral disapproval we shall pass to those springing from moral approval. Foremost among these ranks the concept *good*.

The word "good" is applied to a great variety of objects.[32] The use made of it is in fact so extensive that it has been supposed to be essentially a collection of homonyms, such that the set of things to which it is applied— roughly, those in connection with which we heard it pronounced in early years, like a good bed, a good kick, a good baby, a good God—have no common characteristic at all.[33] Most frequently the concept of goodness has been considered closely related to desire, pleasure, or satisfaction. According to Hobbes, a man calls "good" whatever is the object of his appetite or desire, and "evil" the object of his hate or aversion.[34] Spinoza said that "we deem a thing to be good because we strive for it, wish for it, long for it, or desire it"; [35] but also, that we call a thing "good" or "evil" in so far as we perceive that it affects us with pleasure or pain.[36] Locke [37] and Hume [38] looked upon aptness to produce pleasure as the criterion of goodness. According to Bradley, "we may speak of the good, generally, as that which satisfies desire. It is that which we approve of, and in which we can rest with a feeling of

---

[32] *Cf.* W. D. Ross, *The Right and the Good* (Oxford, 1930), p. 65 *sqq.*

[33] C. K. Ogden and I. A. Richards, *The Meaning of Meaning* (London, 1927), p. 124 *sq.*

[34] Hobbes, *op. cit.,* i. 6, p. 35.

[35] B. de Spinoza, *Ethica,* iii. prop. 9.

[36] *Ibid.,* iv. prop. 8.

[37] J. Locke, *An Essay concerning Human Understanding,* ii. 21. 43, vol. i. (Oxford, 1894), p. 340 *sq.*

[38] D. Hume, *A Treatise of Human Nature,* iii. 1. 2 (Oxford, 1896), p. 472.

contentment. Or we may describe it again, if we please, as being the same as worth." [39] But whatever all other good things may have in common, "goodness," in the emphatically moral sense of the word—and with this alone I am here concerned—has a characteristic of its own, which makes it widely different from any other "good": [40] it is a concept rooted in the tendency to feel the emotion of moral approval, which implies a kindly feeling towards another individual as a cause of pleasure. This was clearly perceived by Hutcheson when he wrote that moral goodness "denotes our idea of some quality apprehended in actions, which procures approbation, attended with desire of the agent's happiness." [41] It is a serious defect of modern theories of value that they so frequently fail to distinguish properly between moral and other values.

"Good" conduct has often been identified with "right" conduct, but this identification is not borne out by the actual use of these terms, which should be our only criterion in fixing their meaning. [42] A father does right in supporting his children, inasmuch as he, by doing so, dis-

[39] F. H. Bradley, *Appearance and Reality* (London, 1915), p. 402.

[40] Professor Sorley (*op. cit.*, p. 120 *sq.*) maintains that "the widespread and unreflective application of moral predicates—of 'good' and 'bad'—to the operations of mere things . . . is really a survival of the primitive animism which attributed to material things a life and mind similar to those of man." But animism, as we know it, certainly does not attribute everything which we should call "good" or "bad" to the activity of volitional or supposed volitional beings, and, generally speaking, I can see no reason whatever for believing that the terms which are used both in a moral and in a non-moral sense were originally expressions for moral qualities only. Language, as already said, is a rough generalizer.

[41] F. Hutcheson, *An Inquiry into the Original of our Ideas of Beauty and Virtue* (London, 1753), p. 105.

[42] That "good" conduct and "right" conduct do not mean the same thing, which I pointed out in my *Moral Ideas,* has been recently emphasized by Dr. Ross (*op. cit., passim*), although he could not of course, from his objectivistic point of view, accept my subjectivistic interpretation of this difference.

charges a duty incumbent on him, but we do not say that he does a good deed by supporting them, or that it is good of him to do so. Nor do we call it good of a man to refrain from killing or robbing his neighbour, although his conduct is so far right. In these cases "good" has an emphatically moral meaning. If the question were put whether it is not always good that a person does his duty, nobody would of course deny that it is good. But then this predicate is used in a wider sense, not as a term of praise derived from the emotion of moral approval: we do not express any tendency to experience a kindly feeling towards a man because he refrains from killing another. The antithesis between "right" and "wrong" is, in a certain sense at least, contradictory, the antithesis between "good" and "bad" is only contrary. Every act—provided that it falls within the sphere of positive moral valuation—that is not wrong is right, but every act that is not bad is not necessarily good. Just as we may say of a thing that it is "not bad" and yet refuse to call it "good," so we may object to praising the discharge of a duty as "good," although the opposite course of conduct would be bad. But at the same time we *may* also very well praise a man for an act the omission of which would have incurred blame. To say of one and the same act that it is "right" and that it is "good," in the strict moral sense, really means that we judge of it from different points of view. Since moral praise expresses a kindly attitude of mind, it is commendable for a man not to be too niggard in his acknowledgment of other people's right conduct; whereas, self-praise being objectionable, only the other point of view is deemed proper when he passes a judgment on himself. He may say, without incurring censure, "I have done my duty, I have done what is right," but it would sound too self-complacent to say, "I have done a good deed," and be actually obnoxious to say, "I am a good man." The best man even refuses to be called good by others:—"Why callest thou me good? there is none good but one, that is, God."[43]

While "goodness" is the general expression for moral praise, the word *virtue* is generally used to denote a disposition of mind that is characterized by some special kind of goodness. He who is habitually temperate possesses the virtue of temperance, he who is habitually brave the virtue of courage, he who is habitually generous the virtue of generosity. Even when a man is simply said to be "virtuous," this epithet is given him, more or less distinctly, with reference to some kind or kinds of goodness attributed to him: it may mean that he has many virtues, or that he has much of one. A Supreme Being who is regarded as all-good is not called virtuous.

Virtue has been said essentially to express effort, resistance, and conquest. According to Kant it is "the moral disposition in struggle";[44] according to others it is the harmony won, while merit is the winning of it.[45] But I do not see that the general concept of virtue presupposes struggle. A virtue, consisting in the disposition to will or not to will a certain kind of conduct, is not even reduced by the fact that no rival impulses make themselves felt. It is true that by struggle and conquest a man may display more virtue, namely, the virtue of self-restraint in addition to the virtue gained by it. The vigorous and successful contest against temptation constitutes a virtue by itself. For instance, the quality of mind that is exhibited in a

[43] *St. Matthew*, xix. 17.
[44] Kant, *Kritik der praktischen Vernunft*, i. 1. 3 (*Gesammelte Schriften*, v. [Berlin, 1913], p. 84; Abbott's translation, p. 178).
[45] J. Dewey, *The Study of Ethics* (Ann Arbor, 1897), p. 133 *sq.* G. Simmel, *Einleitung in die Moralwissenschaft,* i. (Berlin, 1892), p. 228. *Cf.* Shaftesbury, *Characteristicks*, ii. (London, 1733), p. 36 *sqq.*

habitual and victorious effort to subdue strong sexual passions is a virtue distinguishable from that of chastity, and the latter is not made greater thereby; he who exercises more self-restraint in resisting seductive impulses may have more merit, but merit is not necessarily proportionate to virtue. The virtues are broad generalizations of mental dispositions that on the whole are regarded as laudable. Owing to their stereotyped character it easily happens in individual cases that the possession of a virtue confers no merit upon the possessor. A man's virtues are no exact gauge of his general moral worth. In order to form a just opinion of the value of a person's character we must take into account the strength of his instinctive desires and the motives of his conduct; and there are virtues that pay no regard to either. A sober man who has no taste for intoxicants possesses the virtue of sobriety in no less degree than a man whose sobriety is the result of overcoming a strong desire. He who is brave with a view to being applauded is not inferior in courage to him who faces danger merely from a feeling of duty. The only thing that the possession of a virtue presupposes is that it should have been tried and tested. We cannot say that people unacquainted with intoxicants have the virtue of sobriety, and that a man who never had anything to spend distinguishes himself for frugality. To attribute a virtue to somebody is always to bestow upon him some degree of praise, and it is not praise, only irony, to say of a man that he "makes a virtue of necessity."

There has been much discussion about the relation between virtue and duty, and it has been regarded as very complicated. We do not call it a virtue if a man habitually refrains from killing or robbing, or pays his debts, or performs a great number of other duties. We do call temperance and justice virtues, although we regard it as obligatory on a man to be temperate and just. We also call hospitality and charity virtues in cases where their exercise goes beyond the strict limits of duty. It is no wonder that those who consider the notion of duty incapable of being analyzed, or who fail to recognize its true import, are embarrassed by facts like these. But if my analysis of duty and virtue is correct, the relation between them is simple enough. That something is a duty implies that the opposite mode of conduct tends to evoke moral disapproval, that it is a virtue implies that the disposition to practise it tends to evoke moral approval. If the virtues actually cover a comparatively large field of the province of duty, that is due to their being dispositions of mind. We may praise the habits of justice and gratitude, even though we find nothing praiseworthy in an isolated just or grateful act.

There has been no less confusion with regard to the relation between duty and *merit*. Like the notions of goodness and virtue, the "meritorious" derives its origin from the emotion of moral approval; but while the former merely express a tendency to give rise to such an emotion, the "meritorious" implies that the object to which it refers merits praise, that it has a just claim to praise, in other words, that it ought to be recognized as good. This makes the term "meritorious" more emphatic than the term "good," but at the same time it narrows its province in a peculiar way. Just as the expression that something ought to be done implies the idea that it possibly may not be done, so the statement that something is meritorious, in pointing out its goodness, implies the idea that this goodness may fail to receive due recognition. It would be blasphemous to call the acts of a God who is conceived to be infinitely good "meritorious," since it would suggest a thinkable limitation of his goodness.

The emphatic claim to praiseworthiness made by the "meritorious" has led to its identification with the *superobligatory*. But from what has been said above it is manifest that they are not identical. As the discharge of a duty may be praised as a good deed, so it may also be regarded as an act that ought to be recognized as good. Practically, no doubt, there is a certain antagonism between duty and merit. We praise, and especially we regard as deserving praise, only what is above the average,[46] and we censure what is below it. But although thus most acts that are deemed meritorious fall outside the ordinary limits of duty as roughly drawn by the popular mind, we are on the other hand often disposed to attribute merit to a man on account of an act which from a strict point of view is his duty, but a duty that most people in the same circumstances would have left undischarged. This shows that the antagonism between duty and merit is not absolute. And in the concept of merit *per se* no such antagonism is involved.

But while "meritorious" is not identical with "superobligatory," it is obvious that if a course of conduct which is not regarded as a duty is held to be meritorious, it is *eo ipso* admitted that a man can do more than his duty. This is denied both by those who derive goodness from duty and consider that what is good is what ought to be done, and by those who derive duty from goodness and consider that everybody ought to do the best he is able to do. Duty, which is the minimum of morality in so far as it implies that the opposite mode of conduct is wrong, is identified with the supreme moral ideal, which requires the best possible conduct for its realization. As I have

[46] Merit, as Professor S. Alexander (*Moral Order and Progress* [London, 1896], p. 196) says, "expresses the interval which separates the meritorious from the average."

said above, this rigorism is not supported by our practical moral judgments. It is a mere theory, which may be traced either to the direct or indirect influence of Protestant theology with its denial of all works of supererogation, or to the endeavours of normative moralists to preach the most elevated kind of morality they can conceive. For my own part I do not see how such a doctrine could serve any useful purpose at all. The recognition of a "superobligatory" does not lower the moral ideal, on the contrary it tends to raise it; and at the same time it makes it more possible to vindicate the moral law and administer it more strictly. It is nowadays a recognized principle in legislation that a law loses much of its weight if it cannot be enforced. If the realization of the highest moral ideal is commanded by a moral law, such a law will always remain a dead letter, and morality will gain nothing. It seems to me that far above the anxious effort to fulfil the commandments of duty stands the free and lofty aspiration to live up to an ideal, which, unattainable as it may be, threatens neither with blame nor remorse him who fails to reach its summits. Does not experience show that those whose minds are constantly prepossessed with thoughts of duty are apt to become inhuman, intolerant, indeed intolerable?

In the earlier part of the book I have tried to show that there are no moral truths in the ordinary sense of the word, which attributes objective validity to moral judgments. But if I am right in my assertion that the moral concepts intrinsically express a tendency to feel a moral emotion of either approval or disapproval, it is obvious that a judgment which contains such a concept may be said to be true if the person who pronounces it actually has a tendency to feel the emotion in question with reference to the subject of the judgment. Professor Sorley argues against me that if a value-judgment lacked that validity it assumes, the proposition "this is good" could never be either true or false; "it would only express some peculiar state of mind of the person making the assertion and would have no possible validity in itself—would be, indeed, simply an emotion put by mistake into the form of a proposition." [47] I thought it was generally recognized that every proposition is either true or false, and that this must consequently be the case also with the proposition "this is good," whatever be the meaning of its predicate. But whether it is true *or* false just depends on the meaning given to it. If, as I maintain, the objective validity of all moral valuation is an illusion, and the proposition "this is good" is meant to imply such validity, it must always be false. On the other hand, if "good" expresses a tendency to feel moral approval, the proposition in question is, as already said, true if there really is such a tendency with regard to that of which goodness is predicated, and false if there is no such tendency—people are often hypocrites in their moral judgments. The same predicate is thus used in a sense that makes the proposition always false, and in another sense that makes it either true or false—just as the proposition "the sun sets" was always false in those days when everybody believed that it was the sun and not the earth that moved, but may be either true or false when its predicate is used in the present sense of the word. As to the alleged mistake of putting an emotion into the form of a proposition, it should be noticed that all of us, even normative moralists, are guilty of similar "mistakes" when we say that something is fearful, wonderful, hateful, admirable, lovable, or what not.

Professor Moore has raised other objections to my

47 Sorley, *op. cit.,* p. 68.

theory of the emotional origin of the moral concepts. He argues that if one person says "this action is wrong," and another says of the very same action that it is not wrong, and each of them merely makes a judgment about his own feelings towards it, they are not differing in opinion about it at all, and, generally speaking, there is absolutely no such thing as a difference of opinion upon moral questions. "If two persons think they differ in opinion on a moral question (and it certainly seems as if they sometimes *think* so), they are always, on this view, making a mistake, and a mistake so gross that it seems hardly possible that they should make it : a mistake as gross as that which would be involved in thinking that when you say, 'I did not come from Cambridge to-day' you are denying what I say when I say 'I did.' " This seems to Professor Moore to be a very serious objection to my view.[48] But let me choose another, analogous case, to illustrate the nature of his argument. One person says, "This food is disagreeable," and another says of the very same food that it is not disagreeable. We should undoubtedly assert that they have different opinions about it. On Professor Moore's view this shows that the two persons do not merely judge about their feelings but state that the food really is, or is not, disagreeable, and if they admitted that they only expressed their own feelings—as they most probably would if their statements were challenged [49]—and yet thought that they differed in opinion, they would make a mistake almost too great to be possible. For my own part I venture to believe that most people would find it absurd if they *denied* that they had different opinions about the food. This follows from the fact that the subjective experience has been objectivized in

[48] G. E. Moore, *Philosophical Studies* (London, 1922), p. 333 *sq.*
[49] *Cf.* H. Sidgwick, *The Methods of Ethics* (London, 1913), p. 27.

the speech as a quality attributed to the object, and seems the more natural on account of the ambiguous meaning which the word "opinion" has in common parlance, where it is used both for a judgment and for the expression of a feeling.[50] Indeed, in another place Professor Moore himself admits that "a man's *feelings* with regard to an action are not always clearly distinguished from his *opinion* as to whether it is right or wrong," and that "one and the same word is often used, sometimes to express the fact that a man has a *feeling* towards an action, and sometimes to express the fact that he has an *opinion* about it." [51] It seems to me that this admission itself is sufficient to deprive his argument of all evidential value.

Dr. Ross repeats Professor Moore's argument, which he finds unanswerable, and adds the following one of his own against the view that identifies goodness with the presence of some feeling: "If something, without changing its nature, at some moment aroused for the first time the feeling in some mind, we should clearly judge not that the object had then first become good, but that its goodness had then first been apprehended." [52] This is simply implied in the common sense belief in the objectivity of moral values, which I have examined before. But it is certainly in perfect agreement with my theory of moral values that we may judge an act to have been good before it evoked moral approval in us, since our tendency to feel this emotion, which constitutes its goodness, is something quite different from our actual feeling of it. I agree with Dr. Ross that if, for instance, some one were to become aware of an act of self-denial and admire it, he might "pronounce that it had been good even when no one had

[50] See, *e.g.*, H. W. Fowler and F. G. Fowler, *The Concise Oxford Dictionary of Current English* (Oxford, 1929), p. 798.
[51] G. E. Moore, *Ethics* (London, *s.d.*), p. 119.
[52] Ross, *op. cit.*, pp. 11, 82 *sq.*

been admiring it,"[53] inasmuch as he might attribute to
himself a tendency to admire or, as I should say, approve
of it, and consequently to the object a tendency to arouse
in him the emotion of approval. Such a tendency is exactly on a par with that power of producing aesthetic enjoyment which, according to Dr. Ross, is the characteristic
of a beautiful object.[54] And I think that if Professor
Moore's objection to my theory of the subjectivity of
moral values were sound, it would also apply to Dr. Ross'
view of beauty. He says that if the same object produces
genuine aesthetic enjoyment in one individual and genuine
aesthetic repulsion in another, the same object is both
beautiful and ugly, and that consequently our ordinary
ideas about beauty and ugliness require revision, since we
generally mean by "beautiful" and "ugly" attributes which
cannot belong to the same thing.[55] This is quite analogous
to my view that the same act can be both good and bad,
according as it is approved of by one individual and disapproved of by another. And in either case we may cer-

[53] *Ibid.,* p. 89.

[54] Dr. Ross (*op. cit.,* p. 128) says that "we cannot judge an object
to be beautiful till we think we have been aesthetically thrilled by it,"
and that "the judgment, while it is not a judgment about the judger's
state of mind, is one in which, on the strength of his knowledge of
(or opinion about) his state of mind, he ascribes an attribute to an
object. And if we ask ourselves what is the common attribute belonging to all beautiful objects, we can, I believe, find none other than
the power of producing the kind of enjoyment known as aesthetic."
He admits that "we do not *mean* by 'beautiful' an attribute having
even this sort of reference to a mind, but something entirely resi-
dent in the object, apart from relation to a mind"; but suggests that
"we are deceived in thinking that beautiful things have any such
common attribute over and above the power of producing aesthetic
enjoyment." This view of beauty is precisely similar to my view of
moral values, namely, that the moral attributes are ultimately tendencies to feel either moral approval or disapproval interpreted as
dynamic tendencies in the phenomena that gave rise to the emotion,
and that we are deceived if we think they are anything else.

[55] *Ibid.,* p. 129 *sq.*

tainly say that the two individuals differ in opinion about that on which they pronounce their judgments. How, then, can Dr. Ross regard Professor Moore's argument against me as "unanswerable"?

The other critical remark that Professor Moore has made on my theory has also reference to the meaning of words. He says it is commonly believed that some moral rules exhibit a *higher* morality than others, and asks what I could mean by saying that A's morality is higher than B's. He gives himself the answer: I could only mean that "A's morality is *my* morality, and B's is not." There is no inconsistency in this: my denial of objective moral standards does not prevent my pronouncing moral judgments which are expressions of my own moral feelings, and whatever terms I use they have to be interpreted accordingly. "But," he adds, "it seems to me quite clear that when we say one morality is higher than another, we do not merely mean that it is our own. We are not merely asserting that it has a certain relation to our own feelings." [56] I have no doubt that this is the case with most people's judgments, but this does not disprove my view that their assumed objectivity is an illusion. Leslie Stephen says each man thinks that his own morality is the *right* morality, and that any other standard is mistaken.[57] But who could maintain that it is so, because it is thought to be so?

The word "higher" has also incited Dr. Rashdall to an attack on me. He says that in one place I have talked about some emotions as "higher emotions"; but the context in which I did so [58] ought to have made it quite plain that I attached no moral significance at all to this expression.

---

[56] Moore, *Philosophical Studies*, p. 334 *sq.*
[57] L. Stephen, *The Science of Ethics* (London, 1882), p. 37.
[58] *Moral Ideas,* ii. 744.

He asks why I, on my views, should assume that "the emotions of the reflective are higher or truer than those of the unreflective." [59] I have said no such thing—how could an emotion be "true"? But I have said that the moral consciousness has developed from unreflective to reflective, which implies that the moral emotions have come to be more and more influenced by thought and reasoning.

Though all moral judgments are ultimately based on emotions, the influence that intellectual factors exercise on such judgments is very great indeed.[60] Emotions are determined by cognitions and differ in nature or strength according as the cognitions differ. This has been a very important cause of the variations of moral judgments: the same course of conduct is differently judged of because different ideas are held as to its nature or implications. If a person tells an untruth we are apt to feel indignant; but if, on due consideration of facts, we find that his motive was benevolent, for instance, to save the life of the person to whom the untruth was told, our indignation ceases and may be followed by approval. A moral judgment may be said to be more enlightened in proportion as it is influenced by reflection or knowledge, and the so-called moral evolution largely consists in a gradual progress in enlightenment. On this subject I shall have much more to say in the two following chapters.

[59] H. Rashdall, *Is Conscience an Emotion?* (London, 1914), p. 123. Cf. *Idem, The Theory of Good and Evil*, ii. (London, 1924), p. 413.

[60] A statement of mine (*op. cit.,* i. 20) to the effect that if it could be brought home to people that there is no absolute standard in morality they would perhaps be more apt to listen to the voice of reason, has led Dr. Rashdall (*Is Conscience an Emotion?*, p. 124 *sq.*) to the exclamation, "'The voice of reason,' forsooth, when the whole chapter is a diatribe against the notion that Reason has anything to say about conduct." This inaccuracy is astounding. In that very same chapter I have said (*op. cit.,* i. 10), "The influence of intellectual considerations upon moral judgments is certainly immense."

CHAPTER VI

THE SUBJECTS OF MORAL JUDGMENTS

THE moral emotions are not only at the bottom of the predicates of moral judgments, but also account for the general nature of their subjects.

Moral judgments are commonly said to be passed upon conduct and character. This is a convenient mode of expression, but needs explanation. The term "conduct" includes various elements into which the subjects of moral judgments may be resolved. In the first place it may be an act, by which I understand an event together with the intention to produce it. I then maintain that there can be only one intention in one act, and reject as confusing such distinctions as that between the immediate and the remote intentions or the direct and the indirect intentions of an act, which have been made by some moralists. It has been said, for instance, that if a nihilist seeks to blow up a train containing an emperor and others, his direct intention may be simply the destruction of the emperor, but that he indirectly also intends the destruction of the others who are in the train, since he is aware that their destruction will be included along with that of the emperor.[1] In this case we have two intentions and, if the nihilist succeeds in realizing them, two acts, namely, the blowing up of the train and the killing of the emperor; the former of these acts does not even necessarily involve the latter. But I fail to see that there is any intention at all to kill other persons.

[1] J. S. Mackenzie, *A Manual of Ethics* (London, 1929), p. 49. *Cf.* H. Sidgwick, *The Methods of Ethics* (London, 1913), p. 202 n.

The nihilist's non-intention in this respect may not serve
as an extenuation of his guilt, but we must not confound
a moral estimate with the psychical fact to which it refers.
His intention to blow up the train involved an extreme
disregard of the fate of those persons, he knowingly exposed them to extreme danger; and this may have been
held as blamable as if he had intended to kill them.

More strictly speaking, however, the moral judgments
we pronounce on acts do not really relate to the event but
to the intention; and a moral judgment may refer to a
mere intention, independently of its being realized or not.
The event is of moral importance only in so far as it indicates a decision that is final; "the road to hell is paved
with good intentions." External events are generally the
direct causes of our moral emotions; indeed, without the
doing of harm and the *doing* of good the moral consciousness would never have come into existence. Hence the in-
eradicable tendency to pass moral judgments upon acts,
though they really refer to the final intentions involved in
acts. It would be both inconvenient and purposeless to de-
viate, in this respect, from the established usage. And no
misunderstanding can arise if it is borne in mind that by
an "act," as the subject of a moral judgment, is invariably
understood the event *plus* the intention which produced it,
and that the very same moral judgment as is pronounced
on acts would also, on due reflection, be recognized as
valid with reference to final decisions in cases where purely
accidental circumstances prevented the accomplishment of
the act.

It is in their capacity of volitions that intentions are
subjects of moral judgments. But there are certain other
conations that also may be the objects of moral blame or
praise, namely, deliberate wishes, which have been too
little noticed both by psychologists and moralists. In the

realm of conations decisions and deliberate wishes form a province by themselves by being, in contrast to mere impulses, expressions of a man's character or "will."

If moral judgments are passed on intentions and deliberate wishes, it follows that they may, in many cases, be passed on motives. The term "motive" has been defined in different ways. It has been taken to mean an element in deliberation, the selected impulse in the conflict between various impulses, which normally results in a volitional action.[2] More frequently, I believe, it is used in a wider sense. I understand by it the conative cause or reason of an intention or a deliberate wish, a conation that "moves" the will.[3] As such it may itself be, or not be, an intention or a deliberate wish; and if it is, it obviously falls within the sphere of moral valuation. But it should be noticed that if the motive of an act is an intention, it must be an intention belonging to another act. When Brutus helped to kill Caesar in order to save his country, his intention to save it was the reason, and therefore the motive, of his intention to kill Caesar. Some writers have said that the motive of an act is a part of the intention. But if the intention of an act is a part of the act itself, and a motive is the cause of an intention, the motive of an act cannot be a part of its intention, since a part cannot be the cause of the whole of which it forms a part.

But even motives which, being neither intentions nor deliberate wishes, are no proper subjects of moral valuation, may nevertheless indirectly exercise much influence on moral judgments. One such motive is fear; hence compulsion is also in the eye of the law a frequent ground of extenuation.[4] Strictly speaking, a volition can never be

[2] R. H. Thouless, *Social Psychology* (London, 1925), p. 258.
[3] *Cf.* the *Oxford English Dictionary, s. v.* "Motive."
[4] *Moral Ideas,* i. 284 *sq.*

compelled into existence;[5] to act under compulsion really means to act under the influence of a non-voluntary motive which is so powerful that every ordinary human will would yield to it. As Aristotle puts it, pardon is given when "a man has done what he ought not to have done through fear of things beyond the power of human nature to endure and such that no man could undergo them. And yet, perhaps," he adds, "there are some things which a man must never allow himself to be compelled to do, but must rather choose death by the most exquisite torments."[6] There is also what is called "compulsion by necessity." If a person without permission gratifies his hunger with food that is not his own, the impulse which is the motive of his act has by itself no moral value. Nevertheless it must be taken into account by him who judges of the act: other things being equal, the person is less guilty in proportion as his hunger is more intense, and in extreme cases he may incur no blame at all; and this is likewise recognized by many laws.[7] So also, if any one commits a crime in a rage he is less blamable, and punished less severely,[8] than if he commits the same crime in cold blood; in this case, too, the moral judgment is modified by the pressure that a mere impulse exercises upon the agent's will. No man is responsible for such a pressure, unless it be due to choice or it might have been avoided with due foresight, and a thoughtful judge can only blame the agent for not having resisted the impulse, but allowed it to determine his will. In certain cases of mental disease a morbid impulse may take such a despotic possession of the patient as to drive him to the infliction of an injury.

[5] Cf. F. H. Bradley, *Ethical Studies* (Oxford, 1927), p. 44.
[6] Aristotle, *Ethica Nicomachea*, iii. 1. 7 *sq.*
[7] *Moral Ideas*, i. 285 *sqq.*
[8] *Ibid.*, i. 294 *sqq.*

He may be dominated by an impulse to kill somebody which he cannot resist; or he may yield to an impulse to steal or to set fire to houses or other property, without having any purpose to serve by what he does or any ill-feeling against the owner of the property. The deed to which the patient is driven may be one that he abhors, as when a mother kills the child whom she loves most. In such cases the agent is acquitted by an enlightened and scrupulous moral judge, and if he is condemned by the law of his country and its guardians, the reason for this can be nothing but ignorance.

If we more carefully analyze our moral judgments, however, we have to admit that they are not really passed on intentions or deliberate wishes in the abstract, but on the persons who have them: *they* are held blamable or worthy of praise. And the reason for this is that the moral emotions are reactionary attitudes towards living beings. When moral judgments formally refer to intentions or deliberate wishes they intrinsically refer to persons on account of them. Such judgments may then include both the intention of an act and its motive, but they may also have reference to either of them separately. Many judgments take notice only of the intention of an act and say nothing about its motive. This is particularly the case with judgments the predicates of which express no tendency to feel either approval or disapproval if the act is performed, such as "right," both as an adjective and a substantive, and "just." An act is "right" or "just" independently of its motive; so also what a person has "a right" to do he may do from any motive whatever, and when his right is a duty that other persons owe him their motives for fulfilling this duty are not thought of at all. At the same time we may very well blame or praise a man on account of his motive when he does an act that is "right" or "just." If a man saves a fellow creature from drowning in the hope of being paid for the trouble, it would be absurd to deny that his act is right, but his motive may nevertheless be called bad. On the other hand, even if he had done it in circumstances which exposed him to so great a danger that it could not be required of him as a duty, we should hardly call his action good or meritorious, that is, bestow moral praise on a person for an act the motive of which we disapprove.

If the motive is not considered when an act is called right, it may seem natural that it should not be considered either when an act is called wrong. But these cases are not quite analogous. As long as people do what they ought to do, we have generally no reason for inquiring into their motives; and when we call their actions right we neither blame nor praise them. But when we say that a person has acted wrongly we blame him for his act, and a conscientious judge would consider it necessary to examine his motive before condemning him. It has been said that a man is not necessarily blamable because he has acted wrongly.[9] But this is, in my opinion, to dissociate the act from the agent in a way which our moral consciousness cannot easily accept. As already said, there are cases in which even so stereotyped expressions of moral feelings as laws pay regard to the motives of acts, and the tendency of modern criminal law is to do so more and more, just under the influence of men's moral judgments. It would sound strange to hear that a person is a criminal if he has been acquitted by the judge, and it seems scarcely more appropriate to say that he has acted wrongly if he is

[9] See, e.g., G. E. Moore, Ethics, (London, s. d.), p. 193; A. C. Ewing, The Morality of Punishment (London, 1929), p. 9; C. D. Broad, "Critical Notice" of Ewing's book in Mind, N. S. xxxix. (London, 1930), p. 348.

free from blame. But this is a purely formal question of no deeper ethical significance.

A volition may have reference not only to the doing of a thing, but to the refraining from doing a thing. It may form part not only of an act but of a forbearance, and may as such be the subject of moral judgment no less than the intention involved in an act. But willing not to do a thing must be distinguished from not willing to do a thing: forbearances must be distinguished from omissions. An omission, in the restricted sense of the word, is characterized by the absence of volition; it is, as Austin put it, "the not doing a given act, without adverting (at the time) to the act which is not done." [10] Now moral judgments refer not only to willing but to not-willing as well, not only to acts and forbearances but to omissions. It is curious that this important point has been so little noticed by writers on ethics, although it constitutes a distinct and frequent fact in our moral judgments. It has been argued that what is condemned is really a volition, not the absence of a volition; that an omission is bad, not because the person did not do something, but because he did something else, "or was in such a condition that he could not will, and is condemned for the acts which brought him into that condition"; [11] or that moral blame attaches to him only "in so far as his carelessness is the result of some wilful neglect of duty." [12] All this seems to me to be defective analysis. If a person forgets to discharge a certain duty incumbent upon him, say, to pay a debt, he is cen-

---

[10] J. Austin, *Lectures on Jurisprudence*, i. (London, 1873), p. 438.
[11] S. Alexander, *Moral Order and Progress* (London, 1896), p. 34 *sq.*
[12] Sidgwick, *op. cit.*, p. 60. A similar view is taken by expositors of the moral philosophy of Roman Catholicism (F. A. Göpfert, *Moraltheologie,* i. [Paderborn, 1899], p. 113). *Cf.* K. Binding, *Die Normen und ihre Übertretung,* ii. (Leipzig, 1877), p. 105 *sqq.*

sured not for anything he did, but for not doing a thing he ought to have done, because he did not think of it; he is blamed for his forgetfulness. In other words, his guilt lies in his negligence.

Closely related to negligence is heedlessness; the difference between them is seemingly greater than it really is. While the negligent man omits an act that he ought to have done, because he does not think of it, the heedless man does an act from which he ought to have forborne, because he does not consider its probable or possible consequences.[18] In the latter case there is acting, in the former case there is absence of acting; but in both cases the moral judgment refers to want of attention, that is, to not-willing. In rashness, again, the person adverts to the mischief that his act may cause, but from insufficient advertence assumes that it will not ensue; his fault is partial want of attention. Negligence, heedlessness, and rashness, are all included under the common term "carelessness."

Our moral blame, however, is concerned with not-willing only in so far as it attributed to a defect of the will, not to the influence of intellectual or other circumstances for which no man can be held responsible. That power in a person which is called his "will" is regarded as a cause, not only of such events as are intended, but of such events as we think that the person "could" have prevented by his will. And just as, in the case of volitions, the guilt of the party is affected by the pressure of non-voluntary motives, so in the case of carelessness mental facts falling outside the sphere of the will must be closely considered

[18] In the common use of language the word "negligence" often stands for heedlessness as well, or for carelessness. I use it here in the sense in which it was applied by Austin (*op. cit.*, i. 439 *sq.*).

by the conscientious judge. But nothing is harder than to apply this rule in practice.

Equally difficult it is, in many cases, to decide whether a person's behaviour is due to want of advertence or is combined with a knowledge of what his behaviour implies, or of the consequences that may result from it—to decide whether it is due to carelessness, or to something worse than carelessness. For him who refrains from performing an obligatory act, though adverting to it, "negligent" is certainly too mild an epithet, and he who knows that mischief will probably result from his deed is certainly worse than heedless. Yet even in such cases the immediate object of blame may be the absence of a volition—not a want of attention, but a not-willing to do, or a not-willing to refrain from doing, an act in spite of advertence to what the act implies or to its consequences. I may abstain from performing an obligatory act though I think of it, and yet at the same time make no resolution not to perform it. So too, if a man is ruining his family by his drunkenness he may be aware that he is doing so, and yet he may do it without any volition to that effect. In these cases the moral blame refers neither to negligence or heedlessness, nor to any definite volition, but to disregard of one's duty or of the interests of one's family. At the same time the transition from conscious omissions to forbearances, and the transition from not-willing to refrain from doing to willing to do, are easy and natural; hence the distinction between willing and not-willing may be of little or no significance from an ethical point of view. For this reason such consequences of an act as are foreseen as certain or probable have commonly been included under the term "intention," [14] often as a special branch of intention—

14 Cf. Sidgwick, op. cit., p. 202.

"oblique," or "indirect," or "virtual" intention; [15] but, as was already noticed, this terminology is hardly appropriate. I shall call such consequences of an act as are foreseen by the agent, and such incidents as are known by him to be involved in his act, "the known concomitants" of the act. When the nihilist blows up the train containing an emperor and others, with a view to killing the emperor, the extreme danger to which he exposes the others is a known concomitant of his act. So, also, in most crimes, the breach of law, as distinct from the act intended, is a known concomitant of the act, inasmuch as the criminal, though aware that his act is illegal, does not perform it for the purpose of violating the law. As Bacon said, "no man doth a wrong for the wrong's sake, but thereby to purchase himself profit, or pleasure, or honour, or the like." [16] On the other hand, nobody is responsible for such concomitants of his acts as he could not know. Hence certain classes of agents—animals, children, idiots, madmen—who are more or less unable to know or foresee the implications or consequences of their acts are totally or partially exempted from moral blame as well as legal punishment.

Absence of volitions, like volitions themselves, gives rise not only to moral blame, but to moral praise. We may, for instance, applaud a person for refraining from doing a thing beneficial to himself but harmful to others, which in similar circumstances would have proved too great a temptation to any ordinary man; and it does not necessarily lessen his merit if the opposite alternative did not

[15] J. Bentham, *An Introduction to the Principles of Morals and Legislation* (Oxford, 1879), p. 84. Austin, *op. cit.*, i. 480. E. C. Clark, *An Analysis of Criminal Liability* (Cambridge, 1880), pp. 97, 100.

[16] Bacon, "Essay IV. Of Revenge," in *Essays* (London, 1864), p. 59. *Cf.* H. Grotius, *De jure belli et pacis,* ii. 20. 29. 1: "Vix quisquam gratis malus est."

even occur to his mind, and his abstinence, therefore, could not possibly be ascribed to a volition. Very frequently moral praise refers to known concomitants of acts rather than to the acts themselves. The merit of saving another person's life at the risk of one's own really lies in the fact that the knowledge of the danger did not prevent the saver from performing his act; and the merit of the charitable man depends on the loss that he inflicts upon himself by giving his property to the needy. In these and analogous cases of self-sacrifice for a good end, the merit, strictly speaking, consists in not-willing to avoid a known concomitant of a beneficial act. But there are also instances in which moral praise is bestowed on a person for not-willing to avoid a known concomitant which is itself beneficial. Thus it may on certain conditions be magnanimous of a person not to refrain from doing a thing, although he knows that his deed will benefit somebody who has injured him, and towards whom the average man in similar circumstances would display resentment.

All these various elements into which the subjects of moral judgments may be resolved, viewed with reference to all such circumstances as may influence their moral character, are included in the term "conduct." In order to form an accurate idea of these circumstances, it is necessary to consider not only the case itself but the man's character, if by character is understood a person's will regarded as a continuous entity.[17] The subject of a moral judgment is, strictly speaking, a person's will conceived

[17] Cf. Alexander, op. cit., p. 49: "Character is simply that of which individual pieces of conduct are the manifestation"; W. McDougall, An Outline of Psychology (London, 1926), p. 442: "'The Will' is character in action"; M. Scheler, Der Formalismus in der Ethik (Halle a. d. S., 1927), p. 504: "Der Character ist ja weiter nichts als das hypothetische mehr oder weniger konstante X, das wir setzen, um uns einzelne beobachtete Handlungen einer Person zu erklären." To the word character has also been given a broader meaning.

as the cause of his conduct; and since a man's will or character is a continuity, it is necessary that any judgment passed upon him in a particular case should take notice of his will as a whole, his character. We impute a person's conduct to *him* only in so far as we regard it as a result or manifestation of his character, as directly or indirectly due to his will. Hume observes:—"Actions are, by their very nature, temporary and perishing; and where they proceed not from some *cause* in the character and disposition of the person who performed them, they can neither redound to his honour, if good; nor infamy, if evil. . . . The person is not answerable for them." [18] There is thus an intimate connection between character and conduct as subjects of moral valuation. When judging of a man's conduct in a special instance, we judge of his character, and when judging of his character we judge of his conduct in general.

It is sometimes said that moral judgments are also passed on emotions; but I think this implies a misunderstanding of what is actually judged of. A person who feels resentment may be a proper object of moral disapproval, not on account of the resentful impulse as such, but because it has been allowed to develop either into an intention or into a deliberate wish to make the other person suffer or, at any rate, into a wish that he shall have to suffer; and the word resentment may be vaguely used in all these cases. Envy may be condemned in so far as it contains, not merely a wish to be as fortunate as the man towards whom it is felt—the word is often rather playfully used in this sense—but a wish that he should

---

[18] D. Hume, *An Enquiry concerning Human Understanding*, viii. 2. 76 (Oxford, 1902, p. 98). *Cf. Idem, A Treatise of Human Nature*, ii. 3. 2 (Oxford, 1896), p. 411. See also A. Schopenhauer, *Die Freiheit des Willens*, 5 (*Sämmtliche Werke*, iv.² [Leipzig, 1916], p. 93 *sq.*) ; *Idem, Die Grundlage der Moral*, § 20 (*ibid.*, p. 257).

not be so fortunate. The commandment, "Love your enemies," may imply something more than the next commandment, "Do good to them that hate you," [19] it may enjoin you to try to check your anger; but it cannot reasonably make it an obligation for you to have a tender feeling towards your enemy. As Kant said, "love, as an affection, cannot be commanded," [20] and the reason for this is that it cannot be produced by any effort of will. Professor Moore, who maintains that there is a large class of moral rules that are concerned with our "feelings, thoughts and desires," mentions as an instance of this kind of rule the tenth commandment, "Thou shalt not covet thy neighbour's house," etc.; yet he admits himself that although I cannot by any single act of will directly prevent from arising in my mind a desire for something that belongs to some one else, I might by my will prevent its continuance "by forcing myself to attend to other considerations which may extinguish the desire." [21] But what about the censure we pass on a person who rejoices at the misfortune of another? Dr. Broad calls this joy a wrong emotion, the feeling of which is an "emotional moral defect"; [22] but I do not think that even this case gives support to his general view that emotions are right and wrong in exactly the same sense as actions are. [23] It is true that the joy which is the direct cause of our censure contains neither an intention nor a deliberate wish;

[19] St. Luke, vi. 27.

[20] Kant, Grundlegung zur Metaphysik der Sitten, sec. i. (Gesammelte Schriften, iv. [Berlin, 1911], p. 399; Abbott's translation in Kant's Critique of Practical Reason and other Works on the Theory of Ethics [London, 1898], p. 15). See also Kant, Idem, Einleitung zur Tugendlehre, 11 (Gesammelte Schriften, vi. [Berlin, 1914], p. 401; Abbott, p. 312).

[21] G. E. Moore, Philosophical Studies (London, 1922), p. 315 sq.

[22] C. D. Broad, "Analysis of some Ethical Concepts," in Journal of Philosophical Studies, iii. (London, 1928), pp. 296, 294.

[23] Ibid., p. 297.

but it is an indication of a malicious disposition of will, and it is for this reason we blame the person who feels it. If he joyfully contemplates the misfortune which befalls another it may be assumed that he in other circumstances would wish him to suffer; Kant called this emotion "ein geheimer Menschenhass."[24] So also the absence of an emotion may, when viewed as a symptom, give rise to, and be the apparent object of, a moral judgment. We are apt to blame a man whose feelings are not affected by the news of some evil that has befallen his friend, because we regard this as a sign of an uncharitable character.

Few things are more liable to arouse people's indignation than opinions that differ from their own, and when the disagreement is about morals or religion, the indignation may certainly have a claim to the epithet righteous. Even philosophical theories, like egoistic hedonism and ethical subjectivism, do not escape the charge of immorality. But when an opinion as such is morally condemned it can hardly mean anything else than a condemnation of its realization in practice, or of the consequences to which it is supposed to lead; and it may therefore be considered wrong to pronounce or propagate it. At the same time a person who holds a certain opinion, say an atheist, may be supposed to lack the indispensable requirement for a good life; and the very holding of it may be an object of moral disapproval as an assumed effect of the will—there is a will to believe. That a certain belief, or "unbelief," is never by itself a sufficient ground for condemning the person who has it is recognized both by Catholic and Protestant theology. Thomas Aquinas points out that the *sin* of unbelief consists in "contrary opposition to the

[24] Kant, *Metaphysische Anfangungsgründe der Tugendlehre,* § 36 (*Gesammelte Schriften,* vi. [Berlin, 1914], p. 460).

faith, whereby one stands out against the hearing of the faith, or even despises faith," and that, though such unbelief itself is in the intellect, the cause of it is in the will. And he adds that in those who have heard nothing of the faith, unbelief has not the character of a sin, "but rather of a penalty, inasmuch as such ignorance of divine things is a consequence of the sin of our first parent." [25] Dr. Wardlaw likewise observes:—"Ignorance is criminal only when it arises from wilful inattention, or from aversion of heart to truth. Unbelief involves guilt, when it is the effect and manifestation of the same aversion—of a want of will to that which is right and good." [26]—To shut one's eyes to truth may be a great wrong, but nobody is blamable for seeing nothing with his eyes shut.

However obvious it may be that the moral consciousness, when sufficiently influenced by reflection, intrinsically bestows its blame and praise upon the will alone, we must not, of course, assume that moral judgments always and necessarily relate to the will. Let us briefly consider what light early custom, law, and belief may throw on this subject.[27] That custom is a moral rule, and originally the only moral rule, has been pointed out above, and ancient customs are at the foundation of early law-books, in which they were expressly formulated and enforced by a more definite sanction. It is true that while such laws express moral ideas prevalent at the time they are established, they are not, though still in existence, necessarily faithful representatives of the ideas of a later age; for the legal

[25] Thomas Aquinas, *Summa Theologica*, ii.-ii. 10. 1 *sq.*
[26] R. Wardlaw, *Four Sermons: Two on Man's Accountability for his Belief, &c.* (Glasgow, 1830), p. 38.
[27] I have discussed this subject much more fully in my *Moral Ideas*, vol. i. chs. ix.-xii., which also give the authorities for the facts quoted in the present chapter.

form gives the ancient custom such fixity that it may be able to survive, as a law, the change of public opinion and the introduction of a new custom. It may also be said that a law, being a general and at the same time strictly defined rule of conduct, cannot make special provision for every case and therefore may fail to satisfy public feelings in particular instances. But these facts do not affect the general conclusions we may arrive at.

We notice that at the lower stages of civilization there is a considerable lack of discrimination between intentional injuries and accidental ones, in other words, that moral judgments are largely influenced by external events involved in, or resulting from, the conduct of men. The customs of some savage peoples are said to make no distinction at all between those two kinds of harm, and other savages impute at least a certain degree of guilt to persons who in our opinion are perfectly innocent. Nay, even among peoples who have reached a higher level of culture innocent persons are often punished by law for bringing about events without any fault of theirs. Instances of this are found in the laws of the Chinese and the ancient Babylonians, Hebrews, Hindus, and Teutons. In historic times Teutonic peoples treated intentional homicide as worse than unintentional, but even the involuntary manslayer had to pay *wer* to the family of the dead man, and the *wer* to be paid was not merely compensation for the loss sustained but it was punishment as well. And the character of criminality attached to accidental homicide survived the system of *wer*. When homicide became a capital offence, homicide by misadventure was included in the law. It is true that the involuntary manslayer was not executed but recommended to the mercy of the prince, and subsequently, when he no longer was in need of mercy, he nevertheless continued to be treated as a crim-

inal by the law of England. He was punished with forfeiture of his goods; and according to the rigour of the
law such forfeiture might have been exacted as late as
the year 1828, when the law was finally abolished after
having fallen into desuetude in the course of the previous
century.

If men at the earlier stages of civilization generally
attach undue importance to the outward aspect of conduct, the same is still more the case with their gods. According to the Vedic hymns, whoever with or without
intention offends against the eternal ordinances of Varuna,
the All-knowing and Sinless, arouses his anger and is
bound with the bonds of the god—with calamity, sickness, or death. In the Greek literature there are several
cases of guilt incurred by the accidental transgression of
some sacred law, the transgressor being perfectly unaware
of the nature of his deed. The Hebrew psalmist cries out,
"Who can understand his errors? cleanse thou me from
secret faults." Unintentional error, Mr. Montefiore observes, would be as liable to incur divine punishment as
the most voluntary crime, if it infringed the tolerably wide
province in which the right or sanctity of Yahveh was
involved. The rabbis maintained that a false oath, even
if made unconsciously, involves man in sin and is punished as such; and we meet with a similar opinion in
mediaeval Christianity, where various penitentials condemned to penance a person who, in giving evidence,
swore to the best of his belief, in case his statement afterwards proved untrue. In other instances, also, penances
were prescribed for mere misfortune; thus, if a person
killed another by pure accident he had to do penance for
one or several years—if he accidentally killed his father
or mother he might have to do so even for fifteen years.
The Scotists expressly declared that the external deed has

a moral value of its own, which increases the goodness or badness of the agent's intention; and though this doctrine was opposed by Thomas Aquinas, Bonaventura, and other leading theologians, it was nevertheless admitted by them that, according to the will of God, certain external deeds entail a certain accidental reward, the so-called *aureola*.

How shall we explain all these facts? Do they faithfully represent ideas of moral responsibility? Do they indicate that, at the earlier stages of civilization, the outward event as such, irrespectively of the will of the agent, is an object of blame?

Most of the statements that imply a perfect absence of discrimination between accident and intention refer to the system of private redress. While this system is more or less regulated by custom and does not allow the injured party or his kin to treat the offender just as they please, it nevertheless makes considerable allowance for their personal feelings, and these feelings are apt to be neither impartial nor sufficiently discriminate.

In the case of accidental homicide, deference may also have to be shown for the supposed feelings of the dead man's ghost, who angry and bloodless is craving for revenge and thirsting for blood, and ready to persecute his own family if they leave his desires ungratified. At the same time he also attacks the manslayer and cleaves to him like a miasma. The manslayer is consequently regarded as unclean, and has both for his own sake and for the sake of the community in which he lives to undergo some ceremony of purification in order to rid himself of the dangerous and infectious pollution; and this is the case whether the shedding of blood was intentional or accidental. Now, though this state of uncleanness does not intrinsically involve guilt, there can be no doubt that

in various cases the polluting effect attributed to manslaughter has influenced the moral judgment of the act;
the inconvenient restrictions laid on the tabooed man-
slayer easily come to be looked upon in the light of a
punishment and the rites of purification as a means of
removing guilt. Moreover, the notion of a persecuting
ghost may be replaced by the notion of an avenging god;
it is a fact of common occurrence that the doings or functions of one mysterious being are transferred to another.
And what particularly helps to explain the attitude of religion towards unintentional and unforeseen shedding of
human blood is the widespread idea that the infection of
uncleanness is shunned by gods even more than it is by
men.

There are other, more general reasons for the want of
discrimination often displayed by religion in regard to
the accidental transgression of a religious law. When a
thing is *taboo* it is supposed to be charged with mysterious
energy that will injure or destroy the person who comes
into contact with the forbidden thing, whether he does
so wilfully or by mistake. So also, according to primitive
notions, the effect of a curse or an oath is purely me-
chanical; hence a person who swears falsely in ignorance
exposes himself to no less danger than a person who per-
jures himself knowingly. Again, as regards religious offences in the strictest sense of the term—that is, offences
against some god that are supposed to arouse his resentment—it should be remembered that, just as a man who
is hurt is unable to judge the matter as coolly as does the
community at large, so a god whose ordinances are transgressed is thought to be less discriminating in his anger
than a disinterested human judge, and consequently more
apt to be influenced by the external event. There are thus
various reasons why, in the point that we are discussing,

the religious beliefs of a people do not faithfully represent their general notions of moral responsibility.

But though the grossest want of discrimination may be explained from revengeful feelings and superstitious beliefs, there still remain a multitude of cases that must be regarded as genuine expressions of moral disapproval. As to these it should, first, be remembered that the reflecting moral consciousness also may hold a person blamable for the unintentional and unforeseen infliction of an injury, namely, in cases where it assumes want of proper foresight. Now, as we know, it is often difficult enough to discern whether, or to what extent, an unintended injury is due to carelessness on the part of the agent; sometimes it is no easy thing to tell whether an injury was intended or not. It is not to be expected, then, that distinctions of so subtle a nature should be properly made by the uncultured mind, and least of all is it to be expected that such distinctions should be embodied in early custom and law, which are based on average cases and allow of no minute individualization. It has been observed that the roughness of Teutonic justice may be partly explained from the difficulty of getting any proof of intention or of its absence, from the lack of any proper distinctions between misadventure and carelessness, and from the fact that the so-called misadventures of early times covered many a blameworthy act. But, most important of all, the unreflecting mind is shocked by the harm done, and cares little for the rest. It does not press the question whether the harm was caused by the agent's will or not. It does not make any serious attempt to separate the external event from the will, and is inclined to assume that there is a coincidence between the two. This is the main reason for the indiscriminate attitude of early custom and law towards accidental injuries. It does not imply any difference in principle between the enlightened and unenlightened moral consciousness as regards the subject of moral valuation.

This becomes quite obvious when we consider what a great influence the outward event exercises upon moral estimates even among ourselves. "The world judges by the event, and not by the design," says Adam Smith. "Every body agrees to the general maxim, that as the event does not depend on the agent, it ought to have no influence upon our sentiments, with regard to the merit or propriety of his conduct. But when we come to particulars, we find that our sentiments are scarce in any one instance exactly conformable to what this equitable maxim would direct." [28] If, however, it is clearly realized that a certain event is the result of merely external circumstances, that it was neither intended by the agent nor could have been foreseen by him, in other words, that it is absolutely unconnected with any defect of will, then there could be no moral disapproval at all. Such an event could not even call forth a feeling of revenge. Sudden anger itself cools down when it appears that the cause of the inflicted pain was a mere accident. Even a dog distinguishes between being stumbled over and being kicked.

Morally equivalent to accidental injuries is harm caused by agents who on account of their intellectual inferiority are unable to know the implications or consequences of their acts, such as animals, little children, idiots, and madmen. Yet however irresponsible they appear to us, they are not always recognized to be so. At lower stages of civilization animals may be treated as responsible agents. The custom of avenging the violent death of a

[28] Adam Smith, *The Theory of Moral Sentiments* (London, 1887), p. 152.

relative is often extended to cases in which the slayer
was an animal, and animals are even exposed to regular
punishment. In various European countries they have
been judicially sentenced to death and publicly executed
in retribution for injuries inflicted by them. Advocates
were assigned to defend the accused animals, and the
whole proceedings, trial, sentence, and execution, were
conducted with all the strictest formalities of justice.
These proceedings seem to have been particularly common from the end of the thirteenth till the seventeenth
century; the last case in France occurred as late as 1845.
It seems to me probable that this practice of punishing
animals after human fashion had developed from the
earlier European custom of giving up a beast who had
done some serious damage, especially if it had caused
the death of a man, to the injured party or his family
that it might be retaliated upon. And the reason for punishing the animal seems simple enough: the animal was
regarded as responsible for its deed. In early records the
punishment is frequently spoken of as an act of "justice,"
and from various details we can also see how closely the
responsibility ascribed to animals resembled the responsibility of men. A distinction was made between a mischievous dog that entered a room through an open door
and one that committed a burglary. The repetition of a
crime aggravated the punishment. The animal "principal"
was punished more severely than the "accessories"; and,
as in the case of men so in the case of animals, youth was
a ground for acquittal. Once when a sow and her six young
ones were tried on a charge of their having murdered and
partly eaten a child, the sow was condemned to death,
whereas the young pigs were acquitted on account of their
youth and the bad example of their mother. The practice
of punishing animals seems less surprising when we con-

sider that even among ourselves the dog who steals or the horse who kicks arouses a feeling of resentment that almost claims to be righteous. And in earlier times beasts were frequently looked upon as more or less rational beings. In the sixteenth century Benoît wrote that animals often speak. In the middle of the following century Hieronymus Rorarius published a book to prove that animals make better use of their reason than men.

The total or partial irresponsibility of childhood has only been recognized more fully along with a deeper insight into the true nature of the child. According to early custom children who have committed an injury are sometimes retaliated upon; and in English records from the eighteenth century we read of a girl of thirteen who was burned for killing her mistress, and of a boy of eight who was hanged for arson. The irresponsibility of the insane has been slowly recognized in European legislation. Many of them were burned as witches or heretics, others were treated as ordinary criminals. A lunatic was a hateful individual because he was supposed to have the devil in him, or because his affliction was regarded as the visitation of God upon heresy or sin. But to explain the forensic attitude towards insanity it should also be noticed that its mental characteristics have been so little understood that many demented persons have been treated as if they were sane because they were thought to be sane, and that others, though recognized as labouring under insane delusions, have been treated as responsible because they were thought to be sane in other respects.

Considering how little regard is paid to motives in our own laws, we must not expect much notice to be taken of them by early law and custom. Yet we find there cases in which theft committed under stress of great hunger is left unpunished; and the difference between an injury which a person inflicts deliberately, in cold blood, and one which he inflicts in the heat of the moment, under the disturbance of great excitement caused by a wrong done to himself, is widely recognized. Even savages of so low a type as the Australian natives are said to distinguish between murder and manslaughter.

It has often been noticed that in early moral codes the so-called negative commandments, which tell people what they ought not to do, are much more prominent than the positive commandments, which tell them what they ought to do. The main reason for this is that negative commandments spring from the disapproval of acts, whereas positive commandments spring from the disapproval of forbearances or omissions, and that the indignation of men is much more easily aroused by action than by the absence of it. A person who commits a harmful deed is a more obvious cause of pain than a person who causes harm by doing nothing, and this naturally affects the guilt in the eyes of the multitude. The more scrutinizing the moral consciousness, the greater the importance which it attaches to positive commandments. This is well illustrated by a comparison between Old and New Testament morality: the old legal formula began "thou shalt not," the new begins, "thou shalt." Yet to say that the new morality involved the discovery of "a new continent in the moral globe," [29] is an obvious exaggeration. The customs of all nations contain not only prohibitions, but positive injunctions as well. To be generous to friends, charitable to the needy, hospitable to strangers, are rules that may be traced back to the lowest stages of savagery known to us. The difference in question is only one of degree.

That moral indignation and moral approval are from the very beginning felt, not with reference to certain

[29] J. R. Seeley, *Ecce Homo* (London, 1892), p. 179.

modes of conduct in the abstract, but with reference to persons on account of their conduct, is obvious from the intrinsic nature of those emotions. The more a moral judgment is influenced by reflection, the more it scrutinizes the character that manifests itself in that individual piece of conduct by which the judgment is occasioned; but however superficial it be, it intrinsically refers to a will conceived of as a continuous entity, to a person regarded as a cause of pleasure or pain. This holds true of savage and civilized men alike. Even tame animals, in response to a hurt or a benefit, behave differently towards different persons according to their previous experience of the agent.

After what has been said above the answer to the all-important question, so frequently ignored by writers on ethics, *why* moral judgments are passed on conduct and character is not far to seek. These judgments spring from moral emotions. The moral emotions are retributive emotions. A retributive emotion is a reactive attitude of mind, either hostile or kindly, towards a living being (or something taken for a living being), regarded as a cause of pain or pleasure. And a living being is, on due reflection, regarded as a true cause of pain or pleasure only in so far as this feeling is assumed to be caused by its will. The correctness of this explanation I consider to be proved by the fact that not only moral emotions, but also non-moral retributive emotions when sufficiently deliberate, are felt towards objects that are exactly similar in nature to those on which moral judgments are passed. This coincidence cannot possibly be accidental: it must have its ground in the retributive character of the emotions which are at the bottom of all moral valuation.

Like moral indignation, deliberate non-moral resent-

ment can be felt only towards a living being, or towards
something which is taken for a living being. We may be
angry with inanimate things for a moment, but our anger
disappears as soon as we reflect that the thing which gave
rise to it is neither volitional nor sensitive. Even a dog
who, in playing with another dog, hurts himself by run-
ning into a tree, changes his angry attitude immediately
he notices what gave him pain.[30]

Very similar to injuries resulting from inanimate things
are injuries resulting accidentally from animate beings.
If my arm or my foot gives a push to my neighbour,
and he is convinced that the push was neither intended
nor foreseen nor due to any carelessness whatever on my
part, surely he cannot feel angry with me. My neighbour
makes a distinction between a part of my body and myself
as a volitional being, and finds that *I* am no proper object
of resentment when the cause of the hurt was merely
my arm or my foot. An event is attributed to *me* as its
cause only if it is considered to be connected in some way
or other with my will; and *I*, regarded as a volitional and
sentient entity, can be a proper object of resentment only
as a cause of pain. As said before, even a dog distinguishes between being stumbled over and being kicked,
and the reason for this is that the dog scents an enemy
in the person who kicks him, but not in the one who
stumbles. We are told of some Kafirs that they expect a
similar discrimination from the elephant; for if an elephant is killed "they seek to exculpate themselves towards
the dead animal, by declaring to him solemnly, that the
thing happened entirely by accident, not by design." [31]

[30] H. M. Stanley, *Studies in the Evolutionary Psychology of Feeling* (London, 1895), p. 154 *sq.*
[31] H. Lichtenstein, *Travels in Southern Africa,* i. (London, 1812),
p. 254.

We can hardly feel disposed to resent injuries inflicted upon us by animals, little children, or madmen when we clearly recognize their inability to judge of the nature of their acts. "Why," says the Stoic, "do you bear with the delirium of a sick man, or the ravings of a madman, or the impudent blows of a child? Because, of course, they evidently do not know what they are doing. . . . Would any one think himself to be in his perfect mind if he were to return kicks to a mule or bites to a dog?" [32] Hartley observes, "As we improve in observation and experience, and in the faculty of analyzing the actions of animals, we perceive that brutes and children, and even adults in certain circumstances, have little or no share in the actions referred to them." [33]

Non-moral resentment, when sufficiently deliberate, considers motives of acts. If a man tells us an untruth, our feelings towards him are not the same if he did it in order to save our life as if he did it for his own benefit. Moreover, our anger abates, or ceases altogether, if we find that he who injured us acted under compulsion,[34] or under the influence of a sudden impulse, too strong for any ordinary man to resist. Then, the main cause of the injury was not his will, conceived as a continuous entity. It yielded to the will of somebody else, reluctantly, as it were, or to a powerful conation which formed no part of his real self. He was merely an instrument in another's hand, or he was "beside himself," "beyond himself," "out of his mind." When we are angry, says Montaigne, "it is passion that speaks, and not we." [35] So also, what a person does in madness is not an act committed by *him*:

[32] Seneca, *De ira,* iii. 26 *sq.*

[33] D. Hartley, *Observations on Man,* i. (London, 1810), p. 493.

[34] *Cf.* Seneca, *op. cit.,* ii. 30: "Who but an unjust person can be angry with what is done under compulsion?"

[35] M. de Montaigne, *Essais,* ii. 31 (*Œuvres* [Paris, 1837], p. 396).

"Was 't Hamlet wrong'd Laertes? Never Hamlet:
If Hamlet from himself be ta'en away,
And when he's not himself does wrong Laertes,
Then Hamlet does it not, Hamlet denies it.
Who does it, then? His madness: if 't be so,
Hamlet is of the faction that is wrong'd;
His madness is poor Hamlet's enemy." [86]

We resent not only acts and volitions, but also omissions, though generally less severely; and when a hurt is attributed to want of foresight, our resentment is, *ceteris paribus,* proportionate to the degree of carelessness which we lay to the offender's charge. The less foresight could have been expected in a given case, the smaller share has the will in the production of the event. Like moral disapproval, non-moral resentment is not indifferent to the character of the injurer. It reaches its height when he is found to nourish habitual ill-will towards the injured party; while the latter is not deaf to the prayer for forgiveness that springs from genuine repentance.

Passing to the emotion of gratitude, we find a similar resemblance between the facts that give rise to this emotion and those which are objects of moral praise. We may feel some kind of retributive affection for inanimate objects that have given us pleasure: "a man grows fond of a snuff-box, of a pen-knife, of a staff which he has long made use of, and conceives something like a real love and affection for them." [37] But gratitude, involving a desire to please the benefactor, can reasonably be felt towards such objects only as are themselves capable of feeling pleasure. On due deliberation we do not feel grateful to a person who does good to us by pure accident: since gratitude is directed towards the assumed cause of

[86] Shakespeare, *Hamlet,* v. 2.   [37] Adam Smith, *op. cit.,* p. 136.

pleasure and a person is regarded as a cause only in his capacity as a volitional being, gratitude presupposes that the pleasure shall be due to his will. For the same reason motives are taken into consideration by the benefited party. As Hutcheson observes, "bounty from a donor apprehended as morally evil, or extorted by force, or conferr'd with some view of self-interest, will not procure real good-will; nay, it may raise indignation." [38]

The objects towards which non-moral resentment and gratitude are felt are thus in their general nature precisely similar to those which are the subjects of moral judgments. This seems to me definitely to solve a problem which necessarily baffles solution in the hands of those who fail to recognize that moral judgments are based on emotions of a retributive character. It has been argued, for instance, that moral praise and blame are not applied to inanimate things and those who commit involuntary deeds, because they are administered only "where they are capable of producing some effect"; [39] that moral judgment is concerned with the question of compulsion, because "only when a man acts morally of his own free will is society sure of him"; [40] that we do not regard a lunatic as responsible, because we know that "his mind is so diseased that it is impossible by moral reprobation alone to change his character so that it may be subsequently relied upon." [41] The bestowal of moral praise or blame on a person is thus attributed to utilitarian calculation. [42] So consistently did James Mill apply his theory, that their purpose is the encouragement of right conduct

[38] F. Hutcheson, *An Inquiry into the Original of our Ideas of Beauty and Virtue* (London, 1753), p. 157.
[39] James Mill, *A Fragment on Mackintosh* (London, 1835), p. 370.
[40] Th. Ziegler, *Social Ethics* (London, 1892), p. 56 *sq.*
[41] W. K. Clifford, *Lectures and Essays* (London, 1886), p. 296.
[42] See also James Mill, *op. cit.*, pp. 261, 262, 375.

and the discouragement of wrong,[43] that, as his son tells us, he refused to let his praise or blame be influenced by the motive of the agent: "he blamed as severely what he thought a bad action, when the motive was a feeling of duty, as if the agents had been consciously evil doers." [44] But, as Stuart Mill observes (though he never seems to have realized the full import of his objection), while we may administer praise and blame with the express design of influencing conduct, "no anticipation of salutary effects from our feeling will ever avail to give us the feeling itself." [45]

But it is not only with reference to their general nature that there is a coincidence between the subjects of moral judgments and the facts which are apt to give rise to retributive emotions: a detailed inquiry into the moral valuation of the particular modes of conduct shows its obvious connection with the retributive character of the moral emotions. The largest portion of my book on *The Origin and Development of the Moral Ideas* has been devoted to such an inquiry, and its result is to my mind the most conclusive proof possible of my theory of the emotional origin of moral judgments. I do not know that any other theory on their origin, whatever arguments have been adduced in support of it, has been subjected to an equally comprehensive test.

When we more closely scrutinize the fact that the subject of a moral judgment is, strictly speaking, a person's will or character as the cause of his conduct, we notice that the question how his character has become what it

[43] A theory which seems to be shared by Sidgwick (*op. cit.*, p. 428) and Professor Moore (*Ethics* [London, *s. d.*], pp. 188, 189, 193).

[44] J. S. Mill, *Autobiography* (London, 1873), p. 49 *sq.*

[45] *Idem*, in a note to James Mill's *Analysis of the Phenomena of the Human Mind*, ii. (London, 1869), p. 323.

is, though generally not raised at all, has something to
do with the thoroughness of the judgment. I think most
people would admit that a licentious man who has grown
up in corrupt surroundings is less blamable than an equally
licentious man who has always lived under conditions
favourable to virtue, and that a pickpocket who was kid-
napped as a child by a band of pickpockets and trained
to the profession should be looked upon with some indulgence. It may of course be said that though the person's conduct is largely due to the influence of external
circumstances upon his character, this influence was not
irresistible, that he might have overcome it by an effort
of will, and that consequently he is not free from blame;
but in any case the influences of environment and the
circumstances of upbringing are not irrelevant to the degree of his guilt. We do make a distinction between the
original and the acquired character, however impossible
it is in practice to draw a hard and fast line between the
two. As Leslie Stephen observes, there is in the whole
of our lives a constant action and reaction between the
external and internal conditions, and "we cannot disen-
tangle them into two separate series of events, any more
than we can say whether breathing depends more upon
the air or the lungs." [46] But I cannot agree with Professor
Field when he calls it a mere prejudice to say that it would
be unfair to condemn a man for things which are the
result of external circumstances over which he had no
control.[47] We do exempt a man from blame if we know
that he acts under compulsion and hold the compulsion

[46] L. Stephen, *The Science of Ethics* (London, 1882), p. 284.
[47] G. C. Field, *Moral Theory* (London, 1921), p. 171 *sq.* A similar
view has been expressed by F. E. Beneke (*Grundlinien des natürlichen
Systemes der praktischen Philosophie,* i. [Berlin, Posen & Bromberg,
1837], p. 533) and Th. Lipps (*Die ethischen Grundfragen* [Leipzig &
Hamburg, 1912], p. 287 *sq.*).

irresistible for any ordinary man. No doubt, we should consider it overscrupulous to refrain from pronouncing a moral judgment on a person because we do not know or cannot know, how far his character is due to education or environment and how far it is not, but we have nevertheless to admit that our judgment might be different if we had such knowledge. In the very strictest sense of the term, the proper subject of moral judgment is the innate character,[48] and any succeeding change a person's character undergoes is imputable to *him* only in so far as it is caused by the character with which he was born.

But what about the innate character itself? *We* have not made it, it is also the product of something outside ourselves. Is all responsibility, then, a mere delusion? The answer to this question is considered by many to depend on whether the will is free or not: if it is free the origin of the character is a matter of no consequence, if it is not free human beings are said to be no more proper subjects of moral judgment than are inanimate things. The application of moral praise and blame would be "in itself as absurd as to applaud the sunrise or be angry at the rain";[49] the only kind of admiration a virtuous man might deserve would be that "which we justly accord to a well-made machine."[50] Nor are these inferences from determinism only weapons forged by its opponents: they are shared by some of its own adherents. Richard Owen and his followers maintained that, since a man's character

---

[48] This was much emphasized by Schopenhauer, who even maintained that a person's character remains unchanged throughout his life (*Die Freiheit des Willens,* iii. [*Sämmtliche Werke,* iv.² [Leipzig, 1916], p. 50 *sqq.*]; *Die Grundlage der Moral,* § 20 [*ibid.,* iv.² 249 *sqq.*]).

[49] J. Martineau, *Types of Ethical Theory,* ii. (Oxford, 1891), p. 41 *sq.*

[50] A. J. Balfour, *The Foundations of Belief* (London, 1895), p. 25.

is made *for* him, not *by* him, there is no justice in punishing him for what he cannot help.[51] To Stuart Mill responsibility simply means liability to punishment, inflicted for a utilitarian purpose.[52] So also Sidgwick—whose attitude towards the free-will theory is that of a sceptic—argues that the common retributive view of punishment and the ordinary notions of "merit," "demerit," and "responsibility," involve the assumption that the will is free, and that these terms, if used at all, have to be used in new significations. "In this view," he says, "if I affirm that A is responsible for a harmful act, I mean that it is right to punish him for it; primarily, in order that the fear of punishment may prevent him and others from committing similar acts in future." [53]

If these conclusions are correct it is obvious that, whether the infliction of punishment be justifiable or not, the *feeling* of moral indignation or moral approval is, from the deterministic point of view, absurd. And yet we find that these emotions are felt by determinists and indeterminists alike. Apparently the former are not in the least affected by their notion that the human will is subject to the general law of cause and effect. Emotions are determined by specific cognitions, and last only as long as the influence of those cognitions last. It makes me sorry to hear that some evil has befallen my friend, but my sorrow disappears directly I find that the rumour was false. I get angry with a person who hurts me, but my anger subsides as soon as I recognize that the hurt was purely accidental. My indignation is aroused by an atrocious crime; but it ceases completely when I hear that

[51] J. S. Mill, *An Examination of Sir William Hamilton's Philosophy* (London, 1865), p. 506.
[52] *Ibid.,* p. 506 *sqq.*
[53] Sidgwick, *op. cit.,* p. 71 *sq.*

the agent was mad. On the other hand, however convinced I am that a person's conduct and character are in every detail a product of causes, that does not prevent me from feeling towards him retributive emotions—either anger or gratitude, moral resentment or approval. This suggests that a retributive emotion is not essentially determined by the cognition of free-will. At the same time it seems easy to explain the fallacy which is at the bottom of the notion that moral valuation is inconsistent with determinism.

Full responsibility, as we have seen, presupposes freedom from compulsion. Hence the inference that it also presupposes freedom from causation, and that complete determination involves complete irresponsibility. Compulsion is confounded with causation; and this confusion is due to the fact that the cause which determines the will is actually looked upon in the light of a constraining power outside the will. Determinism is confounded with fatalism. When a man's whole conduct is determined by an external power ruling over human affairs, a god or an all-powerful fate, he can obviously not be held responsible for what he does under the influence of such constraint: the logical outcome of radical fatalism is a denial of all moral imputability and a rejection of all moral judgment.

Not so with determinism. While fatalism presupposes the existence of a person who is constrained by an outward power, determinism regards the person himself as in every respect a product of causes. It does not assume any part of his will to have existed previous to his formation by these causes; his will cannot possibly be constrained by them because there is nothing to constrain, it is made by them. When we say of a person that he is influenced by external circumstances or subdued by fate, we regard *him* as existing independently of that which influences or subdues him, we attribute to him an innate character which is acted upon from the outside. He would have been different if he had lived under different conditions of life, or if fate had left him alone. But could we say that he would have been different if the causes to which he owes his existence had been different, if he had been the offspring of different parents? *He* would not have existed at all. This is the pivot of the whole question. A moral emotion and a moral judgment presuppose the existence of a certain individual with an innate character, it is towards him that the emotion is felt, on him that the judgment is passed; beyond that they cannot go. They can consider the influences to which his innate character has been subjected from the outside world, they cannot consider the causes from which it has sprung. To do so would be foreign to their very nature. The moral emotions are no more concerned with the origin of the innate character than the aesthetic emotions are concerned with the origin of the beautiful object. In their capacity of retributive emotions, they are essentially directed towards sensitive and volitional entities conceived, not as uncaused themselves, but only as causes of pleasure or pain.

CHAPTER VII

THE VARIABILITY OF MORAL JUDGMENTS

ETHICAL relativity implies that there is no objective standard of morality, and objectivity presupposes universality.
As truth is one it has to be the same for any one who
knows it, and if morality is a matter of truth and falsity,
in the normative sense of the terms, the same must be the
case with moral truth. If a certain course of conduct *is*
good or bad, right or wrong, it is so universally, and cannot be both good and bad, right and wrong. The universality of truth does not mean, of course, that everybody
knows what is true and false. It has constantly been
argued against ethical subjectivism that the variety of
moral judgments no more justifies the denial of moral
objectivity than the diversity in judgments about the
course of things disproves the objectivity of truth. The
validity or fallacy of this argument depends in the first
place upon the causes to which the variability of moral
judgments is due.

In the last chapter I pointed out that the subjects of
moral judgments present no difference in principle so
far as their general nature is concerned. Such judgments
are passed on conduct and character, and if they were
guided by sufficient knowledge of facts and reflection
there would be no essential difference between them as
regards the general subjective conditions of the modes of
conduct to which they refer. This uniformity as regards
the nature of their subjects is due to the facts that they

are all based on moral emotions, and that the moral emotions are retributive emotions felt towards persons conceived as causes of pleasure or pain.

But the variability of moral valuation depends in a very large measure upon intellectual factors of another kind, namely, different ideas relating to the objective nature of similar modes of conduct and their consequences. Such differences of ideas may arise from different situations and external conditions of life, which consequently influence moral opinion. We find, for instance, among many peoples the custom of killing or abandoning parents worn out with age or disease.[1] It prevails among a large number of savage tribes and occurred formerly among many Asiatic and European nations, including the Vedic people and peoples of Teutonic extraction; there is an old English tradition of "the Holy Mawle, which they fancy hung behind the church door, which when the father was seaventie, the sonne might fetch to knock his father in the head, as effete and of no more use." This custom is particularly common among nomadic hunting tribes, owing to the hardships of life and the inability of decrepit persons to keep up in the march. In times when the food-supply is insufficient to support all the members of a community it also seems more reasonable that the old and useless should have to perish than the young and vigorous. And among peoples who have reached a certain degree of wealth and comfort, the practice of killing the old folks, though no longer justified by necessity, may still go on, partly through survival of a custom inherited from harder times, and partly from the humane intent of putting an end to lingering misery. What appears to most of us as an atrocious practice may really be an act of kindness, and

[1] *Moral Ideas*, i. 386 *sqq.*

is commonly approved of, or even insisted upon, by the old people themselves.

Or take the widespread custom of infanticide.[2] Among the lower races custom often decides how many children are to be reared in each family, and not infrequently the majority of infants are destroyed. This wholesale infanticide is also mainly due to the hardships of savage life. The helpless infant may be a great burden to the parents both in times of peace and in times of war. It may prevent the mother from following her husband about on his wanderings or otherwise encumber her in her work. Moreover, a little forethought tells the parents that their child before long will become a consumer of provisions perhaps already too scanty for the family. Savages, who often suffer greatly from want of food, may have to choose between destroying their offspring or famishing themselves. Urgent want is frequently represented by our authorities as the main cause of infanticide; and their statements are corroborated by the conspicuous prevalence of this custom among poor tribes and in islands whose inhabitants are confined to a narrow territory with limited resources. For a similar reason infanticide is or has been a custom among many peoples who have reached a higher degree of civilization. In ancient times the Semites, or at least some of them, not only practised it but, in certain circumstances, approved of it or regarded it as a duty; according to an old Arab proverb, it was a generous deed to bury a female child. The murder of female infants, either by the direct employment of homicidal means or by exposure to privation and neglect, has for ages been a common practice, or even a genuine custom, among various Hindu castes. Exposure of new-born children was practised by the people of the Vedic age, as

[2] *Ibid.*, i. 394 *sqq.*

also by other so-called Aryan peoples in ancient times. The exposure of deformed or sickly infants was a custom in Greece; at Sparta, at least, it was enjoined by law. Aristotle lays down the rule with respect to the exposing or bringing up of children, that "nothing imperfect or maimed shall be brought up." He proposes that the number of children allowed to each marriage shall be regulated by the State, and that, if any woman be pregnant after she has produced the prescribed number, an abortion shall be procured before the foetus has life. It is necessary, he says, to take care that the increase of the people should not exceed a certain number, in order to avoid poverty and its concomitants, sedition and other evils. Yet the exposure of healthy infants, which was of frequent occurrence in Greece, was hardly approved of by public opinion, although generally tolerated. In Rome, also, custom or law enjoined the destruction of deformed infants; but there was no tendency to encourage infanticide beyond these limits. It has been observed that while the Greek policy was rather to restrain, the Roman policy was always to encourage, population. Being engaged in incessant wars of conquest, Rome was never afraid of being over-populated, but, on the contrary, tried to increase the number of its citizens by according special privileges to the fathers of many children and exempting poor parents from most of the burden of taxation. On the other hand, though the exposure of healthy infants was disapproved of in pagan Rome, it was not generally regarded as an offence of very great magnitude, and during the Empire, when it was practised on an extensive scale, it was spoken of in the literature with frigid indifference. But Christianity brought about a complete change of ideas. The early Fathers of the Church taught that if the abandoned infant died, the unnatural parent was guilty of nothing less than murder; and the enormity of the crime of causing an infant's death was enhanced by the notion that children who had died unbaptized were doomed to eternal perdition. This reminds us of the fact that the moral ideas about infanticide are also determined by factors very different from considerations resulting from economic conditions.

The variability of moral judgments largely originates in different measures of knowledge, based on experience of the consequences of conduct, and in different beliefs. In almost every branch of conduct we notice the influence which the belief in supernatural forces or beings or in a future state has exercised upon the moral ideas of mankind, and the great diversity of this influence. Religion or superstition has on the one hand stigmatized murder and suicide, on the other hand it has commended human sacrifice and certain cases of voluntary self-destruction. It has inculcated humanity and charity, but has also led to cruel persecutions of persons embracing another creed. It has emphasized the duty of truth-speaking, and has itself been a cause of pious fraud. It has promoted cleanly habits and filthiness. It has enjoined labour and abstinence from labour, sobriety and drunkenness, marriage and celibacy, chastity and temple prostitution. It has introduced a great variety of new duties and virtues, quite different from those which are recognized by the moral consciousness when left to itself, but nevertheless in many cases considered more important than any other duties or virtues. From this motley crowd of influences I shall single out a few representative cases, in which it may be worth while to point out the facts that have led to the extraordinary diversity of moral opinion.

Hardly any pagan practice has been more revolting to the moral feelings of Christians than that of human sacrifice, which is found not only among many savages, but occurred in early times among all Indo-European peoples, the Semites, and the Japanese, and in the New World among the Mayas and the Aztecs, who practised it on an enormous scale.[3] The gods were supposed to be gratified by such offerings—because they had an appetite for human flesh or blood, or because they required attendants, or because they were angry and could only be appeased by the death of him or those who aroused their anger or some representative of the offending community, or who could exactly tell why? The chief thing is that people know or believe that on some certain occasion they are in danger of losing their lives; they attribute this to the designs of a supernatural being; and, by sacrificing a man, they hope to gratify that being's craving for human life and thereby avert the danger from themselves. That this principle mainly underlies the practice of human sacrifice appears from the circumstances in which it generally occurs. Human victims are often offered in war, before a battle, or during a siege; for the purpose of stopping or preventing epidemics; as a method of putting an end to a devastating famine or drought; or with a view to averting perils arising from the sea or from rivers. In these cases the offering of human sacrifices is mostly a matter of public concern, a method of ensuring the lives of many by the death of one or a few. But human life is also sacrificed, by way of substitution, for the purpose of preventing the death of some particular person, especially a chief or a king, from sickness, old age, or other circumstances. I do not say that the practice of human sacrifice is in every case based on the idea of substitution, but I think there is sufficient evidence to prove that it is as a rule a method of life-insurance—absurd, no doubt, ac-

[3] *Moral Ideas,* i. 434 *sqq.*

cording to our ideas, but not an act of wanton cruelty. When practised for the benefit of the community or in a case of national distress, it is hardly more cruel than to compel thousands of men to suffer death on the battle-field on behalf of their country or to advocate the in-fliction of capital punishment on the ground of social expediency. The sacrifice of offenders has in fact survived in the Christian world, since every execution performed for the purpose of appeasing an offended and angry god may be justly called a sacrifice. It was a principle adopted by the Christian Church and the Christian governments that it belongs to the king "to avenge God's anger very deeply, according as the deed may be," [4] and this prin-ciple was acted upon till quite modern times and largely contributed to the excessive severity of the penal codes.

Whilst human sacrifice has shocked the feelings of Christians, there are other cases in which Christian morals and legislation have treated as most horrible crimes acts which most peoples have looked upon with considerable moral indifference, if not as altogether blameless. One such case is suicide.[5] It is not often that savages are reported to attach any stigma to it; if they deny self-murderers the ordinary funeral rites or bury them in a separate place, they do so for fear of having anything to do with them or in order to prevent them from mixing with the other dead, because their ghosts are looked upon as dangerous. In China and Japan suicide is in many cir-cumstances regarded as an honourable act. Among the Hindus it has always been considered one of the most acceptable rites that can be offered to their deities. In none of the few cases of suicide mentioned in the Old

[4] *The Laws of Cnut,* ii. 40 (in *Ancient Laws and Institutes of Eng-land* [London, 1840]).
[5] *Moral Ideas,* ii. 229 *sqq.*

Testament is any censure passed on the perpetrator of the deed, nor is there any text that forbids a man to die by his own hand. The Greek tragedians frequently give expression to the notion that suicide is in certain circumstances becoming to a noble mind. But according to the Platonic Socrates, "there may be reason in saying that a man should wait, and not take his own life until God summons him"; and Aristotle maintains that he who from rage kills himself commits a wrong against the State. The opinions of the philosophers, however, were anything but unanimous, and the Stoics, especially, advocated suicide as a relief from all kinds of misery. Throughout the whole history of pagan Rome there was no statute declaring it to be a crime for an ordinary citizen to take his own life; the self-murderer's rights were in no way affected by his deed, his memory was no less honoured than if he had died a natural death, his will was recognized by law, and the regular order of succession was not interfered with.

In no question of morality was there a greater difference between classical and Christian doctrines than in regard to suicide. The earlier Fathers of the Church still allowed, or even approved of, suicide in certain cases, namely, when committed in order to procure martyrdom, or to avoid apostasy, or to retain the crown of virginity; but since the days of St. Augustine no such exceptions have been admitted by the Church. Suicide was assimilated with murder, nay, was declared to be the worst form of murder, "the most grievous thing of all." The self-murderer was deprived of the rights that were granted to all other criminals. In the sixth century a Council enjoined that "the oblations of those who were killed in the commission of any crime may be received, except of such as laid violent hands on themselves"; and a subsequent Council denied the latter the usual rites of Christian burial.

It was even said that Judas committed a greater sin in killing himself than in betraying his master Christ to a certain death. How shall we explain these views?

According to the Christian doctrine, as formulated by Thomas Aquinas, suicide is unlawful for three reasons. It is against a natural inclination and contrary to the charity which a man ought to bear towards himself; by killing himself a person does an injury to the community of which he is a part; and he usurps the office of judge on a point not referred to him, because the judgment of life and death belongs to God alone. The second of these arguments is borrowed from Aristotle, and is entirely foreign to the spirit of early Christianity with its enthusiastic commendation of the hermit life. But the other two are deeply rooted in some of the fundamental doctrines of Christianity—in the sacredness of human life, in the duty of absolute submission to the will of God, and in the extreme importance attached to the moment of death. The earthly life is a preparation for eternity, sufferings which are sent by God are not to be evaded but to be endured. The man who takes away the life given him by the Creator displays the utmost disregard for the will and authority of his Master; and, worst of all, he does so in the very last minute of his life, when his doom is sealed for ever. His deed, as Thomas Aquinas says, is "the most dangerous thing of all, because no time is left to expiate it by repentance." This is the crucial point of the whole question. Considering that this religious view of suicide has been the cause of the extreme severity with which it has been treated in Christian countries, it is strange to be told by a sociologist like Durkheim, that the more lenient judgment passed on it by the public conscience of the present time is merely accidental and transient, because moral evolution is not likely to be retrogressive in this particular point after it has followed a certain course for centuries.[6] This is to ignore the real causes of the extraordinary condemnation of suicide in Christian countries.

Another case in which the difference of moral opinion between Christians and pagans has been equally radical is the attitude towards homosexual practices.[7] In Greece pederasty in its baser forms was censured, though generally, it seems, with no great severity, but the universal rule was apparently that when decorum was observed in the friendship between a man and a youth, no inquiries were made into the details of the relationship. And this attachment was not only regarded as permissible, but was praised as the highest form of love, as the offspring of the heavenly Aphrodite, as a path leading to virtue, as a weapon against tyranny, as a safeguard of civic liberty, as a source of national greatness and glory. In Rome there was an old law of unknown date which imposed a mulct on him who committed pederasty with a free person; but this law, of which very little is known, had lain dormant for ages, and the subject of ordinary homosexual intercourse had never afterwards attracted the attention of the pagan legislators. But when Christianity became the religion of the Roman Empire, a veritable crusade was opened against sodomy. Several emperors made it a capital crime: those who were found guilty of it should be punished with the sword or be burned alive in the presence of all the people. "A sentence of death and infamy," says Gibbon, "was often founded on the slight and suspicious evidence of a child or a servant, . . . and pederasty became the crime of those to whom no crime could be imputed." This attitude towards homosexuality had a profound and lasting influence on European legislation.

---

[6] E. Durkheim, *Le suicide* (Paris, 1897), p. 377.
[7] *Moral Ideas,* ii. ch. xliii.

Throughout the Middle Ages and later, Christian law-
makers thought that nothing but a painful death in the
flames could atone for the sinful act. In France persons
were actually burned for sodomy in the middle and latter
part of the eighteenth century. In England it was pun-
ishable by death till 1861, although in practice the extreme punishment was not inflicted. The latter fact shows
that there was a discrepancy between moral sentiments
and the law.

The enormity of guilt attached to this crime has puzz-
led moral philosophers. Kant looks upon sexual perversion as a pollution of human dignity, but finds the utter
reprobation of it very hard to justify upon grounds of
reason.[8] Schopenhauer gives highly metaphysical explanations, connected with his general theory of the will, both
of the homosexual desire and the condemnation of pederasty;[9] but in one of his works he simply says that the
wrongness of the latter lies in the seduction of the
younger and inexperienced party, who is thereby ruined
both physically and morally.[10] He does not raise the question whether the seduction of a youth is fraught with
so much more terrible consequences than that of a girl
as to justify the enormous difference in the treatment
of the seducer. Others maintain that the attitude towards
perversity is only intelligible on the hypothesis that moral
purity is directly judged to have an intrinsic worth quite

[8] Kant, *Metaphysische Anfangungsgründe der Tugendlehre,* § 7
(*Gesammelte Schriften,* vi. [Berlin, 1914], p. 425). *Cf.* J. Laird,
The Idea of Value (Cambridge, 1929), p. 295.

[9] A. Schopenhauer, *Die Welt als Wille und Vorstellung,* ii.
(*Sämmtliche Werke,* iii. [Leipzig, 1916]), p. 646 *sqq. Idem, Parerga
und Paralipomena,* ii. (*Sämmtliche Werke,* vi. [Leipzig, 1916]), § 168,
p. 340.

[10] *Idem, Die Grundlage der Moral,* § 5 (*Sämmtliche Werke,* iv.[2]
[Leipzig, 1916], p. 128 *sq.*).

independent of hedonic results.[11] To me it seems obvious
that the censure to which homosexual intercourse as such
is frequently subject is in the first place due to that feeling of aversion or disgust which it tends to call forth
in normally constituted adult individuals, whose sexual
instincts have developed under normal conditions. This
feeling tends to abate or disappear where special circumstances, such as absence of the other sex, the seclusion
of women, or other facts, have given rise to widely spread
homosexual practices; and in no case does it seem to have
been sufficiently strong by itself to lead to very drastic
public measures. Among uncivilized peoples such practices
are generally taken little notice of; they may be a subject
for derision or contemptuous remarks wounding the van-
ity of the delinquent by the implication that he must be
unable to procure the full natural enjoyment of his impulse if he has to resort to such substitutes.[12] The laws
of the ancient Scandinavians ignored homosexuality,
though passive pederasts were much despised by them,
being identified with cowards and regarded as sorcerers.
Chinese law makes little distinction between unnatural
and other sexual offences; but as a matter of fact the
former are regarded by the Chinese as less hurtful to
the community than ordinary immorality, and pederasty
is not looked down upon. In Japan there was no law
against homosexual intercourse till the revolution of 1868,
and we are told that in the period of Japanese chivalry
it was considered more heroic if a man loved a person

[11] G. Heymans, *Einführung in die Ethik* (Leipzig, 1914), p. 215 *sq.*
A. E. Taylor, "Critical Notice" of the same work, in *Mind,* N. S. xxv.
(London, 1916), p. 391 *sq. Cf. Idem, The Problem of Conduct* (Lon-
don, 1901), p. 45 *sq.*

[12] See, *e.g.,* B. Malinowski, *The Sexual Life of Savages in North-
Western Melanesia* (London, 1929), p. 395; Margaret Mead, *Growing up in New Guinea* (New York, 1930), p. 166.

of his own sex than if he loved a woman. Mohammed forbade sodomy, and the general theory of his followers is that it should be punished like fornication; but in the Mohammedan world it is practically regarded, at most, as a mere peccadillo.

In a very different light was it looked upon by the Hebrews. Unnatural sins are not allowed to defile the land of the Lord: whosoever shall commit such abominations shall be put to death. The enormous abhorrence of them expressed in this law had a very specific reason, namely, the Hebrews' hatred of a foreign cult. Unnatural vice was the sin of a people who was not the Lord's people, the Canaanites, who thereby polluted their land, so that he visited their guilt and the land spued out its inhabitants. We know that sodomy entered as an element into their religion: besides female prostitutes there were male prostitutes, or *qedēshīm,* attached to their temples. The sodomitic acts committed with the latter seem, like the connections with the female temple prostitutes, to have had in view to transfer blessings to the worshippers; in Morocco supernatural benefits are to this day expected not only from heterosexual, but also from homosexual intercourse with a holy person. The *qedēshīm* are frequently alluded to in the Old Testament, especially in the period of the monarchy, when rites of a foreign origin made their way into both Israel and Judah. And it is natural that the Yahveh worshippers should regard their practice with the utmost horror as forming part of an idolatrous cult.

The Hebrew conception of homosexuality passed into Christianity. The notion that sodomy is a form of sacrilege was here strengthened by the habits of the gentiles, among whom St. Paul found the abominations of Sodom rampant. During the Middle Ages heretics were accused of unnatural vice as a matter of course. Indeed, so closely was sodomy associated with heresy that the same name was applied to both. Thus the French *bougre* (from the Latin *Bulgarus,* Bulgarian), as also its English synonym, was originally a name given to a sect of heretics who came from Bulgaria in the eleventh century and was afterwards applied to other heretics, but at the same time it became the regular expression for a person guilty of unnatural intercourse. In mediaeval laws sodomy was also repeatedly mentioned together with heresy, and the punishment was the same for both. It thus remained a religious offence of the first order. And in this fact and its connection with Hebrew ideas we find the answer to the problem we set out to solve. Like suicide, the kind of sexual perversion of which I have now spoken has been stigmatized as a crime of the greatest magnitude on account of its relation to specific religious beliefs. It is interesting to notice that in one other religion, besides Hebrewism and Christianity, it has been looked upon with the same abhorrence, namely, Zoroastrianism, and there also as a practice of infidels, of Turanian shamanists.

In so far as differences of moral opinion depend on knowledge or ignorance of facts, on specific religious or superstitious beliefs, on different degrees of reflection,[13] or on different conditions of life or other external circumstances, they do not clash with that universality which is implied in the notion of the objective validity of moral judgments. We shall now examine whether the same is the case with other differences that, at least apparently, are not due to purely cognitive causes.

[13] I shall in another connection (*infra,* p. 258 *sq.*) discuss the influence of reason in harmonizing differences of moral opinion springing from sentimental likes and dislikes.

When we study the moral rules laid down by the customs of savage peoples we find that they in a very large measure resemble the rules of civilized nations. In every savage community homicide is prohibited by custom, and so is theft. Savages also regard charity as a duty and praise generosity as a virtue, indeed their customs relating to mutual aid are often much more exacting than our own; and many of them are conspicuous for their avoidance of telling lies. But in spite of the great similarity of moral commandments, there is at the same time a difference between the regard for life, property, truth, and the general well-being of a neighbour which displays itself in savage rules of morality and that which is found among ourselves: it has, broadly speaking, only reference to members of the same community or tribe. Primitive peoples carefully distinguish between an act of homicide committed within their own community and one where the victim is a stranger: while the former is in ordinary circumstances disapproved of, the latter is in most cases allowed and often considered worthy of praise. And the same holds true of theft and lying and the infliction of other injuries. Apart from the privileges granted to guests, which are always of very short duration, a stranger is in early society devoid of all rights. And the same is the case not only among savages but among nations of archaic culture as well.

When we pass from the lower races to peoples more advanced in civilization we find that the social unit has grown larger, that the nation has taken the place of the tribe, and that the circle within which the infliction of injuries is prohibited has been extended accordingly. But the old distinction between injuries committed against compatriots and harm done to foreigners remains. In Greece in early times the "contemptible stranger" had no legal rights, and was protected only if he was the guest of a citizen; and even later on, at Athens, while the intentional killing of a citizen was punished with death and confiscation of the murderer's property, the intentional killing of a non-citizen was punished only with exile. The Latin word *hostis* was originally used to denote a foreigner, and Mommsen suggests that in ancient days the Romans did not punish the killing of a foreigner unless he belonged to an allied nation. The German word *elender* has acquired its present meaning from the connotation of the older word which meant an "outlandish" man. In Teutonic countries the stranger as such, unless he belonged to a friendly neighbouring tribe, had originally no legal rights at all; for his protection he was dependent on individual hospitality, and hospitality was restricted by custom to three days only.[14] Later on, when commerce increased and the stranger was more often seen in Teutonic lands, royal protection was extended to him; but throughout the Middle Ages the position of the stranger was anything but enviable. All Europe seems to have tacitly agreed that foreigners had been created for the purpose of being robbed. In the thirteenth century there were still several places in France in which a stranger who remained there for a year and a day became the serf of the lord of the manor. In England, till upwards of two centuries after the Conquest, foreign merchants were considered only as sojourners who had come to a fair or market, and were obliged to employ their landlords as brokers to buy and sell their commodities; and one stranger was often arrested for the debt or punished for the misdemeanour of another. The custom of seizing the goods of persons who had been shipwrecked seems to have been universal, and in some European countries the

[14] *Moral Ideas,* i. 337 *sq.*

law even permitted the inhabitants of maritime provinces to reduce to servitude people who were shipwrecked on their coast. Along the Baltic coast prayers were offered in the churches that God would bless the shores with many shipwrecks; and it was even argued that as shipwrecks were punishments sent by God, it was impious to be merciful to the victims.[15]

It would be in vain to deny that the old distinction between a tribesman or fellow-countryman and a foreigner is dead among ourselves. The prevailing attitude towards war, the readiness with which wars are waged, and the notions as to what is allowed in warfare indicate the survival in modern civilization of the ancient feeling that the life, property and general well-being of a foreigner are not on a par with those of a compatriot. In times of peace this feeling may disclose itself in the form of national aggressiveness, under the flag of patriotism, or perhaps in the behaviour towards the aborigines of some distant country. But both law and public opinion certainly show a very great advance in humanity with regard to the treatment of foreigners. And if we pass to the rules laid down by moralists and professedly accepted by a large portion of civilized humanity, the change from the savage attitude has been enormous. The doctrine of universal love is not peculiar to Christianity. The Chinese moralists inculcated benevolence to all men, without making any reference to national distinctions. Mih-tsze, who lived in the interval between Confucius and Mencius, even taught that we ought to love all men equally; but this precept called forth protests as abnegating the peculiar devotion due to relatives. Buddhism enjoins the duty of universal love: "As a mother, even at the risk of her own life, protects her son, her only son, so let a man

15 *Ibid.,* ii. 24 *sq.*

cultivate goodwill without measure toward all beings." According to the Hindu work *Panchatantra* it is the thought of little-minded persons to consider whether a man is one of ourselves or an alien, the whole earth being of kin to him who is generously disposed. In Greece and Rome philosophers arose who opposed national narrowness and prejudice. Thus the Cynics attached slight value to the citizenship of any special state, declaring themselves to be citizens of the world. But it was the Stoic philosophy that first gave to the idea of a world-citizenship a definite positive meaning and raised it to historical importance.[16]

It is obvious that the expansion of the moral rules has been a consequence of the expansion of the social unit and of increased intercourse between different societies, and if, as I maintain, the range of the moral emotions varies with the range of the altruistic sentiment, there is every reason to assume that an immediate cause of the greater comprehensiveness of the moral rules has been a corresponding widening of that sentiment. Among gregarious animals it is apt to be felt towards any member of their species that is not an object of their fear or anger. In mankind it has been narrowed by social isolation, by differences in race, language, habits, and customs, by enmity and suspicion. But peaceful intercourse leads to conditions favourable to its expansion, as well as to friendly behaviour for prudential reasons in the relations between those who come into contact with each other. People of different nationalities feel that in spite of all dissimilarities there is much that they have in common; and frequent intercourse makes the differences less marked or obliterates many of them altogether.

Professor McDougall, on the other hand, remarks that the rise of the spirit of nationality in the modern world

[16] *Moral Ideas,* ii. 176 *sq.*

has coincided with the great improvements in means of communication which have multiplied a thousand-fold the contacts between men of different races and nations, and he believes that "this multiplication of contact, instead of destroying or weakening the barriers of nationality, the 'prejudices' of race, the partiality of men for their own kind, has but accentuated these things, fostered their growth, intensified their influences throughout the world." [17] That improved means of communication have made some nations more afraid of some other nations is obvious; but though you do not love those you fear, you may respect them and find it to be your interest to treat them with consideration. In other cases Buckle may be right in saying that ignorance is a powerful cause of national hatred, and that "when you increase the contact, you remove the ignorance, and thus you diminish the hatred." [18] Experience derived from intercourse may certainly strengthen national "prejudices," or bias based on preconceived opinion, but we know that it also may have the very opposite effect. Professor McDougall says "it remains true in general that the more we know of other people the more we prefer our own." [19] The idea that one's own people is the best is very deep-rooted in human nature.[20] In their intercourse with white men savages have often noticed with astonishment the arrogant air of superiority adopted by the latter, because in their own opinion they are vastly superior to the whites. According to Eskimo beliefs, the first man, though made by the Great Being, was a failure and was consequently cast

[17] W. McDougall, *Ethics and some modern World Problems* (London, 1924), p. 55.
[18] H. T. Buckle, *History of Civilization in England*, i. (London, 1894), p. 222.
[19] McDougall, *op. cit.*, p. 56.
[20] *Moral Ideas*, ii. 170 *sqq.*

aside and called "white man," but a second attempt resulted in the formation of a perfect man and he was called *in-nu,* the name which the Eskimo give to themselves. If a South Sea Islander sees a very awkward person he says, "How stupid you are, perhaps you are an Englishman." I once heard a young European affirm that everything made in his own country was better than anything similar made in any other country. Of course, travelling or residence abroad may strengthen our preference to live among our own people—"East or west, home is best"— but it should also be apt to open our eyes to the good qualities of other nations. And, to return to our starting-point, how could even the modern spirit of nationality be compared to the attitude towards foreigners in those times when there was little intercourse between the different nations of Europe?

It has been said that "religious ideas have been largely responsible for the transition from a moral code which includes only duties towards the members of a small and exclusive circle to a moral code which embraces, as persons entitled to the performance of certain services, all mankind"; [21] that when the deity came to be considered the Lord of the world, every human being, independently of nationality and race, was recognized as an object of his care; [22] and that without their belief in God as a Father, the Christians could never have formed the idea of a common human brotherhood. [23] It is true, of course, that when religion ceased to be national and became universal, it helped to widen the boundaries of the moral

[21] A. E. Taylor, *op. cit.,* p. 143.

[22] K. Birch-Reichenwald Aars, *Gut und Böse* (*Skrifter udgivne af Videnskaps-Selskabet i Christiania,* 1907. II. Historisk-filosofisk Klasse, no. 3), p. 226.

[23] T. Bohlin, *Das Grundproblem der Ethik* (Uppsala & Leipzig, 1923), p. 44.

community; but it should be remembered that its "universality" did not imply universal acceptance, and that those who did not accept it, even when recognized in theory as "brothers," were treated as enemies to God and man. While extending the moral community to those who had the same faith, religion thus became a new cause of the differentiation of moral rules affecting those who had another faith. The moral value of a religion is to be judged not by its abstract tenets but by its influence on conduct, and in this respect, as everybody knows, Christianity has been very far from realizing the idea of a human brotherhood. The principle of the Church was, "Omnem hominem *fidelem* judica tuum esse fratrem." The orthodox view that unbelief is a legitimate reason for going to war has been acted upon to an extent which made the history of Christianity for many centuries a perpetual crusade, which turned against infidels and heretics alike, nay, even a slight shade of difference from the liturgy of Rome became a legitimate cause of war. When, in the latter part of the Middle Ages, attempts were made by sovereigns and Councils of the Church to abolish the ancient right of seizing the goods of persons who had been shipwrecked, the robbing of shipwrecked infidels was not included in the prohibitions.[24] In the seventeenth century the Scotch clergy taught that food or shelter must on no occasion be given to a starving man unless his opinions were orthodox.[25]

The expansion of the moral rules has been attributed to reason. "With the rise of reflection," says Professor Sorley, "there comes also a change of the objects valued —chiefly by a modification of the tribal or social limits by which they were at first restricted. The circle of duties is widened until it gradually takes in, or is fitted to take

[24] *Moral Ideas,* ii. 25.   [25] Buckle, *op. cit.,* iii. 277.

in, all mankind." [26] The Stoics actually referred to reason in support of their cosmopolitan ideal. Human society has for its basis the identity of reason in individuals; hence we have no ground for limiting this society to a single nation. "If our reason is in common," says Marcus Aurelius, "there is a common law, as reason commands us what to do and what not to do; and if there is a common law we are fellow-citizens; if this is so, we are members of some political community—the world is in a manner a state." [27] Seneca argues:—"It is a crime to injure one's country; so it is, therefore, to injure any of our countrymen, for he is a part of our country. . . . Therefore it is also a crime to injure any man: for he is your fellow-citizen in a larger state." [28] To this great state, which includes all rational beings, the individual states are related as the houses of a city are to the city collectively; [29] and the wise man will esteem it far above any particular community in which the accident of birth has placed him. [30] But there was presumably also an emotional ground for this abolition of national boundaries in the moral ideal. The citizen of Alexander's huge empire had in a way become a citizen of the world; and national dislikes were so much more readily overcome as the various nationalities comprised in it were united not only under a common government, but also in a common culture; [31] indeed the founder of Stoicism was himself only half a Greek. And the later Stoics were citizens of another world-empire.

[26] W. R. Sorley, *Moral Values and the Idea of God* (Cambridge, 1924), p. 164.
[27] Marcus Aurelius, *Commentarii,* iv. 4.
[28] Seneca, *De ira,* ii. 31.
[29] Marcus Aurelius, *op. cit.,* iii. 11.
[30] Seneca, *De otio,* iv. 1. *Idem, Epistulae,* lxviii. 2. Epictetus, *Dissertationes,* iii. 22. 83 *sqq.*
[31] *Cf.* Plutarch, *De Alexandri Magni fortuna aut virtute,* i. 6, p. 329.

But may we really suppose that the universality of the Christian doctrine was the result of a process of reasoning? May we suppose that the conception of God as a Father has led to the conclusion that all men are brothers? If by his fatherhood is meant that he is *our* father but not every man's father, the argument is of course a fallacy; and if it means that he is every man's father, this proposition implies that all men are brothers. The latter proposition may have served to point out the import of the former, but can hardly be said to have been deduced from it. It seems that the Christian doctrine of the fatherhood of God and the brotherhood of man was the outcome of the altruistic sentiment of its author, which was comprehensive enough to embrace all mankind. It should be noticed that the Eastern tenets of universal love were not connected with any notion of a divine fatherhood.

It will perhaps be argued that the impartiality which is a characteristic of all moral judgments required a universalization of the moral rules, and that this could only be accomplished by a process of reasoning, which gradually extended them to wider and wider circles of men and finally to the whole human race.[32] But let us remember what the impartiality of moral judgments really implies. I have derived it [33] from the fact that the retributive emotions which are expressed in the moral concepts are both disinterested, in the strict sense of the term, and are assumed by those who feel them to be uninfluenced by the particular relationship in which they stand to those who are immediately affected by the acts in question and also to those who perform the acts, or at the very least, that they are not knowingly partial. When a person pronounces an act right or wrong, it implies that *ceteris*

---

[32] *Cf.* H. Höffding, *Etik* (Köbenhavn & Kristiania, 1913), p. 52.
[33] *Supra,* p. 90 *sqq.*

paribus it is so whether he, or some friend or enemy of
his, does it to another; *or* another does it to him, or to
some friend or enemy of his. This impartiality has nothing to do with the question whether the agent and he to
whom the act is done belong to the same or different
families, tribes, nations, or other social groups. If it is
considered wrong of a person to cheat another belonging
to his own group but not wrong to cheat a foreigner,
the impartiality of the moral emotion of disapproval,
which underlies the concept of wrongness, merely leads
to a general rule that applies to all similar cases independently of the nationality of him who holds the view.
If I maintain that a foreigner, or a member of another
class in my own society, has a duty towards me but that
I have not the same duty towards him, my opinion can be
justified only on condition that there is some difference
in the circumstances affecting the morality of the case.
People are certainly only too prone to assume that there
are such differences. When they attribute different rights
to different individuals, or classes of individuals, they are
often in reality influenced by the relationship in which
they stand to them; and reflection may be needed to decide whether the assumed impartiality of their moral judgment is real or illusory. Indeed, some degree of reasoning,
however small, may always be needed in order to know
whether a retributive emotion is felt impartially. I can
quite subscribe to Dr. Rashdall's statement that "it is
only so far as he is a rational being that any one is capable
of impartially judging between the claims of one man
and those of another—whether that other be himself or
a third person." [34] But it seems to me to be a sheer illusion to maintain that reason requires of us an impartiality
in our conduct which makes no difference between one

[34] H. Rashdall, *Is Conscience an Emotion?* (London, 1914), p. 104.

man and another or one sentient being and another—Sidgwick, as we have seen, found no rational ground for restricting our impartiality to mankind alone.[35] I cannot find it unreasonable to endeavour to promote the welfare of my own family or country in preference to that of other families or countries. But my moral emotions tell me that I must allow anybody else to show a similar preference for *his* family or country.

I think that the question, why moral rules should differ because the persons to whom they refer are members of different social groups, would hardly arise unless there were a correspondingly broad altruistic sentiment behind it. Whatever part reflection may have played in the expansion of the moral rules—prudence has also, no doubt, had something to do with the matter—it seems to me obvious that the dominant cause has been the widening of the altruistic sentiment. Beyond its limits the equalization of duties in our moral consciousness cannot go, whatever theorists may have to say on the subject; and the varying strength of this sentiment with regard to its objects will always prevent the rules from being anything like uniform and always make their equalization extremely incomplete. It is after all a very limited number of duties that have been included in the process of expansion. The duties that men owe to some smaller groups have never been, and will never be, absorbed by the duties they owe to mankind at large; and it is a mere theoretical postulate that our concentration of altruistic behaviour upon a smaller circle of men is only justified as the most efficient means of promoting the good of all. Somebody has said that the right kind of patriotism is to do good to one's own country without doing harm to anybody else's country; and it is certainly a fact that the universal duties

[35] *Supra*, p. 10.

reached by the extension of moral rules are nearly all such as are expressed by so-called negative commandments.

The variations of the altruistic sentiment in range and strength are also responsible for other differences of moral opinion. Even among ourselves there is no unanimity as to the dictates of duty in cases where a person's own interests collide with those of his fellow-men. I have previously discussed the utilitarian view, formulated in Sidgwick's axiom of "rational benevolence," that, other things being equal, no one must prefer his own lesser good to the greater good of another.[36] He admits himself that this principle is more rigid than the view of common sense; but, as I pointed out, the diversity of opinion on this point is considerably greater than he appears to have realized. I fail to see that any process of reasoning or any "intuition" could ever harmonize the different views. As Höffding said, no reasoning can change an egoist into a utilitarian; his position is so far unassailable.[37] Kant tried to demonstrate the inconsistency of egoism by arguing that the very selfishness of men must make them wish to act altruistically: a will which resolved that each should be left to take care of himself without the assistance of others would contradict itself, inasmuch as many cases might occur in which one would have need of the sympathy of others, and in which, by such a law sprung from his own will he would deprive himself of all hope of the aid he desires.[38] But whatever else may be said of this much critized argument, it could not possibly be used to prove that we are morally bound to regard the happiness of other individuals as much as we regard our own; nor is there anything else to show that this high priest of ethical rationalism would have assented to the utilitarian

[36] *Supra,* p. 9 *sqq.*   [37] Höffding, *op. cit.,* p. 35.   [38] *Infra,* p. 274.

demand that I am not allowed to prefer my own lesser happiness to the greater happiness of another man.[39] In some men the altruistic sentiment is stronger than in others and, consequently, more apt to influence their consciences with regard to their own conduct and their judgments on other people's conduct. And while everybody will no doubt agree that some amount of self-sacrifice is a duty in certain circumstances, the amount and the circumstances can hardly be fixed in general rules, and on the whole, in cases of conflicting interests the judgment must to a large extent remain a matter of private opinion.

There is further the variety of moral opinion relating to men's conduct towards the lower animals. Among savage peoples, the Eastern nations, and the ancient Greeks and Romans, we find rules inculcating regardful or kind behaviour towards them, which are due partly to cognitive causes, especially religious or superstitious ideas, and partly to kindly feelings; [40] the altruistic sentiment has not necessarily reference to members of the same species only—of this we have instances even among animals in confinement and domesticated animals, which frequently become attached to individuals of a different species with whom they live together.[41] In the Old Testament, on the other hand, we meet with an attitude which fundamentally differs from that of other Eastern religions: man is the centre of creation, for whose sake all other sentient creatures were brought into existence, and they are given over to his supreme and irresponsible control without the slightest injunction of kindness or the faintest suggestion of any duties towards them. Among the Hebrews the harshness of this anthropocentric doctrine was somewhat mitigated by the sympathy which a simple pastoral and agri-

39 *Infra,* p. 281 *sq.*   40 *Moral Ideas,* ii. 490 *sqq.*   41 *Ibid.,* i. 112.

cultural people naturally feels for its domestic animals; whereas in Christianity it was further strengthened by the exclusive importance that was attached to the spiritual salvation of man. He was now more than ever separated from the rest of sentient beings; even his own animal nature was regarded with contempt. St. Paul asks with scorn, "Doth God take care for oxen?" No creed in Christendom teaches kindness to animals as a dogma of religion, nor is there any such allusion in most treatises on ethics which base their teachings upon distinctly Christian tenets. The kindest words, I think, which from a Christian point of view have been said about animals have generally come from Protestant sectarians, Quakers and Methodists, whereas Roman Catholic writers—with a few exceptions,—when they deal with the subject at all, chiefly take pains to show that abstinence from wanton cruelty is a duty not to the animal but to man. This view was shared by Kant [42] and many later philosophers. [43] So also the legal protection of animals has often been vindicated on the ground that cruelty to animals might breed cruelty to men or shows a cruel disposition of mind, or that it wounds the sensibilities of other people.

Indifference to animal suffering has been a characteristic of public opinion in European countries up to quite modern times. In 1798 Thomas Young declared in his *Essay on Humanity to Animals* that he was sensible of laying himself open to no small portion of ridicule in offering to the public a book on such a subject. [44] Till the

[42] Kant, *Metaphysische Anfangungsgründe der Tugendlehre,* § 16 *sq.* (*Gesammelte Schriften,* vi. [Berlin, 1914], p. 442 *sq.*).

[43] *E.g.,* D. G. Ritchie, *Natural Rights* (London, 1895), p. 110 *sq.;* S. Alexander, *Moral Order and Progress* (London, 1896), p. 281. According to F. H. Bradley (*Ethical Studies* [Oxford, 1927], p. 208), a beast is the object of duties, but not the subject of rights.

[44] T. Young, *An Essay on Humanity to Animals* (London, 1798), p. 1.

end of the eighteenth century and even later cock-fighting was a very general amusement among the English and Scotch, entering into the occupations of both the old and young. Other pastimes indulged in were dog-fighting, bull-baiting, and badger-baiting; and in the middle of the eighteenth century Lord Kames described the bear-garden as one of the chief entertainments of the English, though it was held in abhorrence by the French and "other polite nations," being too savage an amusement to be relished by those of a refined taste.[45] As late as 1824 Sir Robert (then Mr.) Peel argued strongly against the legal prohibition of bull-baiting.[46]

About two years previously, however, humanity to animals had, for the first time, become a subject of English legislation by the Act which prevented cruel and improper treatment of cattle. It was afterwards followed by others prohibiting cruelty to domestic animals and wild animals in captivity; and subsequently similar laws were made in most continental countries. In the course of the nineteenth century humanity to animals, from being conspicuous in a few individuals only, became the keynote of a movement gradually increasing in strength. It found philosophical expression in Utilitarianism: Bentham, Mill, and, I believe, the utilitarian school generally, applied their doctrine to all beings capable of feeling pleasure and pain.[47]

This rapidly increasing sympathy with animal suffering was no doubt to a considerable extent due to the declining faith in the anthropocentric doctrine and to the influence of another theory, which regards man not as separated

[45] Kames, *Essays on the Principles of Morality and Natural Religion* (Edinburgh, 1751), p. 7.

[46] T. C. Hansard, *Parliamentary Debates*, N. S., x. (London, 1824), p. 491 *sqq.*

[47] J. S. Mill, *Dissertations and Discussions*, ii. (London, 1859), p. 482. Sidgwick, *op. cit.*, p. 414.

from the lower animals by a special act of creation, but as a being generally akin to them and only representing a higher stage in the scale of mental evolution; the orthodox contempt for the dumb brutes was superseded by feelings of affinity and kindly interest. But apart from any theory, growing reflection has also taught men to be more considerate in their treatment of animals by producing a more vivid idea of their sufferings. Human thoughtlessness has been responsible for much needless pain inflicted on them, and in spite of some improvement it is so still. On the other hand, the movement advocating greater humanity to animals is itself by no means free from inconsistencies and lack of discrimination. Take for instance the present crusade against vivisection, as compared with the general indifference to the sufferings caused to wild animals in sport. The vivisector, who in cold blood torments his helpless victim in the interest of science and for the benefit of mankind is called a coward, whereas the sportsman who inflicts agonies on the creature he pursues for sheer amusement escapes all censure and is rather looked up to. The pursued animal, it is argued, has "free chances of escape." [48] This is an excellent argument—provided we share the North American Indian's conviction that an animal can never be killed without its own permission.

The extreme views about our duties to animals may still be modified, on one side by a clearer representation of animal suffering and on the other side by the recognition of certain facts, often overlooked, which make it unreasonable to regard conduct towards dumb creatures in exactly the same light as conduct towards men. Apart from the difference in grades of sentience, it should be

[48] F. P. Cobbe, *The Modern Rack. Papers on Vivisection* (London, 1889), p. 10.

remembered that animals have none of those long-pro-
tracted anticipations of future misery or death which we
have.[49] If they are destined to serve as meat they are not
aware of it; and many domestic animals would never have
come into existence and been able to enjoy what appears
a very happy life, but for the purpose of being used as
food. Yet though greater intellectual discrimination may
lessen the divergencies of moral opinion on the subject,
nothing like unanimity may be expected, for the simple
reason that humanity to animals is ultimately based on the
altruistic sentiment, and sympathy with the animal world
is a feeling which varies greatly in different individuals.
The utilitarian proposition that it is our duty to aim at the
good *universal,* interpreted and defined as "happiness" or
"pleasure," certainly makes it "arbitrary and unreasonable
to exclude from the end, as so conceived, any pleasure of
any sentient being";[50] but that proposition could never
have been made if there had been no tendency to sympathize with the feelings of animals. And even if it be universally admitted that we ought to pay *some* regard to
their feelings, it is impossible to suppose that the same
could ever be the case with the claim that they should be
regarded equally with the feelings of men.

To ethical writers who believe in the objective validity
of moral judgments moral evolution implies a progressive
discovery of values as a matter of reflection or thought,
which follows in the wake of experience. They are fond
of arguing that the changes of moral opinion are on a
par with the discoveries made in mathematics, physics,
and other sciences, which have been disputed quite as

[49] *Cf.* J. Bentham, *An Introduction to the Principles of Morals and
Legislation* (Oxford, 1879), p. 311 n.
[50] Sidgwick, *op. cit.,* p. 414.

fiercely as any differences of moral valuation.[51] "Moral principles," says Locke, "require reasoning and discourse, and some exercise of the mind, to discover the certainty of their truth. They lie not open as natural characters engraven on the mind; which, if any such were, they must needs be visible by themselves, and by their own light be certain and known to everybody. But this is no derogation to their truth and certainty; no more than it is to the truth or certainty of the three angles of a triangle being equal to two right ones, because it is not so evident as, 'the whole is bigger than a part,' nor so apt to be assented to at first hearing. It may suffice that these moral rules are capable of demonstration: and therefore it is our own faults if we come not to a certain knowledge of them." [52] We are reminded of the fact that "in the physical region the existence of divergent ideas does not throw doubt upon the existence of a reality independent of our ideas," [53] and that in speculative philosophy, history, social science, politics, where opinions differ still more widely, "nobody seriously doubts that there is a truth to be found, and that it is discoverable by a proper use of the intellectual faculties which we possess." [54] Professor Sorley remarks that the progress of moral ideas shows

[51] Sorley, *op. cit.*, pp. 136, 137, 163 *sqq.* Heymans, *op. cit.*, p. 20 *sq.* Laird, *The Idea of Value* (Cambridge, 1829), p. 234.

[52] Locke, *An Essay concerning Human Understanding*, i. 2. 1, vol. i. (Oxford, 1894), p. 64 *sq. Cf. ibid.*, iv. 3. 18, vol. ii. 208. According to N. Hartmann (*Ethik* [Berlin & Leipzig, 1926], p. 142), "die Wertblindheit . . . steht vollkommen auf einer Linie mit dem theoretischen Nichteinsehenkönnen des mathematisch Ungeschulten oder Unbegabten."

[53] H. Rashdall, *The Theory of Good and Evil*, ii. (Oxford, 1924), p. 211. *Cf.* Th. Lipps, *Die ethischen Grundfragen* (Leipzig & Hamburg, 1912), p. 2.

[54] Rashdall, *op. cit.*, ii. 152. *Cf.* A. C. Ewing, *The Morality of Punishment with some Suggestions for a general Theory of Ethics* (London, 1929), p. 10 *sq.*

no greater transformation than the theories of science, which at one time seemed firmly established but "have given place to other theories which include a wider sweep, and a better understanding of each portion, of experience." [55] Some earlier writers have gone much farther. Buckle wrote:—"There is, unquestionably, nothing to be found in the world which has undergone so little change as those great dogmas of which moral systems are composed. . . . If we contrast this stationary aspect of moral truths with the progressive aspect of intellectual truths, the difference is indeed startling." [56] According to Mackintosh, "morality admits no discoveries. . . . The facts which lead to the formation of moral rules are as accessible, and must be as obvious, to the simplest barbarian, as to the most enlightened philosopher. . . . The case of the physical and speculative sciences is directly opposite." [57] In spite of their obvious exaggerations, I think there is this much truth in these statements that the changes of moral ideas appear small when compared with the enormous progress in knowledge our race has made on its path from savagery to modern civilization. And the reason for this is that while intellectual evolution has been a perpetual succession of new discoveries, the changes of moral ideas have been no discoveries at all, but only been due to more or less varying reactions of the moral emotions.

But while the objectivists cannot be accused of exaggerating the changes in our theoretical knowledge as compared with those in moral opinion, they have failed to see that the causes of these changes are in a large measure fundamentally different. The theoretical differences can be removed by sufficient observation and reflection, owing

[55] Sorley, *op. cit.*, p. 106.
[56] Buckle, *op. cit.*, p. 180 *sq.*
[57] *Memoirs of the Life of Sir James Mackintosh,* edited by his son, R. J. Mackintosh, i. (London, 1835), pp. 119, 121.

to the general uniformity of our sense-perceptions and intellect. It has been said that "the moral convictions of thoughtful and well-educated people are the data of ethics just as sense-perceptions are the data of a natural science. Just as some of the latter have to be rejected as illusory, so have some of the former; but as the latter are rejected only when they are in conflict with other more accurate sense-perceptions, the former are rejected only when they are in conflict with other convictions which stand better the test of reflection." [58] But, surely, there is an enormous difference between the possibility of harmonizing conflicting sense-perceptions and that of harmonizing conflicting moral convictions. When the sense-perceptions vary in the presence of the same object, as when the object looks different under different objective conditions or if the beholding eye is normal or colour-blind, the variations can be accounted for by reference to the external conditions or the structure of the organ, and they in no way affect our conceptions of things as they really are. So also a hallucination is easily distinguished from a perception when we learn by experience that its object does not exist, whereas the perception has an existing object. On the other hand we all know that there often is a conflict between the moral convictions of "thoughtful and well-educated people," nay, even between the moral "intuitions" of philosophers, which proves irreconcilable. This is just what may be expected if moral opinions are based on emotions. The moral emotions depend upon cognitions, but the same cognitions may give rise to emotions that differ, in quality or intensity, in different persons or in the same person on different occasions, and then there is nothing that could make the emotions uniform. Certain cognitions inspire fear into nearly every breast, but there

[58] W. D. Ross, *The Right and the Good* (Oxford, 1930), p. 41.

are brave men and cowards in the world, independently
of the accuracy with which they realize impending danger.
Some cases of suffering can hardly fail to call forth compassion in the most pitiless heart; but men's disposition
to feel pity varies greatly, both in regard to the beings
for whom it is felt and as to the intensity of the emotion. The same holds true of the moral emotions. To a
large extent, as we have seen, their differences depend
upon the presence of different cognitions, but very frequently the emotions also differ though the cognitions are
the same. The variations of the former kind do not interfere with the belief in the universality of moral judgments, but when the variations of the moral emotions may
be traced to different persons' tendencies to feel differently
in similar circumstances on account of the particular nature of their altruistic sentiments, the supposed universality of moral judgments is a delusion.

It will perhaps be argued that, with sufficient insight
into facts, there would be no diversity of moral opinion
if only the moral consciousness of all men were "sufficiently developed"; this in fact was the explanation given
by Sidgwick in a conversation which I had with him on
his moral axioms. But what is meant by a sufficiently developed moral consciousness? Practically, I suppose, nothing else than agreement with the speaker's own moral
convictions. The expression is faulty and deceptive, because, if intended to mean anything more, it presupposes
a universality of moral judgments which they do not possess, and at the same time may appear to prove what it
presupposes. We may speak of an intellect sufficiently developed to grasp a certain truth, because truth is one; but
it is not proved to be one by the fact that it is recognized
as such by a "sufficiently" developed intellect. The universality of truth lies in the recognition of judgments

as true by all who have a *full* knowledge of the facts concerned, and the appeal to a *sufficient* knowledge rightly *assumes* that truth is universal.

That moral judgments could not possibly possess that universality which is characteristic of truth becomes particularly obvious when we consider that their predicates vary not only in quality but in quantity. There are no degrees of truth and falsehood; [59] but there are degrees of goodness and badness, virtues and merits may be greater or smaller, a duty may be more or less stringent, and if there are no degrees of rightness, the reason for it is that right simply means conformity to the rule of duty. This difference between truth and moral values has been expressly recognized even by writers who uphold the objectivity of the latter, such as Brentano [60] and Martineau. The latter writes:—"Good and Evil, in will and character, cannot be reduced to the True and False; because the latter are unsusceptible of degrees, which attach to the very essence of the former. . . . Truth has no comparative or superlative: it can never be less than true, and never more: its existence is its perfection." [61]

The quantitative differences of moral estimates are plainly due to the emotional origin of all moral concepts. Emotions vary in intensity almost indefinitely, and the moral emotions form no exception to this rule. Indeed, it may be fairly doubted whether the same mode of conduct ever arouses exactly the same degree of approval or disapproval in any two individuals. Many of these differences are of course too slight to manifest themselves in the

[59] *Cf.* H. H. Joachim, *The Nature of Truth* (Oxford, 1906), p. 87; L. A. Reid, *Knowledge and Truth* (London, 1923), p. 39.

[60] F. Brentano, *Vom Ursprung sittlicher Erkenntnis* (Leipzig, 1921), p. 23.

[61] J. Martineau, *Types of Ethical Theory,* ii. (Oxford, 1891), p. 472.

moral judgment; but very frequently the intensity of the emotion is indicated by some special word, or by the tone in which the judgment is pronounced. It should be noticed, however, that the quantity of the estimate expressed in a moral predicate is not identical with the intensity of the moral emotion which a certain course of conduct arouses on a particular occasion. We are liable to feel more indignant if an injury is committed before our eyes than if we read of it in a newspaper, and yet we admit that the degree of badness is in both cases the same. The comparative quantity of moral estimates is determined by the intensity of the emotions which their objects tend to evoke in exactly similar circumstances.

CHAPTER VIII

THE EMOTIONAL BACKGROUND OF NORMATIVE THEORIES

ALL ethical theories are based on facts of the moral consciousness. Without such an empirical foundation none of them could have come into existence and, least of all, gained any supporters. The normative theories have uniformly adopted the common sense idea of the objectivity of moral judgments, which I have tried to prove to be a mistaken interpretation of certain data of our moral experience. But apart from this idea there must be in the moral consciousness facts that account for the origin of all the various theories; and if my view of the emotional basis of moral judgments is correct, these facts must of course be in agreement with it. I shall now proceed to a discussion of the psychological background of normative theories in other points than their claim to objective validity.

Most ethical theories have recognized that there is some connection between moral valuation and the production of pleasure or pain; indeed I think there is none that has completely failed to do so, if not expressly at least by implication. This is just what must be expected if all moral valuation ultimately springs from moral emotions and the moral emotions are by nature retributive, either a kindly attitude of mind towards a person as a cause of pleasure or a hostile attitude of mind towards a person as a cause of pain; and I know no other satisfactory explanation of the connection between moral judgments and the feelings of pleasure and pain. This connection is most directly expressed in the theories of egoistic and universalistic hedonism. The former has been generally repudiated, the latter very widely accepted. This seems to indicate that the support which egoistic hedonism derives from the moral consciousness must be very scanty, and the support which universalistic hedonism derives from it must be very considerable.

I have previously pointed out that if by egoistic hedonism is meant the doctrine that it is everybody's *duty* to seek his own happiness as the ultimate end of his actions and to treat all other objects as subservient to this end, it is doubtful whether it may be found anywhere outside the scope of theological hedonism, and there only on the understanding that happiness means everlasting happiness in the world to come. This doctrine, however, may, if its theological assumptions are accepted, be defended even from the universalistic point of view, since the total amount of happiness which a man can produce in this world would be utterly insignificant in comparison with the infinite reward in store for him hereafter, if he obeys the law of God, and the tremendous penalty of disobeying it. Moreover, the doctrine in question may also be styled universalistic hedonism owing to the assumption that God wishes the happiness of his creatures and consequently will make men happy or miserable according as they designedly increase or decrease the happiness of their fellow-men. Apart from all theological considerations it has been argued, for example, by Bentham in his *Deontology,* that a man best promotes his own happiness by promoting the general happiness. But in this untenable argument the supposed general effect seems rather to serve as a justification of egoism than egoism as the moral basis of universalism.

Most moralists who are commonly looked upon as egoistic hedonists do not say that it is a man's *duty* always
to aim at his own happiness. According to Aristippus, the
Cyrenaic, every one desires pleasure and seeks to avoid
pain; this is the case even with infants, nay, with all living
beings.[1] All pleasure is of the same kind as a feeling,
independently of the source from which it comes;[2] and the
wise man seeks the pleasure which lies directly in his
way, the pleasure of the moment, without troubling himself about the future.[3] So also Epicurus looked upon pleasure as the end towards which all beings in the world tend
as their natural condition.[4] It is the only thing that is
unconditionally good, while the only thing that is unconditionally evil is pain.[5] But true pleasure is satisfaction, tranquillity of soul, freedom from pain, not a yearn-
ing which, though momentarily stilled, bursts forth again.[6]
In order to reach the ideal of life—a mind released from
perturbation—a man requires the assistance of others;
hence friendship is the best of all good things.[7] But to
aim at the desirable state of mind is not represented by
Epicurus either as a duty or a virtue. He expressly says
that virtue is of value only as a means of obtaining it,
only as a source of pleasure.[8] Virtue as such is nothing
but an empty word.[9]

According to a later doctrine of egoism, the one set

---

[1] Diogenes Laertius, *De clarorum philosophorum vitis,* ii. 87 *sq.*
[2] *Ibid.,* ii. 87.
[3] M. Wundt, *Geschichte der griechischen Ethik,* i. (Leipzig, 1908),
p. 412.
[4] Diogenes Laertius, *op. cit.,* x. 129, 137. Cicero, *De finibus,* i. 7. 23;
i. 9. 30.
[5] Diogenes Laertius, *op. cit.,* x. 128 *sq.* Cicero, *op. cit.,* i. 9. 29 *sq.*
[6] Diogenes Laertius, *op. cit.,* x. 131, 132, 136, 139. Cicero, *op. cit.,*
i. 11. 37 *sq.* W. Wallace, *Epicureanism* (London, 1880), p. 147.
Wundt, *op. cit.,* ii. (Leipzig, 1911), p. 188 *sqq.*
[7] Diogenes Laertius, *op. cit.,* x. 148.
[8] *Ibid.,* x. 138. Cicero, *op. cit.,* i. 13. 42 *sqq.* Seneca, *Epistulae,* 85. 18.
[9] Wundt, *op. cit.,* ii. 184.

forth by Mandeville, that which we call virtue is merely selfishness masquerading. All untaught animals are only solicitous of pleasing themselves. The chief thing, therefore, that legislators and politicians were intent upon was to try to make the people they were to govern believe that it was most beneficial for everybody to conquer his appetites, to forgo his own interests, and to pursue those which they themselves had in view. They discovered that flattery was the most powerful instrument for inducing the people to do so. Virtue was the name given to every performance by which man, contrary to the impulse of nature, endeavours to benefit others or to subdue his own passions. "The moral virtues are the political offspring which flattery begot upon pride." [10]

Max Stirner, the arch-egoist, says that to him the words good and bad are devoid of all meaning.[11] People have so long been taught that they ought to suppress their selfishness, that they at last have come to believe it, or in any case try to give the impression of doing so. But they thereby sacrifice their inalienable property, their freedom. They need not refrain from acting as they have been told by religion or morality, from loving their fellow-men and trying to make them happy; but the free man does so only because it gives satisfaction to himself. There is no duty to do anything, a man may do whatever he has power to do.[12]

While the doctrine that it is a man's duty to seek his own happiness as the ultimate end of his actions is not a characteristic of all theories that might be comprised under the heading "egoistic hedonism," it is very widely

[10] B. de Mandeville, "An Enquiry into the Origin of Moral Virtue," in *The Fable of the Bees: or, Private Vices, Publick Benefits* (London, 1724), p. 27 *sqq.*

[11] M. Stirner, *Der Einzige und sein Eigentum* (Leipzig, 1901), p. 8.

[12] *Ibid., passim.*

held outside the limits of any theory that may be called by this name, that it is a man's duty in many cases and many ways to look after his own interests. According to current ideas men owe to themselves a variety of duties resembling those they owe to their fellow-men. They are forbidden to take their own lives, they are in some measure considered to be under an obligation to support their existence, to take care of their bodies, to preserve their personal freedom, not to waste their property, to exhibit self-respect, and in general to promote their own happiness or welfare. And closely related to these self-regarding duties there are self-regarding virtues, such as diligence, thrift, temperance. But the duties which we are considered to owe to ourselves are generally much less emphasized than those we are considered to owe to others, and a prudential virtue does not receive the same praise as one springing from a desire to promote the welfare of a fellow-man. Many moralists even maintain that, properly speaking, there are no self-regarding duties and virtues at all; that useful action which is useful to ourselves alone is no matter for moral notice; that in every case duties towards oneself may be reduced to duties towards others; that intemperance and extravagant luxury, for instance, are blamable only because they tend to the public detriment, and that prudence is a virtue only in so far as it is employed in promoting public interest.[13] In Positivism all moral questions are referred to the well-being of Humanity, and by "duty" is understood a useful social func-

[13] F. Hutcheson, *An Inquiry into the Original of our Ideas of Beauty and Virtue* (London, 1738), pp. 133, 201. J. Grote, *A Treatise on the Moral Ideals* (Cambridge, 1876), p. 77 *sqq.* W. K. Clifford, *Lectures and Essays* (London, 1886), pp. 298, 335. R. von Jhering, *Der Zweck im Recht,* ii. (Leipzig, 1883), p. 225. J. E. Heyde, " 'Ich' und das Sittliche," in *Studier tillägnade Efraim Liljeqvist,* i. (Lund, 1930), pp. 210, 219 *sq.*

tion voluntarily discharged.[14] Fichte said, "There is only one virtue—to forget one's own person, and only one vice —to think of oneself." [15]

It is true that any kind of conduct which in a considerable degree immediately affects a person's own welfare is at the same time apt to affect, to some extent, the well-being of other individuals, and that the moral ideas concerning such conduct as is called self-regarding are more or less influenced by considerations as to its bearing upon others. But this is certainly not the only factor that determines the judgment passed on it. There are circumstances which give rise to moral judgments with direct reference to the effect a person's behaviour has on his own well-being. In the education of children various courses of self-regarding conduct are strenuously insisted upon by parents and teachers. What they censure or punish is regarded as wrong, what they praise or reward is regarded as good; for, as we have noticed before, men have a tendency to sympathize with the retributive emotions of persons for whom they feel regard.[16] Moreover, in cases of self-inflicted harm the injury committed may excite sympathetic resentment towards the agent, although the victim is his own self. Plato asks in his *Laws*, "What ought he to suffer who murders his nearest and so-called dearest friend? I mean, he who kills himself." [17] And the same point of view is conspicuous in St. Augustine's argument, that the more innocent the self-murderer was before he committed his deed the greater is his guilt in taking his life [18]—an argument of particular force in connection

[14] J. K. Ingram, *Human Nature and Morals according to Auguste Comte* (London, 1901), p. 57 *sqq.*

[15] J. G. Fichte, *Die Grundzüge des gegenwärtigen Zeitalters,* 3 (*Sämmtliche Werke,* vii. [Berlin, 1846], p. 35).

[16] *Supra,* p. 106 *sq.*

[17] Plato, *Leges,* ix. 873.

[18] St. Augustine, *De Civitate Dei,* i. 17.

with a theology which condemns suicides to everlasting torments, and regards it as a man's first duty to save his soul. It should also be noticed that disinterested likes or dislikes lead to moral approval or disapproval of conduct which is essentially self-regarding. But at the same time it is not difficult to see why self-regarding duties and virtues only occupy a subordinate place in our moral consciousness. The influence which self-regarding conduct exercises upon other persons' welfare is mostly too remote to attract attention. In education there is no need to emphasize any other self-regarding duties and virtues but those which, for the sake of the individual's general welfare, require some sacrifice of his immediate pleasure or comfort. The compassion we are apt to feel for the victim of an injury is naturally much lessened by the fact that it is self-inflicted—it is his own fault. And, on the other hand, indignation against the offender is disarmed by the fact that he has got his punishment.

I have now spoken of self-regarding conduct that does not perceptibly interfere with the interests of other individuals. Sometimes it is looked upon as a duty, sometimes as praiseworthy, but in the large majority of cases it is treated with moral indifference, whatever theorists may have to say about it.[19] It becomes a matter of acute moral concern mainly when it affects other individuals' well-being, and then a problem may arise which the agent finds very difficult to solve. The conflict is not generally between what he may consider to be a duty to himself and what he may consider to be a duty to others, but between his right to promote his own well-being and his duty to respect the right of somebody else. Universalistic hedonism or utilitarianism has laid down the rule that it is a duty for each person to aim at the greatest amount

[19] *Moral Ideas,* i. 154 *sqq.*

of happiness on the whole, taking into account all whose happiness is affected by the conduct and at his own happiness as an element of the whole. It has, from the point of view of common sense, greatly exaggerated the *duty* of promoting one's own happiness by putting it on a par with the duty of promoting the happiness of others. Who would really consider it a duty for a person to seek his own happiness in every case where it implies a sacrifice of the lesser happiness of another? Who would consider it to be in the same degree my duty to refrain from doing harm to myself as to refrain from doing the same amount of harm to another, for instance, to avoid causing an economic loss to myself as to avoid causing a similar loss to another? At the same time, I may, according to current moral ideas, have a *right* to seek my own happiness in many cases where it involves a lessening of some other person's happiness, even though I could claim no counterbalancing gain to anybody else as an excuse for my action.[20] Utilitarianism, on the other hand, requires the sacrifice of the agent's private interests where they are incompatible with the greatest happiness of the greatest number. And it also requires that the happiness of every other individual should be considered as much as that of any one else, unless there are special grounds for believing that a greater amount of happiness is likely to be realized in the one case than in the other.

Generally speaking, the origin of utilitarianism may be traced to the nature of the moral emotions. In the first place, as we have seen, they are retributive emotions, moral approval being a kindly attitude of mind towards a cause of pleasure and moral disapproval a hostile attitude of mind towards a cause of pain: we approve a person who causes pleasure and condemn one who causes

[20] See *supra,* p. 13 *sq.*

pain. Thus our moral emotions are produced by exactly the same facts, the giving of pleasure and the infliction of pain, as utilitarianism considers the criteria of moral and immoral conduct. In the second place, moral approval and disapproval, in distinction from other retributive emotions, such as gratitude and anger, are disinterested, in the strict sense of the term, and apparently impartial; in other words, they are felt independently of any reference that the conduct causing them may have to the interests of those who feel them, and are also assumed by these persons to be uninfluenced by the particular relationship in which they stand both to those who are immediately affected by the acts in question and to those who perform them. But these essential characteristics of the moral emotions do not lead, for reasons already indicated, to the exaggerated ideas expressed in the utilitarian formula as to the duty of promoting one's own happiness; nor are they, on the other hand, sufficient to explain either its reduction of a person's rights when his interests conflict with those of others, or its requirement that the happiness of every other individual shall be considered as much as that of any one else. The disinterestedness of the moral emotions cannot admit that one person has a right to promote his own happiness in circumstances where another similar person has no such right; but it is not opposed to the rule that every similar person may in similar circumstances seek his own happiness on an occasion when it involves a decrease of happiness on the whole. So also the impartiality of the moral emotions does not allow a person to treat another differently from any one else on account of the particular relationship in which he stands to him personally, unless every similar person is admitted to have a similar right in similar circumstances. It does not prevent us from paying greater attention to the in-

terests of our own family or nation than to the interests
of other families or nations, quite apart from its effect
on happiness as a whole. The utilitarian formula is not
a mere expression of the disinterestedness and impartiality
of the moral emotions, and cannot therefore be regarded
as anything like a moral axiom: its universalism, as I
have said before, is undoubtedly closely connected with a
corresponding expansion of the altruistic sentiment. This
sentiment is an important cause of the moral emotions,
but its scope may vary indefinitely without affecting their
essential nature, and may consequently give rise to very
different moral judgments; and if extended to the whole
sentient creation, universalistic hedonism may be the result. These facts, in addition to the specific nature of the
moral emotions, help us to understand the great popularity
of utilitarianism in a world imbued with the ethics of the
New Testament. As Stuart Mill pointed out, "to do as
one would be done by, and to love one's neighbour as
oneself, constitute the ideal perfection of utilitarian morality." [21]

Though widely accepted, especially by earlier generations, utilitarianism has been subjected to much criticism.
It has been argued that it is impossible to foresee all the
hedonic consequences of one's own or any other person's
conduct in a certain case; that different people often feel
differently in the same circumstances, that one man's feelings cannot, therefore, be estimated and dealt with as if
they were identical with another man's feelings, and that
it is impossible to know the differences between them;
that neither pleasure nor pain admit of a rigid application of the rules of arithmetic and algebra; and so forth.
Much of this criticism has no bearing upon the question
I am now discussing, but a few remarks, besides those

[21] J. S. Mill, *Utilitarianism* (London, 1895), p. 24 *sq.*

already made, are appropriate in the present connection.

The first and most fundamental assumption involved in the very conception of "greatest happiness" as an end of action is the commensurability of pleasures and pains. The pleasures sought and the pains shunned are assumed to have determinate quantitative relations to each other, since otherwise they cannot be conceived as possible elements of a total of which we are to seek the maximum, and in the comparison and balancing between them pain is reckoned as the negative quality of pleasure. It is strange, however, that the expounders of utilitarianism, who have taken so much trouble to vindicate the psychological commensurability of pleasures and pains should have failed to notice that they are far from commensurable in the moral valuation of conduct. There the production of a certain amount of pain is not *eo ipso* counterbalanced by what may be psychologically regarded as an equal, nay, a greater amount of pleasure; not even a cock-fight is nowadays considered justified by the amusement it gives to any number of people. The large majority of duties enjoin abstinence from the infliction of pain, or alleviation or prevention of pain, and these are practically the only duties to fellow-creatures that the customs and laws of all peoples insist upon. To promote the positive happiness of others is mostly looked upon as laudable, not as a duty. This is not in agreement with the utilitarian view that "it is always wrong for a man knowingly to do anything other than what he believes to be most conducive to universal happiness"; [22] but it is in perfect agreement with my theory of the emotional origin of moral judgments. The hostile attitude of mind towards a cause of pain is a much more frequent and a much stronger emotion than the kindly attitude of mind towards a cause of pleasure, and the

[22] H. Sidgwick, *The Methods of Ethics* (London, 1913), p. 492.

altruistic sentiment, which plays such an important part in the formation of moral resentment and moral retributive kindly emotion, is much more readily moved by the sight of pain than by the sight of pleasure. Indeed, the latter emotion has powerful rivals in the feelings of jealousy and envy, which may even excite anger against him who bestows the benefit upon the other individual.[23] The author of the utilitarian formula "the greatest happiness of the greatest number" laid all stress on positive happiness, which he looked upon as "far superior to misery, even in this world."[24] But we may rather second Dr. Goldscheid's proposition that the chief moral criterion is "the smallest pain of the smallest number."[25]

Utilitarianism would, of course, be utterly incompatible with the morality of common sense if it taught that we are to determine the morality of a particular mode of conduct by computing its probable effects in each individual case. Such a doctrine would be as absurd as to maintain, on the principle I am advocating, that the moral judgments depend upon the emotions felt by persons at the moment they pronounce them. Those judgments are largely expressions of tendencies in certain classes of conduct to arouse moral emotions; to say of a theft that it is wrong implies that an act of this kind has a tendency to call forth moral disapproval. So also a utilitarian does not hold that it is wrong because it in this particular case produces more pain than pleasure; it is not at all certain that it really does so. But he insists on the necessity of acting according to general rules instead of attempting to show that we may calculate the consequences in each

[23] *Supra*, p. 98.

[24] F. Hutcheson, *A System of Moral Philosophy*, i. (London, 1755), p. 190.

[25] R. Goldscheid, *Zur Ethik des Gesamtwillens*, i. (Leipzig, 1902), p. 383.

special case. Dr. Albee believes that no utilitarian but Bentham in his *Deontology,* where the object is to guide the individual agent in his moral life, has failed to recognize the need of depending upon such rules; at least there is no passage in that book which points out their importance, as opposed to particular computations.[26] But at the same time the utilitarian admits that there are emergencies in which a general rule may be transgressed; as in a case of special need—"necessity knows no law," —or when the general utility of truth-speaking is outweighed by particular, bad consequences, or when the keeping of a promise ceases to be a duty if it has been procured by fraud or unlawful violence, or if the performance of it would be injurious to the promisee.[27] This, too, is in full agreement with the emotional theory of moral judgments and has the support of common sense. But I want to emphasize that the relaxation of general rules in individual cases serves the object, not of increasing pleasure, but of diminishing pain—unless we consider as such a case like the telling of harmless stories to children in order to amuse them.

It has been contended that utilitarianism cannot adequately account for certain duties, such as justice, veracity, and chastity. So far as criminal justice is concerned I agree: I have previously tried to show that those theorists who think it possible to base punishment on utilitarian considerations alone, independently of the emotion of moral resentment, are victims of an illusion.[28] As for veracity, there is also some truth in the imputation.

In a large measure this duty undoubtedly has a utilitarian foundation: he who tells a lie generally commits an

[26] E. Albee, *A History of English Utilitarianism* (London, 1902), pp. 188, 320.
[27] Sidgwick, *op. cit.,* p. 443.
[28] *Supra,* p. 78 *sqq.*

injury against another person; his act consequently calls forth sympathetic resentment, and becomes an object of moral censure. Men have a natural disposition to believe what they are told, but they also like to know the truth; curiosity is displayed even by many of the higher animals. In our endeavour to learn the truth we are frustrated by him who deceives us, and he becomes an object of our resentment. Nor are we injured by a deception merely because we like to know the truth, but, chiefly, because it is of much importance for us that we should know it. Our conduct is influenced by ideas; hence the erroneous notion as regards some fact in the past, present, or future, which is produced by a lie, may lead to unforeseen events detrimental to our interests. Moreover, on discovering that we have been deceived, we have the humiliating feeling that another person has impertinently made our conduct subject to his will. This is a wound on our pride, a blot on our honour. "The lie," says Sainte-Palaye, "has always been considered the most fatal and irreparable affront that a man of honour could receive." [29] How largely the condemnation of falsehood is due to the harm suffered by the victim appears from the fact that a lie is held more condemnable in proportion to the magnitude of the harm caused by it. But even in apparently trifling cases the reflective mind insists upon the necessity of truthfulness. Every lie may have a tendency to lessen mutual confidence, to predispose the perpetrator to commit a similar offence in the future, and to serve as a bad example for others.[30] Contrariwise, as Aristotle observes, he who is truthful in unimportant matters will be all the more so in important ones.[31] Similar considerations, how-

[29] De la Curne de Sainte-Palaye, *Mémoires sur l'ancienne chevalerie*, i. (Paris, 1781), p. 78.
[30] *Cf.* J. Bentham, *Theory of Legislation* (London, 1882), p. 260.
[31] Aristotle, *Ethica Nicomachea,* iv. 7. 8.

ever, require a certain amount of reflection and far-sightedness; hence intellectual development tends to increase the emphasis laid on the duty of veracity. At the earlier stages of civilization it is frequently considered good form to tell an untruth to a person in order to please him, and ill-mannered to contradict him, however much he be mistaken, for the reason that farther consequences are left out of account. The utilitarian basis of the duty of truthfulness also accounts for those extreme cases in which deception is held permissible or even a duty, either in self-defence or when promoting the true interests of the person deceived.

But untruthfulness is not merely condemned on utilitarian grounds, on account of the harm it is apt to cause: it is an object of disinterested, moral resentment also because it is intrinsically antipathetic. Lying is a cheap and cowardly method of gaining an undue advantage, and is consequently despised where courage is respected. It is the weapon of the weak, the woman, and the slave. Fraud, says Cicero, is the property of a fox, force that of a lion; "both are utterly repugnant to society, but fraud is the more detestable." [32] "To lie is servile," says Plutarch, "and most hateful in all men, hardly to be pardoned even in poor slaves." [33] On account of its cowardliness, lying was incompatible with Teutonic and knightly notions of manly honour; and among ourselves the epithets "liar" and "coward" are equally disgraceful to a man. "All . . . in the rank and station of gentlemen," says Sir Walter Scott, "are forcibly called upon to remember that they must resent the imputation of a voluntary falsehood as the most gross injury." [34] Fichte asks, "Whence comes that in-

[32] Cicero, *De officiis*, i. 13.
[33] Plutarch, *De educatione puerorum*, 14.
[34] W. Scott, "Essay on Chivalry," in *Miscellaneous Prose Works*, vi. (Edinburgh, 1827), p. 58.

ternal shame for one's self which manifests itself even stronger in the case of a lie than in the case of any other violation of conscience?" And his answer is, that the lie is accompanied with cowardice, and that nothing so much dishonours us in our own eyes as want of courage.[35] According to Kant, "a lie is the abandonment, and, as it were, the annihilation, of the dignity of a man." [36]

The duty of chastity is a more complicated matter. I shall first discuss moral ideas concerning sexual relations between men and women falling outside the recognized marriage institution. Among many uncivilized peoples both sexes enjoy perfect freedom previous to marriage; but it seems that those who look upon unchastity in a girl as a disgrace or punish it as a crime are, roughly speaking, as numerous as those who condone it, and among the former the man who seduced her is also censured or punished. Among the simpler peoples the standard of pre-nuptial chastity in a tribe is not proportionate to its degree of culture, but it appears, on the contrary, that in the lowest tribes chastity is more respected than in the higher ones. Where free intercourse prevails between unmarried people, sexual connections between a boy and a girl are a frequent preliminary to their marriage, and may be a regular method of courtship or a trial before establishing more permanent relations; and if they lead to pregnancy or the birth of a child they often make marriage compulsory.[37]

Passing to more advanced races, we find that chastity is regarded as a duty for unmarried women, whilst a dif-

[35] J. G. Fichte, *Das System der Sittenlehre* (Jena & Leipzig, 1798), p. 370.

[36] Kant, *Ethische Elementarlehre*, § 9 (*Gesammelte Schriften*, vi. [Berlin, 1914], p. 429).

[37] *The History of Human Marriage*, i. (London, 1921), pp. 72 *sqq.*, 126 *sqq.*

ferent standard of morality is generally applied to men.[38]
"Confucianism," says Mr. Griffis, "virtually admits two
standards of morality, one for man, another for woman.
. . . Chastity is a female virtue, it is a part of womanly
duty, it has little or no relation to man personally." [39]
Yet it is said that in youth, when the physical powers are
not yet settled, the superior man guards against lust.[40]
Among the ancient Hebrews fornication was forbidden to
women [41] but not to men. The action of Judah towards
the supposed harlot on the way to Timnath is mentioned
as the most natural thing in the world,[42] even though
the perpetrator was a man whom his brethren "shall
praise" and before whom his "father's children shall bow
down." [43] Throughout the Mohammedan world chastity
is regarded as a stringent duty in the case of a woman,
for the breach of which she has often to pay with her life,
whereas in the case of a man it is at most held as an
ideal, almost out of reach. Among the Hindus sexual
impurity is scarcely considered a sin in the men, but in
women nothing is held more execrable or abominable. In
one of the Pahlavi texts continence is recommended from
the point of view of prudence: "Commit no lustfulness, so
that harm and regret may not reach thee from thine own
actions." [44] But in Zoroastrianism, also, chastity is chiefly
a female duty. Among the ancient Teutons an unmarried
woman who belonged to an honourable family was severely punished for incontinence, and the seducer was

[38] *Moral Ideas,* ii. 427 *sqq.*

[39] W. E. Griffis, *The Religions of Japan* (London, 1895), p. 149.

[40] *Lun Yü,* xvi. 7 (in J. Legge, *The Chinese Classics,* i. [Oxford, 1893]).

[41] *Leviticus,* xix. 29. *Deuteronomy,* xxiii. 18.

[42] *Genesis,* xxxviii. 15 *sqq.*

[43] *Ibid.,* xlix. 8.

[44] *Dinâ-î-Maînôgî Khirad,* ii. 23 *sq.* (in *The Sacred Books of the East,* xxiv. [Oxford, 1885]).

exposed to the revenge of her family, or had to pay compensation for his deed. In Greece the chastity of an unmarried girl was anxiously guarded, and according to Athenian law the relatives of a maiden who had lost her virtue could with impunity kill the seducer on the spot. It is true that a certain class of courtesans occupied a remarkably high position in the social life of Greece, being admired and sought after even by the principal men; but they did so on account of their extraordinary beauty or their intellectual superiority. The Romans, on the other hand, regarded the courtesan class with much contempt. But both in Greece and Rome pre-nuptial unchastity in men, when it was not excessive [45] or did not take some especially offensive form, was hardly censured by public opinion. The elder Cato expressly justified it; [46] and Cicero says that "if there be any one who thinks that youth is to be wholly interdicted from amours with courtesans, he certainly is very strict indeed." [47] A few other writers, however, were more exacting. [48] Such opinions grew up especially in connection with the Neo-Platonic and Neo-Pythagorean philosophies, and may be traced back to the ancient masters themselves. We are told that Pythagoras inculcated the virtue of chastity so successfully that when ten of his disciples, being attacked, might have escaped by crossing a bean-field, they died to a man rather than tread down the beans, which were supposed to have a mystic affinity with the seat of impure desires. [49] Plato, again, is in favour of a law to the effect that "no one

[45] Valerius Maximus, *Facta dictaque memorabilia*, ii. 5. 6.

[46] Horace, *Satirae*, i. 2. 31 *sq.*

[47] Cicero, *Pro Coelio*, 20 (48).

[48] Musonius Rufus, quoted by Stobaeus, *Florilegium*, vi. 61. J. Denis, *Histoire des théories et des idées morales dans l'antiquité*, ii. (Paris, 1856), p. 133 *sqq.*

[49] Jamblichus, *De Pythagorica vita*, 31 (191).

shall venture to touch any person of the freeborn or noble class except his wedded wife, or in barren and unnatural lusts." [50]

Much stronger was the censure which Christianity passed on pre-nuptial connections. While looking with suspicion even on the life-long union of one man with one woman, the Church pronounced all other forms of sexual intercourse to be mortal sins. In the Penitentials sins of unchastity were the favourite topic; and the horror of them finds an echo in the secular legislation of the first Christian emperors. Even the innocent offspring of illicit intercourse were punished for their parents' sins with ignominy and loss of certain rights which belonged to other, more respectable, members of the Church and the State. Persons of different sex who were not united in wedlock were forbidden by the Church to kiss each other; nay, the sexual desire itself, though unaccompanied by any external act, was regarded as sinful in the unmarried.[51] In this standard of purity no difference of sex was recognized, the same obligation being imposed upon man and woman.

In this, as in many other points of morals, there has always been a considerable discrepancy between Christian doctrine and public opinion in Christian countries. The influence of the ascetic doctrine of the Church was in one respect quite contrary to its aspirations: the institution of clerical celibacy created a large class of people to whom illicit love was the only means of gratifying a natural desire, and this could hardly be favourable to the ideal of chastity. During the Middle Ages incontinence was largely an object of ridicule rather than censure, and in the comic

---

[50] Plato, *Leges*, viii. 840 *sq*. Cf. Xenophon, *Memorabilia*, i. 3. 8.

[51] "Perit ergo et ipsa mente virginitas." E. Katz, *Ein Grundriss des kanonischen Strafrechts* (Berlin & Leipzig, 1881), p. 114 *sq*. For the subject of kissing see also Thomas Aquinas, *Summa theologica*, ii.-ii. 154. 4.

literature of that period the clergy are represented as the
great corrupters of domestic virtue. Whether the tenet of
chastity laid down by the code of Chivalry was taken more
seriously may be fairly doubted. For a mediaeval knight
the chief object of life was love, he who did not understand how to win a lady was but half a man; and the difference between a lover and a seducer was apparently
slight. The Reformation brought about some change, if
in no other respect at least by making marriage lawful
for the clergy. In fits of religious enthusiasm even the secular legislators busied themselves with acts of incontinence in which two unmarried adults of different sex were
consenting parties. In the days of the Commonwealth, in
cases of less serious breach of chastity than adultery and
incest, each man or woman was for each offence to be
committed to the common gaol for three months; and in
Scotland, after the Reformation, fornication was punished with a severity nearly equal to that which attended
the infraction of the marriage vow. But the fate of these
and similar laws has been either to be repealed or to become invalid. For ordinary acts of incontinence public
opinion is, practically at least, the only judge. In the case
of female unchastity its sentence is severe enough among
the upper ranks of society, while, so far as the lower
classes are concerned, it varies considerably even in different parts of the same country, and is in many cases regarded as venial. As to similar acts committed by unmarried men, the words which Cicero uttered on behalf of
Coelius might be repeated by any modern advocate who,
in defending his client, ventured frankly to express the
popular opinion on the subject. It seems to me that with
regard to sexual relations between unmarried men and
women Christianity has done little more than establish a
standard which, though accepted perhaps in theory, is

hardly recognized by the feelings of the large majority of people—or at least of men—in Christian communities, and has introduced the vice of hypocrisy, which apparently was little known in sexual matters by pagan antiquity.

After this survey of facts, which are of importance for our discussion, we now come to the main points of it. Why has sexual intercourse between unmarried people, if both parties consent, come to be regarded as wrong? Why are the moral opinions relating to it so variable? Why is the standard commonly so different for man and woman?

If marriage, as I consider most probable, is based on an instinct, tending to preserve the next generation and thereby the species, which has been derived from some apelike progenitor,[52] it would from the beginning be regarded as the natural form of sexual intercourse in the human race, whilst other, more transitory connections would appear abnormal and consequently be disapproved of. Some feeling of this sort, however vague, may still be very general in the race. But it has been more or less or almost totally suppressed by social conditions which make it impossible for men to marry at the first outbreak of the sexual passion.

I believe that the censure passed on pre-nuptial connections may be principally traced to the preference which a man gives to a virgin bride. This preference, which is probably very ancient, seems to spring partly from a feeling akin to jealousy towards women who have had previous connections with other men, and partly from an instinctive appreciation of female coyness. Each sex is attracted by the particular characteristics of the other sex, and coyness is a female quality. In mankind, as among

[52] *The History of Human Marriage,* i. ch. i.

other mammals, the female requires to be courted, often endeavouring for a long time to escape from the male; not only in civilized countries may courtship mean a prolonged making of love to the woman. And it is certainly not the woman who most readily yields to the desires of a man that is most attractive to him; as an ancient writer puts it, all men love seasoned dishes, not plain meats, or plainly dressed fish, and it is modesty that gives the bloom to beauty.[53] Conspicuous eagerness in a woman appears to a man unwomanly, repulsive, contemptible. His ideal is the virgin; the lustful woman he despises.

Where marriage is the customary form of sexual intercourse pre-nuptial incontinence in a woman, as suggesting lack of modesty, is therefore apt to disgrace her. At the same time it is a disgrace to, and consequently an offence against, her family, especially where the ties of kinship are strong. Moreover, where wives are purchased the unchaste girl, by lowering her market value, deprives her father or parents of part of their property. This commercial point of view is found not only among savage peoples, but is expressed in the Mosaic rule :—"If a man entice a maid that is not betrothed, and lie with her, he shall surely endow her to be his wife. If her father utterly refuse to give her unto him, he shall pay money according to the dowry of virgins." [54] The girl, however, is not the only offender: the offence against her family is divided between her and the seducer, who is regarded in the light of a robber spoiling their merchandise. Marriage by purchase has thus raised the standard of female chastity, and also, to some extent, checked the incontinence of the men. But in numerous instances where a seduction is followed by more or less serious consequences for the seducer, the

[53] Athenaeus, *Deipnosophistae,* xiii. 16.
[54] *Exodus,* xxii. 16 *sq.*

penalty he has to pay is evidently something else than the mere market value of the girl.

Thus the men, by demanding that the women whom they marry shall be virgins, indirectly give rise to the demand that they themselves shall refrain from intercourse with unmarried girls, which is considered offensive to the families of the latter. To him who duly reflects upon the matter it is clear that the seducer does a wrong to the woman also; but I find no indication that this idea occurs to the savage mind. Where the seducer is censured the girl also is censured, being regarded not as the injured party but as an accomplice in the crime. Even in the case of rape the harm done to the girl herself is often little thought of; and if the girl's feelings are thus disregarded when she is an unwilling victim of violence, it can hardly be expected that she should be an object of pity when she is a consenting partner. Does not public opinion in the midst of civilization turn against the dishonoured one rather than the dishonourer?

There is yet another party to be considered, namely, the offspring. One would imagine that to a thinking mind, not altogether destitute of sympathetic feelings, the question what is likely to happen to the child if the woman becomes pregnant should present itself as one of the greatest gravity. But in judging of matters relating to sexual morality men have generally made little use of their reason, and been guilty of much thoughtless cruelty. Although marriage has come into existence for the sake of the offspring, it rarely happens that in sexual relations much unselfish thought is bestowed upon unborn individuals. Legal provisions in favour of illegitimate children have made men somewhat more careful, for their own sake, but they have also nourished the idea that the responsibility of fatherhood may be bought off by the small sum the man has to pay for the support of his natural child. The law may exempt him even from this duty. "La recherche de la paternité est interdite." [55]

The great authority on the ethics of Roman Catholicism, Thomas Aquinas, tries to prove that simple fornication is a mortal sin chiefly because it "tends to the hurt of the life of the child who is to be born of such intercourse," or more generally, because "it is contrary to the good of the offspring." [56] But this tender care for the welfare of illegitimate children seems strange when we consider the manner in which such children have been treated by the Catholic Church herself. It is obvious that the horror of fornication which is expressed in the Christian doctrine is in the main a result of the same ascetic principle that declared celibacy superior to marriage and tolerated marriage only because it could not be suppressed.

Moral ideas regarding unchastity have also been influenced by the close association which exists in a refined mind between the sexual impulse and a sentiment of affection which lasts long after the gratification of the bodily desire. We find an outcome of this feeling in the distinction drawn between the prostitute and the woman who yields to temptation because she loves. To indulge in mere sexual pleasure, unaccompanied by higher feelings, appears brutal in a man and still more so in the case of a woman. After all, love is generally only an episode in a man's life, whereas for a woman it is often the whole of her life. The Greek orator said that at the moment when a woman loses her chastity her mind is changed.[57] On the other hand, when a man and a woman, tied to each other

---

[55] *Code Napoléon,* § 340.
[56] Thomas Aquinas, *op. cit.,* ii.-ii. 154. 2.
[57] Lysias, quoted by L. Schmidt, *Die Ethik der alten Griechen,* i. (Berlin, 1882), p. 273.

by deep and genuine affection, decide to live together as husband and wife, though not joined in legal wedlock, the censure which public opinion passes upon their conduct seems to an unprejudiced mind justifiable at most only in so far as it may be considered to have been their duty to comply with the laws of their country and to submit to a rule of some social importance.

Among ourselves an act of incontinence assumes a different aspect if one of the parties, either the man or the woman, is married. Involving a breach of faith, adultery is an offence against him or her to whom faith is due, and at the same time the seducer commits an offence against the husband of the adulteress. But here again our own views are not universally shared. Among savage and barbarous tribes it is obviously the rule that conjugal fidelity, while considered a stringent duty in the wife, is not generally considered so in the husband, although there are interesting exceptions to the rule; and among the peoples of ancient civilization the law requires faithfulness of the wife alone. Among the Hebrews adultery was a capital offence, but it presupposed that the guilty woman was another man's wife.[58] The Aryan nations in early times generally saw nothing objectionable in the unfaithfulness of a married man, whereas an adulterous wife was punished with the greatest severity.[59] Until some time after the introduction of Christianity among the Teutons their law-books made no mention of the infidelity of husbands, because it was permitted by ancient custom.[60] The Romans defined adultery as sexual intercourse with another man's wife; the intercourse of a married man with an unmar-

---

[58] *Leviticus,* xx. 10. *Deuteronomy,* xxii. 22.

[59] O. Schrader, *Prehistoric Antiquities of the Aryan Peoples* (London, 1890), p. 388.

[60] W. E. Wilda, *Das Strafrecht der Germanen* (Halle, 1842), p. 821. H. Brunner, *Deutsche Rechtsgeschichte,* ii. (Leipzig, 1892), p. 662.

ried woman was not regarded as adultery.[61] The ordinary Greek feeling on the subject is expressed in the oration against Neaera, ascribed to Demosthenes, where the license accorded to husbands is spoken of as a matter of course:—"We keep mistresses for our pleasures, concubines for constant attendance, and wives to bear us legitimate children and to be our faithful housekeepers."[62] In classical literature, however, the idea that fidelity in marriage ought to be reciprocal is not altogether unknown.[63]

In its condemnation of adultery Christianity made no distinction between husband and wife.[64] If continence is a strict duty for unmarried persons independently of their sex, the observance of the sacred marriage vow must be so in a still higher degree. But here again there is a considerable discrepancy between the actual feelings of Christian peoples and the standard of their religion. Even in their laws relating to divorce and judicial separation we often find an echo of the popular notion that adultery is a smaller offence in a husband than in a wife.[65] That a married man enjoys more liberty than a married woman is largely due to the same causes as make him the more privileged partner in other respects; but there are also special reasons for this inequality between the sexes. It was a doctrine of the Roman jurists that adultery is a crime in the wife, and the wife only, on account of the danger of introducing strange children to the husband. Moreover, the temptation of infidelity and the facility in indulging

[61] A. Vinnius, *In quatuor libros institutionum imperialium commentarius,* iv. 18. 4, p. 993. *Cf. Digesta,* I. 16. 101. 1.

[62] *Oratio in Neaeram,* p. 1386. *Cf.* L. Schmidt, *op. cit.,* ii. 196 *sq.*

[63] Aristotle, *Oeconomica,* p. 341, vol. ii. (Oxonii, 1810), p. 679. Plutarch, *Conjugalia praecepta,* 16. Plautus, *Mercator,* iv. 5. L. Schmidt, *op. cit.,* ii. 195 *sq.*

[64] Gratian, *Decretum,* ii. 35. 5. 23.

[65] *The History of Human Marriage,* iii. (London, 1921), pp. 343, 344, 357 *sq.*

in it are commonly greater in the case of the husband than in that of the wife; and actual practice is always apt to influence moral opinion. And a still more important reason for the inequality is undoubtedly the general notion that unchastity of any kind is more discreditable for a woman than for a man.

There is one form of unchastity that is universally condemned in man and woman alike, namely, incest; but in this case the prohibition is not restricted to non-matrimonial intercourse, it refers in the first place to marriage itself. Among all peoples there are exogamous rules, which forbid the members of a particular group to marry any other member of it. In most cases this group is composed of persons who are, or consider themselves to be, related by blood or of the same kin; and the nearer the relationship, the more frequently is it a bar to intermarriage, at least within the same line of descent. The most frequent of all exogamous rules are those which prohibit a son from marrying his mother and a father from marrying his daughter; these rules seem, in fact, to be universally prevalent in mankind. Hardly less universal is the rule which forbids marriages between brothers and sisters who are children of the same father and mother; the best authenticated exceptions to this rule are generally found in the families of kings or ruling chiefs, and there can be little doubt that they are due to the aim of maintaining the purity of the royal blood. Among peoples unaffected by modern civilization the exogamic rules are probably in the large majority of cases more extensive than among ourselves; very often they refer to all the members of the clan, and the rule that a man may not marry a woman of his own clan is usually supplemented by a further prohibition of marrying other women who are nearly related to him.[66]

[66] *The History of Human Marriage,* ii. ch. xix.

Many attempts have been made to account for the exogamous rules; [67] I doubt whether any other question in the history of social institutions has given rise to more controversy. They have been ascribed to a pristine habit of female infanticide; to the vain desire of savage men to have trophies in their wives; to experience of the injurious influence of in-breeding (which must have been made at an earlier stage of human development than that represented by any living savages, but afterwards forgotten); to marriage by capture originating in the hypothetical period of primitive promiscuity; to marriage by purchase; to a superstitious belief that incest blights the crops, prevents the multiplication of edible animals, and renders the women of the community sterile; to totemism; or to the furious jealousy of a gorilla-like ancestor. I have elsewhere tried to show that the gravest objections may be raised to each of these theories, and that in addition there are other objections that may be raised to all of them. They all regard the exogamous rules as social survivals from very remote ages. They all suppose that these rules have originated in social conditions which no longer exist, or in ideas which have been found among a few savages or which have never been found anywhere. Now, is it really reasonable to believe that a law like that against incest among ourselves could be traced to similar sources? The exogamous rules have not remained unaltered; on the contrary, they differ even among peoples of the same stock, and we know that in Europe, in the course of a few centuries, they have been greatly changed in spite of the religious sanction given them by the Church. This proves that those rules are not dead fossils, but living parts of the social organism, subject to modifications according to the circumstances.

Moreover, the theories in question imply that the home

[67] *Ibid.,* ii. ch. xx.

is kept free from incestuous intercourse by law, custom, or education. But even if social prohibitions might prevent unions between the nearest relatives, they could not prevent the desire for such unions. The sexual instinct can hardly be changed by prescriptions; I doubt whether all laws against homosexual intercourse, even the most draconic, have ever been able to extinguish the peculiar desire of anybody born with homosexual tendencies. Nevertheless, our laws against incest are scarcely felt as a restraint upon individual feelings. And the simple reason for this is that in normal cases there is no desire for the acts which they forbid. Generally speaking, there is a remarkable absence of erotic feelings between persons living closely together from childhood; among the lower animals, also, there are indications that the pairing instinct fails to be stimulated by companions and seeks strangers for its gratification. Hume committed a curious psychological error in his utilitarian explanation of the prohibition of incest when he wrote, "Those who live in the same family have so many opportunities of licenses of this kind, that nothing could preserve purity of manners, were marriage allow'd amongst the nearest relations, or any intercourse of love betwixt them ratify'd by law and custom." [68] Plato showed a sharper eye for the problem of incest in his observation that an unwritten law defends as sufficiently as possible parents from incestuous intercourse with their children and brothers from intercourse with their sisters, and that the thought of such a thing does not enter at all into the minds of most of them.[69]

Sexual indifference, however, is not by itself sufficient to account for exogamous prohibitions. But such indif-

[68] D. Hume, *An Enquiry concerning the Principles of Morals,* sec. iv. (London, 1751), p. 67.
[69] Plato, *Leges,* viii. 838.

ference is very generally combined with sexual aversion when the act is thought of; indeed, I believe that this is normally the case whenever the idea of sexual intercourse occupies the mind with sufficient intensity and a desire fails to appear. An old and ugly woman, for instance, would in such circumstances become sexually repulsive to most men, and to many male inverts any woman, as an object of sexual desire, is not merely indifferent but disgusting. And, as I have pointed out above, aversions which are generally felt readily lead to moral disapproval and prohibitory customs or laws. This I take to be the fundamental cause of the exogamous prohibitions. Persons who have been living closely together from childhood are as a rule near relatives. Hence their aversion to sexual relations with one another displays itself in custom and law as a prohibition of intercourse between near kin. This interpretation of their aversion in terms of kinship is exactly analogous to another case of equally world-wide occurrence, namely, the process which has led to the association of all sorts of social rights and duties with kinship, though ultimately depending upon close living together. Parental, filial, and fraternal duties and rights, and those referring to relatives more remotely allied, are not in the first instance rooted in considerations of kinship. If men, instead of remaining in the circle where they were born and keeping with their kindred, had isolated themselves or united with strangers, there would certainly be no blood-bond at all.

Innumerable facts show that the extent to which relatives are forbidden to intermarry is nearly connected with their close living together; and among various peoples marriage is prohibited even between all persons belonging to the same village or other local group, whether they are related by blood or not. At the same time the members of an exogamous clan very frequently do not live in the same locality. The exogamous rules, though in the first place associated with kinship because near relatives normally live together, have come to include relatives who do not do so—just as social rights and duties connected with kinship, although ultimately depending upon local proximity, have a strong tendency to last after the local tie is broken. Clan exogamy has its counterpart, for instance, in the blood-feud as a duty incumbent on the whole clan, whether the members of the clan live together or not. In this process the influence of a common name has undoubtedly been of great importance. As kinship is traced by means of a system of names, the name comes to stand for blood-relationship. This system is naturally one-sided, keeping up the record of descent either on the father's or the mother's side, but not on both sides at once; hence the prohibited degrees, like the social rights and duties generally connected with clanship, extend much farther on the one side than on the other.

It has been said by Professor Heymans, seconded by Professor Taylor,[70] that the attitude of mankind towards sexual perversion is absolutely critical for the utilitarian theory. It is argued that, so far as utilitarian consequences are concerned, voluntary celibacy and sexual perversion, both being detrimental to the propagation of the species, stand on much the same footing, whereas it is clear that the unsophisticated moral verdict of the *orbis terrarum* makes a distinction between them which the utilitarian cannot explain and has no right to explain away. Perversion is generally and strongly condemned, celibacy has been praised as the height of moral perfection. This argu-

---

[70] G. Heymans, *Einführung in die Ethik auf Grundlage der Erfahrung* (Leipzig, 1914), p. 215 *sq.* A. E. Taylor, "Critical Notice" of the same work, in *Mind*, N. S. xxv. (London, 1916), p. 391 *sq.*

ment, which shows no great knowledge of actual moral ideas and their causes, takes us to a discussion of celibacy and compels me to add a few words about homosexuality to what was said of it in the preceding chapter.

Among an enormous number of peoples celibacy *is* condemned, to some extent for sentimental reasons but very largely on utilitarian grounds.[71] In the savage world nearly every man endeavours to marry when he has reached the age of puberty—if he has not been betrothed before—and practically every woman gets married; and very frequently we are told that a person who does not marry is looked upon as an unnatural being or is an object of contempt or ridicule. So also among peoples of archaic culture celibacy is a great exception and marriage is regarded as a duty. In China it is considered one of the greatest misfortunes that could befall a man to die without leaving a son to perpetuate the family cult, and at the same time an offence against the whole line of ancestors. For it would doom father, mother, and all the ancestry in the Nether-world to a pitiable existence without descendants enough to serve them properly, to worship at the ancestral tombs, to take care of the ancestral tablets, and duly to perform all rites connected with the dead. Among the Semites we meet with the idea that a dead man who has no children will miss something in Shĕol through not receiving that kind of worship which ancestors in early times appear to have received. The Hebrews looked upon marriage as a religious duty. According to the Shūlḥān ʿĀrūkh, the recognized Jewish code, he who abstains from marrying is guilty of bloodshed, diminishes the image of God, and causes the divine presence to withdraw from Israel; hence a single man past twenty may be compelled

71 *The History of Human Marriage,* i. ch. x.

by the court to take a wife.[72] Although Islam considers marriage a civil contract, it enjoins it as a religious duty "incumbent on all who possess the ability." The Aryan nations in ancient times, as Fustel de Coulanges and others have pointed out, regarded celibacy as an impiety and a misfortune: "an impiety, because one who did not marry put the happiness of the manes of the family in peril; a misfortune, because he himself would receive no worship after his death." [73] The old idea still survives in India, and we meet with it in Zoroastrianism and in ancient Greece.[74] But the Greeks regarded marriage as a matter not only of private but also of public importance: in various places criminal proceedings might be taken against celibates.[75] So also the conviction that the founding of a house and the begetting of children constituted a moral necessity and a public duty had a deep hold on the Roman mind in early times.[76]

Modern civilization looks upon celibacy in a different light. The religious motive for marriage has ceased to exist: the lot of the dead is no longer supposed to depend upon the devotion of the living. It is said, in a general way, that marriage is a duty to the nation or the race, but this argument is hardly applied to individual cases. According to modern ideas the union between man and woman is too much a matter of sentiment to be properly classified among civic duties. Nor does the unmarried state strike us as particularly unnatural; such a feeling is incompatible with the large proportion of people who never marry. Nay, far from enjoining marriage as a duty in-

[72] *Shūlhān ʿĀrūkh,* iv. (Ebhen ha-ʿezer), i. 1, 3.
[73] N. D. Fustel de Coulanges, *La cité antique* (Paris, 1864), p. 54 *sq.*
[74] Isaeus, *Oratio de Apollodori hereditate,* 30, p. 66.
[75] Pollux, *Onomasticum,* iii. 48.
[76] Th. Mommsen, *The History of Rome,* i. (London, 1908), p. 74.

cumbent on all, enlightened opinion seems to agree that it is, on humanitarian—*i.e.,* utilitarian—grounds, a duty for many persons to remain unmarried. In some European countries the marriages of persons in receipt of poor-law relief have been legally prohibited, and in certain cases the legislators have gone further still and prohibited all marriages until the contracting parties can prove that they possess the means of supporting a family.[77] There is a growing opinion that persons suffering from certain kinds of disease, which are likely to be transmitted to the off-spring, ought not to marry. People are beginning to feel that it entails a heavy responsibility to bring a new being into existence, and that many persons are wholly unfit for such a task. Future generations will probably with a kind of horror look back at a period when the most important, and in its consequences the most far-reaching, function which has fallen to the lot of man was entirely left to individual caprice and lust.

Side by side with the notion that marriage is a duty for all ordinary men and women, however, we find among many peoples the rule that persons whose function it is to perform religious or magical rites must be celibates.[78] To these belong both savage and barbarous tribes and peoples of a higher civilization. In ancient Peru there were virgins dedicated to the sun, who lived in perpetual seclusion to the end of their lives. Among the Hindus, in spite of the great honour in which marriage is held, celibacy has always commanded respect in instances of extraordinary sanctity; and a feeling of this kind led in Buddhism and Jainism to the obligatory celibacy of monks and priests. In ancient Persia there were sun priestesses who were

[77] W. E. H. Lecky, *Democracy and Liberty,* ii. (London, 1899), p. 181.
[78] *The History of Human Marriage,* i. ch. xi.

obliged to refrain from intercourse with men. The Romans had their vestal virgins. In Greece priestesses were not infrequently required to be virgins, if not for their whole life, at any rate for the duration of their priesthood. A small class of Hebrews, the Essenes, held the idea that marriage is impure and neglected wedlock. This doctrine exercised no influence on Judaism, but perhaps much upon Christianity. "He that gives her (his virgin) in marriage doeth well; but he that gives her not in marriage doeth better." [79] "It is good for a man not to touch a woman. Nevertheless, to avoid fornication, let each man have his own wife, and let each woman have her own husband." [80] This and other passages in the New Testament inspired a general enthusiasm for virginity. It works miracles; it is like a spring flower, always softly exhaling immortality from its white petals. The Lord himself opens the kingdoms of the heavens to eunuchs. If Adam had preserved his obedience to the Creator he would have lived for ever in a state of virgin purity, and some harmless mode of vegetation would have peopled paradise with a race of innocent and immortal beings. But this opinion, expressed by Gregory of Nyssa and John of Damascus, was opposed by Thomas Aquinas, who maintained that the human race was from the beginning propagated by means of sexual intercourse, although such intercourse was originally free from all carnal desire, which is the real root of all sexual sinfulness.[81] Ideas of this sort led by degrees to the obligatory celibacy of the Christian clergy.

Religious celibacy springs from various sources. In many cases the priestess is regarded as married to the god

---

[79] *1 Corinthians,* vii. 38.

[80] *Ibid.,* vii. 1 *sq.*

[81] H. von Eicken, *Geschichte und System der mittelalterlichen Weltanschauung* (Stuttgart, 1887), p. 437 *sq.*

whom she is serving. A trace of this idea is even found in
early Christianity. St. Cyprian speaks of women who have
dedicated themselves to Christ and live with him in a
spiritual matrimony; and if any of these women is guilty
of impure connections she is "an adulteress, not against a
husband, but Christ." [82] According to the gospel of
Pseudo-Matthew, the Virgin Mary had in a similar manner dedicated herself as a virgin to God.[83] Religious celibacy is further enjoined or commended as a means of
self-mortification supposed to appease an angry god, or
with a view to raising the spiritual nature of man by sup-
pressing one of the strongest of all sensual appetites. It
has also been argued that marriage prevents a person from
serving God perfectly, because it induces him to occupy
himself too much with worldly things; and this was one,
but certainly not the only, cause of the obligatory celibacy
which the Christian Church imposed upon her clergy. A
further, and extremely important, cause of religious celibacy is the idea that sexual intercourse is defiling and in
certain circumstances a mysterious cause of evil. This
idea is particularly conspicuous in connection with religious observances. It is a common rule that he who
performs a sacred act or enters a holy place must be
ceremonially clean, and no kind of uncleanness is to be
avoided more carefully than sexual pollution. Holiness is
a delicate quality which is easily destroyed if anything
polluting comes into contact with the holy object or person, and it may also injure them in a more positive manner. In self-defence, therefore, gods and holy persons try
to prevent polluted individuals from approaching them,

---

[82] St. Cyprian, *Epistola LXII., ad Pomponium de virginibus,* 3 *sq.*
(J. P. Migne, *Patrologia,* iv. [Parisiis, 1844], p. 368 *sqq.*).

[83] *The Gospel of Pseudo-Matthew,* 8 (*Ante-Nicene Christian Library,* xvi. [Edinburgh, 1870], p. 25).

and their worshippers are naturally anxious to do the
same. And apart from the resentment that the sacred
being naturally feels against the defiler, it appears that
holiness is supposed to act quite mechanically against pollution, to the destruction or discomfort of the polluted person. It should also be noticed that, owing to the injurious
effect of pollution upon holiness, an act generally regarded
as sacred would, if performed by an unclean individual,
lack that magic efficacy which would otherwise be attached
to it. Mohammed described the ablution, which is a necessary preparation for prayer, as "the half of faith and the
key of prayer." The Syrian philosopher Jamblichus speaks
of the belief that "the gods do not hear him who invokes
them, if he is impure from venereal connections"; [84] and
a similar notion prevailed among the early Christians.

If freedom from sexual pollution is required even of
the ordinary worshipper, it is of course all the more indispensable in those whose special office is to attend to the
sacred cult. The Hebrew priest had to avoid all unchastity;
he was not allowed to marry a harlot or a divorced wife,
and the high-priest was also forbidden to marry a widow.[85]
But for a nation like the Jews, whose ambition was to
live and to multiply, celibacy could never become an ideal.
The Christians, on the other hand, who professed the
most perfect indifference to all earthly matters, found no
difficulty in glorifying a state which, however opposed it
was to the interests of the race and the nation, made men
pre-eminently fit to approach their god. It was even argued
that sexual intercourse, far from being a benefit to the
kingdom of God by propagating the species, was on the
contrary detrimental to it by being the great transmitter
of the sin of our first parents. Thus the view that celibacy
is the height of moral perfection is simply the outcome of

[84] Jamblichus, *De mysteriis,* iv. 11.   [85] *Leviticus,* xxi. 7, 14.

some specific religious and magical beliefs of a rather primitive character; and utilitarianism can therefore hardly be blamed for being at variance with it.

Nor can it be blamed if it does not condemn sexual perversion—which has been said to stand on much the same footing as celibacy—on the ground that it is unfavourable to propagation. Utilitarianism does not consider reproduction as a duty for a man; nor does it condemn sexual acts that are unproductive of offspring, unless there are other reasons for condemning them. If it did, it would, to be consistent, have to accept the Christian doctrine, laid down by Athenagoras, that the procreation of children is the measure of a man's indulgence in appetite, just as the husbandman throwing the seed into the ground awaits the harvest, not sowing more upon it.[86] Utilitarians have found reasons for condemning perversion as harmful, at least in certain cases, and refused to recognize any other reasons.[87] But utilitarian considerations can certainly not account for the great variety of moral attitudes towards homosexuality. It seems quite obvious, as I have pointed out in another connection, that where homosexual intercourse is an object of censure it is so in the first place on account of the aversion it is apt to call forth; while the view that it is a crime of the utmost gravity is due to its association with unbelief or heresy.[88]

From this discussion—which has been somewhat lengthy on account of the extremely complicated nature of the subject and its great theoretical importance from the ethical point of view—it should be obvious that the moral ideas relating to chastity partly rest on a utilitarian basis, partly are influenced by specific religious ideas, and to a

[86] Athenagoras, *Legatio pro Christianis,* 33 (Migne, *op. cit.,* Ser. Graeca, vi. [Parisiis, 1857], p. 966).

[87] G. Mehlis, *Probleme der Ethik* (Tübingen, 1918), p. 42 *sqq.*

[88] *Supra,* p. 194 *sqq.*

large extent spring from sentimental likes and dislikes, which in no branch of morality have been allowed a greater scope than here. Generally speaking, sentimental preferences and aversions are largely responsible for that divergence which exists between actual moral ideas and a consistently utilitarian code of morality. But instead of recognizing this divergence moralists have only too often disguised it by advancing utilitarian pretexts for sentimental requirements, and have thereby missed an opportunity to act as moral educators. It is a strong point in consistent utilitarianism that it cannot accept such requirements on their own merits. Although the origin of instinctive likings and aversions, which are still more or less generally felt, may be sought for in their specific usefulness, civilization has brought about changed conditions so far removed from the state of nature that such feelings can by no means serve as utilitarian criteria of morality. If we clearly realize that a certain act is productive of no other harm but the aversion or disgust it causes, we can hardly look upon it as a proper object of moral censure, provided that the agent has not in an indelicate manner shocked anybody's feelings. When sufficiently discriminating, resentment, whether moral or non-moral, is too much concerned with the will of the agent to be felt towards a person who obviously neither intends to offend any one nor is guilty of culpable oversight. Even when the person knows that his behaviour is repulsive to others, he may, on utilitarian grounds, be considered to be justified in acting as he does; some degree of reflection should lead to the thought that antipathies are no sufficient ground for interfering with other individuals' liberty of action either by punishing them or subjecting them to moral censure. Nobody has more vehemently denounced such interference than Stuart Mill. He insisted on "liberty of tastes and pursuits; of framing the plan of our life to suit our own character; of doing as we like, subject to such consequences as may follow: without impediment from our fellow-creatures, so long as what we do does not harm them, even though they should think our conduct foolish, perverse, or wrong." [89] Bain wrote, "When one man endeavours to impose his likings or dislikes upon another, or when a mere sentimental preference entertained by the majority is made the law for every one, there is a very serious infringement of individual freedom on the one hand, with nothing legitimate to be set against it in the way of advantage." [90]

An often adduced argument against utilitarianism, and hedonism generally, is that it considers the motive of all action to be a desire to feel pleasure or avoid pain, although every desire aims directly at an objective end and not, at least in the first instance, at the attainment of the subjective feeling of pleasure or relief from pain. Hunger is directed to food, ambition to honour, benevolence to the good of others, and similarly with other desires. Butler wrote long ago that "all particular appetites and passions are towards external things themselves, and distinct from the pleasure arising from them." [91] An act may be desired though it is not known by the agent to be attended with pleasure. As Professor McDougall remarks, "we may observe numberless instances of action, of persistent striving towards ends, on the part of lowly animals which cannot be credited with the power of anticipating or desiring the pleasure that may accrue from success." [92] Nor is an-

[89] J. S. Mill, *On Liberty* (London, 1859), p. 26 sq.

[90] A. Bain, *The Emotions and the Will* (London, 1880), p. 279.

[91] J. Butler, *Sermon XI.—Upon the Love of our Neighbours,* §6 (Works, i. [London, 1903], p. 139).

[92] W. McDougall, *An Introduction to Social Psychology* (London, 1926), p. 314.

ticipation of pleasure always connected with an act which is known to be pleasurable. But the doctrine of psychological hedonism, according to which volition is always determined by pleasure or pain actual or prospective, is not inseparably joined with utilitarianism, and has even been expressly rejected by some of its expounders. As an ethical theory utilitarianism is essentially concerned, not with the psychology of desire, but with the moral valuation of acts. In our moral consciousness pleasure and pain certainly play a dominant rôle, in so far as moral approval is a kindly attitude of mind towards a person as a cause of pleasure, and moral disapproval a hostile attitude of mind towards a person as a cause of pain. But this has nothing whatever to do with the psychological question of pleasure and pain as motives of action.

The distinction between the desire for pleasure and the desire for something pleasant is emphasized by those theories which have been included under names like energism, welfare theory, or eudemonism. The moral value lies not in pleasure as such but in pleasurable functions. The preservation and promotion of individual and social life is the highest good, because the individual being strives to preserve and advance both himself and other persons with whom he sympathizes, and though pleasure is not the direct object of desire it is a necessary concomitant of the realization of the desire to promote individual and racial welfare. The theories belonging to this class do not present the same definiteness as utilitarianism, which regards pleasure as the common standard of all that is desirable, and they often differ in details. What is "welfare"? Höffding defines it as a durable state of pleasure, or "true" happiness, which is not a state of passivity but one consisting in activity, work, development.[93] Accord-

[93] H. Höffding, *Etiske undersögelser* (Köbenhavn, 1891), p. 31. *Idem, Etik* (Köbenhavn & Kristiania, 1913), pp. 137, 139, 143.

ing to other eudemonists, pleasure is an indication of the successful attainment of the general end, welfare.[94] But however welfare is defined, it is always something which we desire, and all psychologists agree that the fulfilment of a desire brings pleasure while the frustration of it brings pain.[95] This is the case whatever the object of the desire may be—pleasure, welfare, self-realization, or any other "good." And thus every ethical theory that regards any course of conduct which promotes the attainment of a certain desired end as good and any course of conduct which obstructs it as bad, is so far in agreement with my view that moral judgments are ultimately based on emotional reactions against causes of pleasure or pain. I have no reason, then, to examine the attempts of the rival theories to fix the nature of the desire concerned.

Among teleological moralists, both hedonists and non-hedonists, there are, as we have seen, some who derive their criterion of morality directly from the general prevalence of a certain kind of desire, and others who found their theories on intuitions. These intuitions are nowadays generally referred to reason, or practical or moral reason, as a special faculty or a part of the general faculty of reason, by which we apprehend moral truths immediately without the drawing of inferences. Now it is very significant that the conduct which the supposed moral intuitions pronounce good or bad at the same time has a tendency to arouse emotions of moral approval or disapproval. The intuitionist maintains that it does so, and has always done so, *because* it is good or bad; whereas in my opinion it is, or was originally, held to be good or

---

[94] W. K. Wright, *General Introduction to Ethics* (New York, 1929), p. 327.

[95] *Cf.* G. F. Stout, *A Manual of Psychology* (London, 1901), p. 245; H. Maier, *Psychologie des emotionalen Denkens* (Tübingen, 1908), p. 764 *sq.;* W. McDougall, *An Outline of Psychology* (London, 1926), p. 269.

bad on account of its tendency to arouse the emotion. Intuitionists are fond of comparing moral judgments to mathematical propositions; but they have ignored the fact that while the former are correlated with certain definite emotions, there is in the case of the latter no similar correlation at all. Richard Price, it is true, argued that our perceptions of virtue and vice ought no more to be confounded with the feelings which are their effects and concomitants "than a particular truth (like that for which Pythagoras offered a hecatomb) ought to be confounded with the pleasure that may attend the discovery of it." [96] This is, of course, an altogether different matter: the pleasure caused by the *discovery* of a truth is not comparable to the emotions felt in connection with the attribution of moral qualities to conduct or character. As a "plausible" explanation of this connection it has been suggested that the emotions of approval and disapproval may "furnish the necessary occasions on which Reason recognizes ethical characteristics, such as *goodness* and *rightness*." [97] If this were the case, we should have to admit that the emotions, owing to their variability, would frequently beguile Reason into transgression of its own "law of non-contradiction," by declaring the very same course

[96] R. Price, *A Review of the Principal Questions in Morals* (London, 1787), p. 63.

[97] C. D. Broad, *Five Types of Ethical Theory* (London, 1930), p. 270. In speaking of self-evident moral judgments, Dr. H. Rashdall (*The Theory of Good and Evil*, ii. [Oxford, 1924], p. 402 *sq.*) says that a large class at least of them cannot be made at all without the presence of certain emotions. He finds it difficult to distinguish mere feelings or aversions from real judgments of value, although he is clear that the two things must be distinguished. The only approach to a test he can suggest is to put the question, whether "an intuition—an apparently unaccountable repugnance to some kind of conduct—" persists after a due consideration of all the consequences of yielding to it. If it does, he says, "it may probably be taken to represent not merely a feeling, but a feeling to which the moral Reason attributes intrinsic value" (*ibid.*, i. 211 *sq.*).

of conduct sometimes right or good and at other times wrong or bad. This would no doubt explain the irreconcilable conflict between intuitions of different moralists, but at a cost too terrible to be conceived. The only reasonable explanation of the intimate connection between so-called intuitions and the presence of emotional tendencies is, so far as I can see, that the intuitions actually *are* these tendencies formulated as judgments that are calculated to give moral values an objectivity they do not in reality possess.[98] If this be admitted, an enormous advance is made towards our understanding of the moral consciousness. For while a moral intuition can be no more explained than a mathematical axiom, a moral emotion *can* be explained, as a particular emotional attitude arising under definite conditions. We can say *why* it arises, our mental constitution being such as it is, and the moral judgment may thereby be traced to its ultimate source.

[98] *Cf. supra,* p. 61.

CHAPTER IX

THE EMOTIONAL BACKGROUND OF NORMATIVE THEORIES (*concluded*)

IN HIS ethical theory Kant differs both from those who maintain that the general prevalence of a desire leads directly to the duty of satisfying it, and, apparently at least, from those who base moral laws on intuitions which they discover in their own consciousness. He founds his ethics on conceptions of pure reason without any appeal to experience of any kind: "reason of itself, independent of all experience, ordains what ought to take place." [1] In his *Grundlegung zur Metaphysik der Sitten* he says that we cannot make out empirically whether there is an imperative of morality, a categorical imperative, at all; and not having the advantage of its reality being given in experience, we have to investigate its possibility *a priori.* [2] The basis of obligation must be sought *a priori* in the conceptions of pure reason and not in the nature of man, or in the circumstances in the world in which he is placed, because all moral laws must be valid with absolute necessity. They must be so for all rational creatures generally, and for this reason only also for men. In other words, "we must derive them from the general concept of a rational being." [3]

[1] Kant, *Grundlegung zur Metaphysik der Sitten,* sec. ii. (*Gesammelte Schriften,* iv. [Berlin, 1911], p. 408; T. K. Abbott's translation in *Kant's Critique of Practical Reason and other Works on the Theory of Ethics* [London, 1898], p. 24).

[2] *Ibid.,* sec. ii. (iv. 419 *sq.;* Abbott, p. 36 *sq.*).

[3] *Ibid.,* Vorrede (iv. 389; Abbott, p. 3 *sq.*), sec. ii. (iv. 408, 412,

In order that Kant's conception of obligation shall hold good for a rational being it is not enough that this being is endowed with reason. In the first place, the moral law applies to all rational beings "in so far as they have a will, that is, a power to determine their causality by the conception of rules." For the Infinite Being, however, there is no obligation or duty, because its will is a holy will, which would be incapable of any maxim conflicting with the moral law, and obligation implies a constraint to an action by the law, while duty is the name given to this action. On the other hand, for all created rational beings, affected as they are with wants and physical motives, the moral law is a law of duty, of moral constraint, and of the determination of their actions by respect for this law and reverence for its duty.[4] This implies that these beings have not only reason and a will, but also desires which tempt them to transgress the moral law. Kant has thus attributed human feelings and inclinations, which he knows by experience, to rational beings of whom he can have no experience.[5] But apart from this, what is the use of the proposition that the conception of duty holds good for all finite rational beings, if these beings are presumed to have just those characteristics of

425, 442; Abbott, pp. 25, 28, 43, 60 sq.), sec. iii. (iv. 447 sq.; Abbott, p. 66 sq.).

[4] Kant, *Kritik der praktischen Vernunft*, i. 1. 1. 7 (*Gesammelte Schriften*, v. [Berlin, 1913], p. 32; Abbott, p. 120 sq.), i. 1. 3 (v. 82; Abbott, p. 175).

[5] In his *Einleitung zur Tugendlehre*, 1 (*Gesammelte Schriften*, vi. [Berlin, 1914], p. 379; Abbott, p. 290), Kant seems to have discovered his mistake, when he writes that the constraint announced by the moral imperative "does not apply to all rational beings (for there may also be holy beings), but applies to men as rational physical beings who are unholy enough to be seduced by pleasure to the transgression of the moral law, although they themselves recognize its authority." In his *Kritik der praktischen Vernunft* (i. 1. 1. 7 [v. 32; Abbott, p. 121]) he had said that the holiness of will is "a practical idea which

humanity which Kant was so anxious to eliminate in his deduction of duty from reason?

The proposition in question, which Kant never gets tired of repeating, was intended to give emphasis and support to his contention that the moral law has its foundation in pure reason; he does not even shrink from an argument like this: "Since moral laws ought to hold good for every rational creature, we must derive them from the general concept of a rational being." [6] His main thesis is that no experience can explain a law which must carry with it absolute necessity, and that it consequently must be based on reason. The moral law, he says, "is conceived as objectively necessary, only because it holds for everybody that has reason and will." [7] That it possesses objective validity was an idea that Kant, like all other normative moralists, shared with common sense. He found this idea in his moral experience in the form of a categorical imperative preserving the mysterious awfulness of the old "Thou shalt," as an echo from another world.[8] When he says that we cannot make out empirically whether there is such an imperative at all, he refers in proof of this to our inability to show with certainty in any example that the will was determined merely by the law, without any other spring of action.[9] But surely, our inability to do so does not involve that we have no notion of the law itself. In his *Kritik der praktischen Vernunft* he has evidently himself come to the same conclusion; for he says there, "The moral law is given as a fact of pure

must serve as a type to which finite rational beings can only approximate indefinitely."

[6] *Grundlegung*, sec. ii. (iv. 412; Abbott, p. 28).

[7] *Kritik der praktischen Vernunft*, i. 1. 1. 8 (v. 36; Abbott, p. 126).

[8] See *supra*, p. 55 sq. Cf. *Kritik der praktischen Vernunft*, i. 1. 2 (v. 71; Abbott, p. 163): "Mysticism is quite reconcilable with the purity and sublimity of the moral law."

[9] *Grundlegung*, sec. ii. (iv. 407, 419; Abbott, pp. 23, 24, 36 sq.).

reason of which we are *a priori* conscious, and which is apodictically certain, though it be granted that in experience no example of its exact fulfilment can be found." [10] And when he speaks of the two things which fill the mind with ever new and increasing admiration and awe, the starry heavens above and the moral law within, he adds :— "I have not to search for them and conjecture them as though they were veiled in darkness or were in the transcendent region beyond my horizon; I see them before me and connect them directly with the consciousness of my existence. . . . The second begins from my invisible self, my personality, and exhibits me in a world which has true infinity, but which is traceable only by the understanding." [11]

While deriving the moral law from reason, Kant was overwhelmed by the awe and reverence it aroused in him.[12] He writes, "The majesty of the law (like that on Sinai) inspires (not dread, which repels, nor yet a charm, which invites to familiarity, but) *awe*, which awakes *respect* of the subject for his law-giver, and in the present case the latter being within ourselves, a feeling of the sublimity of our own destiny.[13] It is in this powerful emotional response to the notion of duty that we have to look for the ultimate ground of his theory of the moral motive. The notion of duty "requires in the action, objectively, agreement with the law, and, subjectively in its maxim, that respect for the law shall be the sole mode in which the will

[10] *Kritik der praktischen Vernunft,* i. 1. 1. 8 (v. 47; Abbott, p. 136). *Cf. ibid.,* i. 1. 1. 8 (v. 55; Abbott, p. 145) : "The objective reality of a pure will, or, what is the same thing, of a pure practical reason, is given in the moral law *a priori,* as it were, by a fact."

[11] *Ibid.,* ii. (v. 161 *sq.;* Abbott, p. 260).

[12] *Cf. ibid.,* i. 1. 3 (v. 86; Abbott, p. 180).

[13] *Von der Einwohnung des bösen Princips neben dem guten,* Anmerkung (*Gesammelte Schriften,* vi. [Berlin, 1914], p. 23 n.; Abbott, p. 330 n. 1).

is determined thereby. . . . Moral worth can be placed only in this, that the action is done from duty, that is, simply for the sake of the law." [14] No act done from inclination has any moral worth, and this is true whatever be the nature of the inclination. All human inclinations are desire for pleasure: "to be happy is necessarily the wish of every finite rational being, and this, therefore, is inevitably a determining principle of its faculty of desire." [15] And the feeling of pleasure is always of one and the same kind and can only differ in degree: it is of no consequence what the pleasing object is, but only how much it pleases. [16] Kant illustrates his doctrine by the following example. A man is beneficent simply because his mind is so sympathetically constituted that he, without any other motive, finds a pleasure in spreading joy around him and takes delight in the satisfaction of others so far as it is his own work. However proper, however amiable an action of this kind may be, it has nevertheless no true moral worth, but is on a level with any other that is done from inclination and not from duty. On the other hand, if nature has put little sympathy in the heart of this or that man, if he is by temperament cold and indifferent to the sufferings of his fellowmen, "would he not still find in himself a source from whence to give himself a far higher worth than that of a good-natured temperament could be? Unquestionably. It is just in this that the moral worth of the character is brought out which is incomparably the highest of all, namely, that he is beneficent, not from inclination, but from duty." [17] So also actions which are done with great sacrifice may be praised as

[14] *Kritik der praktischen Vernunft,* i. 1. 3 (v. 81; Abbott, p. 174).
[15] *Ibid.,* i. 1. 1. 3 (v. 25; Abbott, p. 112).
[16] *Ibid.,* i. 1. 1. 3 (v. 22 *sqq.;* Abbott, p. 109 *sqq.*).
[17] *Grundlegung,* sec. i. (iv. 398 *sq.;* Abbott, p. 14 *sq.*).

noble and sublime, "only so far as there are traces which suggest that they were done wholly out of respect for duty and not from excited feelings." [18]

Thus, then, while Kant agreed with the psychological hedonists that all human inclinations are desire for pleasure, the ethical conclusion he drew from this assumption was the exact opposite of hedonism. Instead of deriving moral worth from desire for pleasure, he regarded this desire as the great obstacle to morality. But then the question arose: How shall we explain that respect for the moral law which is the condition for its fulfilment? How can it be a spring to action? This is a problem with which Kant grapples without being able to solve it. Respect for the law is a feeling which is produced by an intellectual cause, a rational concept, and therefore specifically distinct from all feelings that may be referred either to inclination or fear.[19] In order that "a rational being who is also affected through the senses should will what reason alone directs such beings that they ought to will, it is no doubt requisite that reason should have a power to infuse a feeling of pleasure or satisfaction in the fulfilment of duty, that is to say, that it should have a causality by which it determines the sensibility according to its own principles." But at the same time it seems to him quite impossible to discern how a mere thought, which itself contains nothing sensible, can itself produce a sensation of pleasure or pain—quite impossible to explain how man can take an interest in the moral law. In other words, "how pure reason can be practical—to explain this is beyond the power of human reason, and all the labour and pains of seeking an explanation of it are lost." [20]

[18] *Kritik der praktischen Vernunft,* i. 1. 3 (v. 85; Abbott, p. 178 *sq.*).
[19] *Ibid.,* i. 1. 3 (v. 73; Abbott, p. 166). *Grundlegung,* sec. i. (iv. 401 n.*; Abbott, p. 17 n. 2).
[20] *Ibid.,* sec. iii. (iv. 460 *sq.;* Abbott, p. 80 *sqq.*).

It has often been pointed out that the radical distinction which Kant makes between "the respect for the moral law" and "inclination" is a psychological error, and that conscientious action springs from a desire or inclination just as any other action. The incompatibility of his proposition, that there is no moral worth in any act that is not done simply for duty's sake, with current moral ideas is equally evident. The point which is of particular interest in this connection is the question how he came to form such a view. Besides the extraordinarily strong hold the feeling of duty had on his mind, his defective psychology, and his aversion to the ethical hedonism and eudemonism which flourished in his days, there are some other facts to be considered. Kant had the perfectly correct idea of the conception of duty that it implicitly contains a prohibition of that which ought *not* to be done, that there would be no moral law if there were no possibility of its transgression.[21] But this does not imply that whenever a person behaves in conformity to it, the idea of transgression presents itself to his mind. In the enormous majority of cases there is no thought of it at all. Most of us are throughout our lives obedient to the rules which forbid murder, theft, adultery, and what not, and who would say that we are so from that respect for the law which, according to Kant, "implies fear, or at least apprehension of transgression"?[22] The same applies to most of the numberless duties which we perform in our daily life as a matter of course; it is only in rare cases that we think of the contrary course of conduct at all. There is chiefly an apprehension of it when a desire conflicting with the law tempts the person to be disobedient to it; and it is on such cases of conflict that Kant has concentrated his at-

[21] Cf. *supra,* p. 123.
[22] *Kritik der praktischen Vernunft,* i. 1. 3 (v. 81 *sq.;* Abbott, p. 174).

tention in his doctrine of duty. If the respect for the moral law implies apprehension of its transgression and at the same time is a necessary condition for doing one's duty, it is certainly quite consistent to assert that the doing of a dutiful action necessarily involves a conscious resistance to inclination; but it is to restrict the meaning of duty within much narrower limits than is justified by the ordinary usage of the word.

The notion of duty, as commonly conceived, implies that the contrary mode of conduct is wrong. The man who refrains from doing his duty is disapproved of, he who does his duty is not disapproved of. This is the essential fact contained in the notion of duty.[23] But what moral worth could there be, under all circumstances, in refraining from doing wrong? Yet, though the notion of duty involves no applause, there are cases in which we applaud a man for doing his duty. The performance of an act may of course be praised, although the omission of it is disapproved of; and, besides, "duty" is often used as the name for a course of conduct the omission of which is generally, though not necessarily in every instance, an object of disapproval.[24] Now we are particularly apt to bestow moral praise on a person who has done his duty in unusually difficult circumstances, when he had a strong interest in acting differently and his conduct involves a high degree of self-restraint. This explains why Kant attributes moral worth only to dutiful acts that result from a successful struggle against contrary inclinations. For him "duty," the "sublime and mighty name," [25] is an expression of admiration and reverence, of the emotion of moral approval aroused by obedience to duty, and not

[23] *Supra*, p. 123.
[24] *Supra*, p. 124 *sq.*
[25] *Kritik der praktischen Vernunft,* i. 1. 3 (v. 86; Abbott, p. 180).

merely of the emotion of disapproval aroused by transgression. He takes no notice of any other duty, or, as he
would say, action objectively conformable to the law, but
that which "gains reluctant reverence," [26] except that he
pronounces it devoid of all moral worth. He does not
say that it is wrong because it is performed from some
other motive than respect for the law. He even finds it
a very beautiful thing to do good to men from love of
them and from sympathetic goodwill, or to be just from
love of order.[27] And he applies the term "fantastically
virtuous" to the man who will admit nothing to be indifferent in respect of morality, and "who strews all his
steps with duties, as with traps." [28] At the same time, his
notion of the sublimity of duty implies that he can assign
no superiority to other concepts based on the emotion of
moral approval. What is good is what ought to be done;
however virtuous any one may be, all the good he can ever
do is only duty; [29] and "when we can bring any flattering
thought of merit into our action, then the motive is already
somewhat alloyed with self-love." [30] He speaks, however,
of "imperfect duties" that are "duties of virtue" and the
fulfilment of which is "merit," though their transgression
is not necessarily demerit but only moral unworth.[31]

In the case of all finite beings that possess reason and
will, says Kant, the moral law has the form of an imperative which commands categorically.[32] The categorical
imperative lays down the rule that you ought to obey the
law whatever be the consequences of your action; and "the

[26] *Kritik der praktischen Vernunft,* i. 1. 3 (v. 86; Abbott, p. 180).
[27] *Ibid.,* i. 1. 3 (v. 82; Abbott, p. 175).
[28] *Einleitung zur Tugendlehre,* 17 (vi. 409; Abbott, p. 320).
[29] *Von der Einwohnung des bösen Princips neben dem guten,* Allgemeine Anmerkung (vi. 48 *sq.;* Abbott, p. 357).
[30] *Kritik der praktischen Vernunft,* ii. (v. 159; Abbott, p. 257).
[31] *Einleitung zur Tugendlehre,* 7 (vi. 390; Abbott, p. 300).
[32] *Kritik der praktischen Vernunft,* i. 1. 1. 7 (v. 32; Abbott, p. 121).

moral worth of an action does not lie in the effect expected from it, nor in any principle of action which requires to borrow its motive from this expected effect." [33] Hence the moral worthlessness of all hypothetical imperatives, which say that you ought to do so or so if you desire such or such an end.[34] Kant's doctrine of moral imperatives is in agreement with the fact, recognized both by moralists and common sense, that duties are expressed in rules which command general obedience, but it is singular in its insistence that there must be no modification of these rules to meet exceptional cases. Even Schleiermacher, who tried to organize ethically the whole of life, had to refrain from formulating precepts applicable in all situations.[35] That Kant refused to allow any exceptions to moral rules was due to his peculiar idea that they could have no other ground but the individual's desire to modify the rule in his own favour. He says that the specific criterion of categorical as distinguished from hypothetical imperatives is that all interest is renounced.[36]

As the content of the categorical imperative Kant gives the formula, "Act only on that maxim whereby thou canst at the same time will that it should become a universal law." [37] What is meant here by the word "will"? If Kant

[33] *Grundlegung*, sec. i. (iv. 401; Abbott, p. 17).

[34] *Ibid.*, sec. ii. (iv. 414, 427, 428, 441, 444; Abbott, pp. 31, 45, 46, 60, 63). *Kritik der praktischen Vernunft*, i. 1. 1. 1. (v. 20; Abbott, p. 106).

[35] F. Schleiermacher, *Grundlinien einer Kritik der bisherigen Sittenlehre* (Berlin, 1834), p. 110. *Cf.* E. Laas, *Idealismus und Positivismus*, ii. (Berlin, 1882), p. 259. H. Driesch (*Die sittliche Tat* [Leipzig, 1927], pp. 67, 77) admits exceptions to the moral rules, but calls them "excuses" (*Entschuldigungen*), which means that they are "zwar nicht gut, aber weniger nicht-gut als das Gegenteil. . . . Denn unerbittlich ist des Gewissens Sprache."

[36] *Grundlegung*, sec. ii. (iv. 431; Abbott, p. 50). *Cf. ibid.*, sec. ii. (iv. 424; Abbott, p. 42).

[37] *Ibid.*, sec. ii. (iv. 421; Abbott, p. 38). *Cf. ibid.*, sec. i. (iv. 402; Abbott, p. 18), sec. ii. (iv. 436 *sq.;* Abbott, p. 55); *Kritik der praktischen Vernunft*, i. 1. 2 (v. 69; Abbott, p. 161).

has used it in its ordinary psychological sense the consequences are appallingly inconsistent with the most fundamental principle of his ethical theory. One person may will that one maxim should become a universal law and another person may will that the opposite maxim should become so, and if anybody's will in that respect is recognized as a criterion of duty, both the conflicting maxims are right. In other words, whatever any one thinks is right is right, and there is no objectively valid moral law at all.[38] In the argument by which Kant tries to show that it is impossible to adopt the egoistic maxim as a universal law, he evidently speaks of will as a psychological fact. He maintains that the very selfishness of men, for whom happiness is by nature the first and unconditional object of their desire,[39] must make them wish to act altruistically. Although it is possible that a universal law of nature might exist in accordance with the maxim that each should be left to take care of himself without the assistance of others, "it is impossible to *will* that such a principle should have the universal validity of a law of nature. For a will which resolved this would contradict itself, inasmuch as many cases might occur in which one would have need of the love and sympathy of others, and in which, by such a law of nature, sprung from his own will, he would deprive himself of all hope of the aid he desires." [40] What else could Kant in this instance mean by will but the "elective will," as he calls it, which "implies a wish that arises from subjective causes, and there-

---

[38] *Cf.* H. Sidgwick, *The Methods of Ethics* (London, 1913), p. 210.
[39] *Von der Einwohnung des bösen Princips neben dem guten,* Allgemeine Anmerkung (vi. 46 n.; Abbott, p. 355 n.).

[40] *Grundlegung,* sec. ii. (iv. 423; Abbott, p. 41). See also *Einleitung zur Tugendlehre,* 8 (vi. 393; Abbott, p. 303 *sq.*) ; *Metaphysische Anfangungsgründe der Tugendlehre,* § 30 (*Gesammelte Schriften,* vi. [Berlin, 1914], p. 453).

fore may often be opposed to the pure objective determining principle"?[41] A will whose maxim that one should help others springs from the selfish wish to be helped by them cannot be said to be a will the universal legislation of which "is not based on any interest,"[42] or "an absolutely good will," the principle of which must be a categorical imperative, and the maxims of which are capable of making themselves a universal law, "which the will of every rational being imposes on itself, without needing to assume any spring or interest as a foundation."[43] Nevertheless, it may very well be that Kant, when framing his formula, thought of a rational will, of the capability to act in accordance with practical reason as the guide of one's action, and in this case there could be nothing illogical or self-contradictory in one's maxim.[44] This interpretation is suggested by the formula in *Kritik der praktischen Vernunft,* "Act so that the maxim of thy will can always at the same time hold good as a principle of universal legislation."[45]

A host of critics have pointed out the impossibility of deriving moral obligation from the principle of mere formal self-consistency.[46] "A principle that is suitable for universal legislation," said Hegel, "already presupposes a content. . . . The criterion that there should be no con-

---

[41] *Kritik der praktischen Vernunft,* i. 1. 1. 7 (v. 32; Abbott, p. 121).
[42] *Grundlegung,* sec. ii. (iv. 432; Abbott, p. 50).
[43] *Ibid.,* sec. ii. (iv. 444; Abbott, p. 63).
[44] *Cf.* A. Hägerström, *Kants Ethik* (Uppsala & Leipzig, 1902), p. 315 *sqq.*
[45] *Kritik der praktischen Vernunft,* i. 1. 1. 7 (v. 30; Abbott, p. 119). See also *Einleitung in die Metaphysik der Sitten,* 4 (*Gesammelte Schriften,* vi. [Berlin, 1914], p. 225; Abbott, p. 281) ; *Einleitung zur Tugendlehre,* 5, 9 (vi. 389, 395; Abbott, pp. 299, 306).
[46] Among the early critics F. E. Beneke deserves special mention (*Grundlegung zur Physik der Sitten* [Berlin & Posen, 1822], p. 27 *sqq.; Grundlinien des natürlichen Systemes der praktischen Philosophie,* i. [Berlin, Posen & Bromberg, 1837], p. 19 *sqq.*).

tradiction produces nothing." [47] Even in the cases which Kant has carefully selected to demonstrate his principle he cannot help considering human nature, social conditions, and the consequences of acts, however much he deprecates a morality that depends on experience. Lotze [48] and others have remarked that without a consideration of consequences almost any maxim might be suitable to be presented as a universal rule; it is its consequences that decide whether it is suitable or not. Kant says that even common sense considers the maxim of an action morally impossible if it does not stand the test of "the form of a universal law of nature"; [49] and in a certain sense he is right. It has been said that the weakness of his imperative of duty is that it "lacks all organic filling," that it is an empty form without contents, an unconditional command which commands nothing; but, as it seems to me, his fault was just that he attempted to fill it by deriving from it particular rules of duty. If he had left it alone it would have amounted to this: there is a moral law, which like every law has the character of universality, in so far that what is right or wrong for me to do is also right or wrong to do for all similar persons in similar circumstances. This is no discovery of Kant, [50] it is as old as morality itself. It is an expression of the disinterestedness or impartiality of the moral emotions, which distinguishes them from other retributive emotions; and this characteristic, as we have seen, has its root in primitive custom as a rule of conduct, in the public indignation aroused by

---

[47] Hegel, *The Philosophy of Right* (London, 1896), § 135, p. 129.

[48] Lotze, *Grundzüge der praktischen Philosophie* (Leipzig, 1884), § 5, p. 10.

[49] *Kritik der praktischen Vernunft*, i. 1. 2 (v. 69 *sq.*; Abbott, p. 161).

[50] Professor Th. Lipps (*Die ethischen Grundfragen* [Leipzig & Hamburg, 1912], p. 171) calls Kant's supreme law of morality an important discovery, the most important one ever made by him.

its transgression. Kant's categorical imperative has thus a deep foundation in the nature of the moral emotions, and could therefore serve as a moral law claiming universality. He had himself the notion that this claim implied a tautology. He wrote, "A practical law which I recognize as such must be qualified for universal legislation; this is an identical proposition, and therefore self-evident." [51]

Very different from what Kant calls "the general formula of the categorical imperative" is another which he thinks he can deduce from it, namely, "So act as to treat humanity, whether in thine own person or in that of any other, in every case as an end withal, never as means only." [52] The former is a purely formal law of logical consistency, the latter is a special rule of duty, which enjoins a certain course of conduct and requires experience for its observance. If interpreted as an injunction referring to one's action in a given situation only, it is a rule which is neither followed nor regarded as a duty by anybody. As Professor Laird says, "when I send letters by the post, letter-sorters and engine-drivers *are* mere instruments so far as I am concerned, and similarly I may make a mere instrument of myself." [53] Against this it has been argued that "I am not treating postmen and sorters as *mere* tools when I post a letter, as is sufficiently proved by the consideration that we should all refuse to staff the Post Office with public slaves to be used up, regardless of humanity, for our own convenience." [54] This implies

[51] *Kritik der praktischen Vernunft,* i. 1. 1. 4 (v. 27; Abbott, p. 115).
[52] *Grundlegung,* sec. ii. (iv. 429; Abbott, p. 47). See also *Kritik der praktischen Vernunft,* i. 1. 3 (v. 87; Abbott, p. 180 *sq.*) ; *Einleitung zur Tugendlehre,* 9 (vi. 395; Abbott, p. 306).
[53] J. Laird, *A Study in Moral Theory* (London, 1926), p. 234.
[54] A. E. Taylor, "Critical Notice" on Laird's *A Study in Moral Theory,* in *Mind,* N. S. xxxv. (London, 1926), p. 488. Kant's formula has been criticized from various points of view, *e.g.,* by Schopenhauer, *Die Grundlage der Moral,* § 8 (*Sämmtliche Werke,* iv.²

that they are recognized by me as persons having certain claims to consideration or rights, and, although this recognition can hardly be said to form part of my treatment of them when I post my letter, Kant would no doubt have accepted such an interpretation of his formula. It was the expression of a broad humanitarian feeling, which was in agreement with the spirit of an age profoundly influenced by the teaching of Rousseau and the new ideas of human worth and dignity and rights as something belonging to every man independently of his station.[55] Kant's endeavour to found it upon a purely rational principle[56] cannot conceal its eudemonistic origin. In one place he himself recognizes a connection between his conception of humanity as an end in itself and the duty of promoting the happiness of others, though he deduces the latter from the former: the natural end which all men have is their own happiness, and "the ends of any subject which is an end in himself, ought as far as possible to be *my* ends also." [57]

In spite of his aversion to eudemonism, Kant cannot keep out the notion of happiness as an end. He describes it as "the general well-being and contentment with one's

[Leipzig, 1916], p. 160 *sq.*) ; Sidgwick, *op. cit.,* p. 390; D. G. Ritchie, *Natural Rights* (London, 1895), p. 152 *sq.;* C. D. Broad, *Five Types of Ethical Theory* (London, 1930), p. 132; W. Freytag, *Die Aufgaben der Ethik* (Halle a. S., 1916), p. 149 *sqq.* The last-mentioned writer raises the question whether it is possible to use another person merely as means. He argues that if I want to induce some one to render me a service, I can succeed in doing so only if he consents, and his consent implies that he directly or indirectly pursues some end of his own.

[55] F. Paulsen, *Immanuel Kant* (Stuttgart, 1899), p. 346.

[56] On his failure to do so see Hägerström, *op. cit.,* p. 416 *sqq.;* H. Höffding, *Den nyere Filosofis Historie,* ii. (Köbenhavn, 1904), p. 83. In *Kritik der praktischen Vernunft* (i. 1. 1. 3 [v. 87; Abbott, p. 180 *sq.*]) he has made no such attempt.

[57] *Grundlegung,* sec. ii. (iv. 430; Abbott, p. 48 *sq.*).

condition," [58] or as "a rational being's consciousness of
the pleasantness of life uninterruptedly accompanying his
whole existence," [59] or as a man's "satisfaction with his
condition, with certainty of the continuance of this satisfaction." [60] To be happy is necessarily the wish of every
man,[61] and pure practical reason does not require that we
should renounce all claim to happiness, but only that the
moment duty is in question we should take no account of
happiness.[62] On the other hand, to seek one's own happiness is not an end that is also a duty. A command that
every one should try to make himself happy would be foolish, for one never commands any one to do what he of
himself infallibly wishes to do.[63] Such a thing does not
come under the notion of duty at all, because this is a
constraint to an end reluctantly adopted, and it is therefore a contradiction to say that a man is in duty bound to
advance his own happiness.[64] At the same time he may be
indirectly bound to do so: discontent with one's condition,
under a pressure of many anxieties and amidst unsatisfied
wants, might easily become a great temptation to transgression of duty, and in order to remove such hindrances
to morality it may be our duty to promote our own happiness. In that case the end is not happiness but the morality
of the agent, and his conduct acquires true moral worth

[58] *Ibid.*, sec. i. (iv. 393; Abbott, p. 9).

[59] *Kritik der praktischen Vernunft*, i. I. I. 3 (v. 22; Abbott, p. 108).

[60] *Einleitung zur Tugendlehre*, 5 (vi. 387; Abbott, p. 298).

[61] *Kritik der praktischen Vernunft*, i. I. I. 3 (v. 25; Abbott, p. 112).
Einleitung zur Tugendlehre, 4 *sq.* (vi. 386 *sq.;* Abbott, pp. 296, 298).
Supra, pp. 268, 274.

[62] *Kritik der praktischen Vernunft*, i. I. 3 (v. 93; Abbott, p. 186).
Einleitung in die Metaphysik der Sitten, 2 (vi. 216; Abbott, p. 271).

[63] *Kritik der praktischen Vernunft*, i. I. I. 8 (v. 37; Abbott, p. 126).

[64] *Einleitung zur Tugendlehre*, 4 (vi. 386; Abbott, p. 296).

only if he secures his happiness not from inclination but from duty.[65]

If happiness, then, is in question, which it is to be my duty to promote as my end, it must be the happiness of other men, whose permitted end I hereby make also mine. It still remains left to themselves to decide what they shall reckon as belonging to their happiness; "only that it is in my power to decline many things which *they* so reckon, but which I do not so regard, supposing that they have no right to demand it from me as their own." [66] Kant's doctrine of duties is thus to a large extent utilitarian. But at the same time it differs in various points from the theory which generally goes under the name of utilitarianism, according to which it is a duty for each person to aim at the greatest amount of happiness on the whole, taking into account all whose happiness is affected by the conduct and his own happiness also, though only as an element of the whole. As we just saw, Kant does not regard it as a duty at all to promote one's own happiness as an end in itself. In his argument that one does not command anybody to do what he of himself inevitably wishes to do, he fails to notice that people do not always will to do what is most conducive to their greatest happiness; that for the sake of the latter they may have to sacrifice their immediate happiness; and that this even may require such reluctance and self-restraint as is implied in his own notion of duty. In his denial of any obligation to promote one's own happiness as an end in itself Kant differs from the morality of common sense; but the difference between the latter and the orthodox utilitarian view which puts the hedonistic duty which a man owes

[65] *Grundlegung,* sec. i. (iv. 399; Abbott, p. 15). *Einleitung zur Tugendlehre,* 5 (vi. 388; Abbott, p. 298 *sq.*).
[66] *Ibid.,* 5 (vi. 388; Abbott, p. 298).

to himself on a par with that which he owes to others, is more striking. It is, on the other hand, doubtful whether Kant would have assented to the utilitarian demand that I am not *allowed* to prefer my own lesser happiness to the greater happiness of another man. In the examples he gives to demonstrate the inconsistency of the egoistic maxim he only speaks of assistance in distress or help in case of necessity, and his argument could not possibly be used to prove that we are morally bound to regard the happiness of other individuals as much as we regard our own. Indeed, he says expressly that "many a one would gladly consent that others should not benefit him, provided only that he might be excused from showing benevolence to them." [67] In his *Tugendlehre* he writes that it is impossible to assign definite limits how far I am bound to sacrifice to others a part of my own welfare without hope of recompense. "Much depends on what would be the true want of each according to his own feelings, and it must be left to each to determine this for himself. For that one should sacrifice his own happiness, his true wants, in order to promote that of others, would be a self-contradictory maxim if made a universal law. This duty, therefore, is only indeterminate; it has a certain latitude within which one may do more or less without our being able to assign its limits definitely." [68] As another instance of an indeterminate duty—by which he means the permission to limit one maxim of duty by another—he mentions the permission to limit the general love of our neighbour by the love of parents,[69] without any attempt to justify it by its effect upon the general happiness. In his doctrine of the duty to contribute to the happiness of others there is no

[67] *Grundlegung*, sec. ii. (iv. 430 n.*; Abbott, p. 48 n. 1).
[68] *Einleitung zur Tugendlehre*, 8 (vi. 393; Abbott, p. 304).
[69] *Ibid.*, 7 (vi. 390; Abbott, p. 300).

reference to the greatest happiness on the whole. Sidgwick imputes to Kant the view that "it can only be stated
as a *duty* for me to seek my own happiness so far as I
consider it as a part of the happiness of mankind in general"; [70] but there is nothing whatever to show that he
ever held such a view. He says that we may be indirectly
bound to secure our own happiness in order to avoid
"temptation to transgression of duty" or to remove "hindrances to morality," not in order to increase the happiness of mankind.

I have already, in another connection, stated Kant's
attempt to establish the duty of beneficence by alleging
that the egoistic maxim would contradict itself.[71] Every
man in need wishes for the aid of others, and it is therefore impossible for any one to will that each should be left
to take care of himself without such assistance. He maintains that the duty of beneficence may consequently be
deduced from the imperative, "Act only on that maxim
whereby thou canst at the same time will that it should
become a universal law." In one place he has deduced the
duty to promote the happiness of others from his conception of "humanity as an end in itself," [72] but this deduction is quite inconsistent with his denial of any obligation to promote one's own happiness; for humanity,
according to his definition, comprises both one's own
person and that of any other, and "the natural end which
all men have is their own happiness." But who could believe that the duty of beneficence really was an inference
from the categorical imperative? Kant, like everybody
else, found the notion of it in his moral consciousness,
and he had to explain it, to the best of his ability, in
accordance with his general principle of morality; it was
not the principle that led him to that notion. It is vaguely

[70] Sidgwick, *op. cit.,* p. 386.   [71] *Supra,* p. 274.   [72] *Supra,* p. 278.

or distinctly found, though greatly varying in comprehensiveness, in the moral consciousness of all men, because it springs from emotions common to them all.

Another notion in Kant's ethics, of which the idea of happiness is a component part, has obviously a similar origin. Although he declares, in the opening sentence of his *Grundlegung,* that "nothing can possibly be conceived in the world, or even out of it, which can be called good without qualification, except a good will," [73] he found that there is something still better, namely, the *summum bonum,* which is a combination of two elements, morality and happiness, the latter as conditioned by and proportioned to the former.[74] This combination is recognized as *a priori,* and therefore as practically necessary: it is indispensably required by practical reason, which cannot assume the one of these elements without the other also being attached to it. Now an accurate correspondence between happiness and moral worth is not to be expected, but must on the contrary be regarded as impossible, in a mere course of nature in the world; the possibility of the *summum bonum* can therefore only be admitted on the supposition of a moral and all-powerful Supreme Being who establishes such correspondence. But "although the conception of the *summum bonum* as a whole, in which the greatest happiness is conceived as combined in the most exact proportion with the highest degree of moral perfection (possible in creatures), includes my own happiness, yet it is not this that is the determining principle of the will which is enjoined to promote the *summum bonum,* but the moral law, which on the contrary limits by strict conditions my unbounded desire of happiness. Hence also

[73] *Grundlegung,* sec. i. (iv. 393; Abbott, p. 9).
[74] *Kritik der praktischen Vernunft,* i. 2. *passim* (v. 107 *sqq.;* Abbott, p. 202 *sqq.*).

morality is not properly the doctrine how we should *make* ourselves happy, but how we should become *worthy* of happiness . . . ; for it has to do simply with the rational condition (*conditio sine qua non*) of happiness, not with the means of attaining it." [75] The virtuous man is thus in a very precarious position. Even though he know that he is worthy of happiness, and even may hope to participate in it,[76] he must not allow any such hope to slip in as a motive for his conduct; for if he does so he ceases to be virtuous and will not get the happiness he hopes for.

We have previously heard from Kant that the desire for happiness, which springs from our sensuous nature, is the great obstacle to morality, and now happiness has been raised to the rank of an element of the *summum bonum,* side by side with morality itself. Nay more, their combination is said to be recognized *a priori,* as indispensably required by practical reason. Paulsen remarks that this is an inconsistency to which it would be difficult to find a parallel in the whole history of philosophical thought.[77] Yet there must be some explanation of it. The following passages are significant:—"Virtue (as worthiness to be happy) is the supreme condition of all that can appear to us desirable, and consequently of all our pursuit of happiness, and is therefore the supreme good. But it does not follow that it is the whole and perfect good as the object of the desires of rational finite beings; for this requires happiness also, and that not merely in the partial eyes of the person who makes himself an end, but even in the judgment of an impartial reason, which regards persons in

[75] *Kritik der praktischen Vernunft,* i. 2. 5 (v. 129 *sq.;* Abbott, p. 227).

[76] *Kritik der reinen Vernunft,* Transcendentale Methodenlehre, ii. 2 (*Gesammelte Schriften,* iii. [Berlin, 1911], p. 525 *sqq.*).

[77] Paulsen, *op. cit.,* p. 327.

general as ends in themselves. For to need happiness, to deserve it, and yet at the same time not to participate in it, cannot be consistent with the perfect volition of a rational being possessed at the same time of all power, if, for the sake of experiment, we conceive such a being." [78] Why can it not be consistent with it? The answer is not far to seek: such a being would naturally feel the moral emotion of retributive kindliness towards a virtuous person worthy of happiness and, being not only perfectly good but also all-powerful, would distribute to him happiness in proportion to his virtue. The emotional background is visible in the following statement:—"The sight of a being who is not adorned with a single feature of a pure and good will, enjoying unbroken prosperity, can never give pleasure to an impartial rational spectator. Thus a good will appears to constitute the indispensable condition even of being worthy of happiness." [79] Kant takes care to point out that the happiness attached to virtue in the *summum bonum* is not a reward based on the justice of God, but a favour due to his goodness and love. Even the best man only does his duty and has therefore no claim to divine benevolence: "a remunerative justice (*iustitia brabeutica*) is in God's relation to men a contradiction." [80] Nevertheless, in one place he says exactly the reverse, namely, that a disproportion between virtue and happiness is contrary to the divine justice.[81] His feelings seem to have got the upper hand of his theory.

[78] *Kritik der praktischen Vernunft,* i. 2. 2 (v. 110; Abbott, p. 206).
[79] *Grundlegung,* sec. i. (iv. 393; Abbott, p. 9).
[80] *Metaphysische Anfangungsgründe der Tugendlehre,* Schlussanmerkung (vi. 489). "Über das Misslingen aller philosophischen Versuche in der Theodicee," in *Gesammelte Schriften,* viii. (Berlin, 1912), p. 258 n.
[81] *Ibid.,* viii. 261 *sq.*

In any case the justice of God requires that the wicked shall be punished.[82] Punishment "is a physical evil, which, though it be not connected with moral evil as a natural consequence, ought to be connected with it as a consequence by the principles of a moral legislation." [83] The sole object of punishment is retribution. Juridical punishment "can never be administered merely as a means for promoting another good, either with regard to the criminal himself or to the civil society, but must always be inflicted only because he has committed a crime. . . . The penal law is a categorical imperative; and woe to him who creeps through the serpent-windings of the happiness theory in order to discover something which, in virtue of the advantage it promises, may release him from the duty of punishment or even from a fraction of it." [84] Kant asks what principle should be followed in fixing the kind and degree of punishment, and his answer is: no other principle but that of requital (*jus talionis*), which requires equivalence both in quality and quantity. Thus the only rightful punishment for murder is death. Even if a civil society decides to dissolve itself with the consent of all its members, the last murderer lying in the prison ought to be executed before the resolution is carried out. If several persons are implicated in a murder, including any one who has been an accessory to it, they shall all die; this is decreed by justice as represented by the judicial power, "in accordance with universal laws which have *a priori* origin." [85] Yet we are told that in one case this categorical imperative may be suspended out of utilitarian considerations: if the num-

<hr/>

[82] *Ibid.*, viii. 261. *Metaphysische Anfangungsgründe der Tugendlehre*, Schlussanmerkung (vi. 489).

[83] *Kritik der praktischen Vernunft*, i. 1. 1. 8 (v. 37; Abbott, p. 127).

[84] *Metaphysische Anfangungsgründe der Rechtslehre*, § 49 (*Gesammelte Schriften*, vi. [Berlin, 1914], p. 331).

[85] *Ibid.*, § 49 (vi. 332 *sq.*).

ber of offenders is so large that the infliction of the death-penalty might be very dangerous to the State, the sovereign must be entitled, in agreement with his right of pardon, to substitute some other penalty.[86] In two other cases, where a person's honour is concerned, Kant doubts whether the law is justified in applying capital punishment: the one is the duel, the other is infanticide committed by the mother of an illegitimate child. In the latter case one might suppose that the motive for relinquishing the law of talion was pity felt for the unfortunate mother, but the categorical imperative could, of course, never allow such a feeling to interfere with its command; so Kant had to devise another explanation, which better agreed with its rationality. He argues that the infant has been born outside the law, and consequently is not protected by the law. It has, as it were, crept into the community as contraband (*verbotene Waare*), and as it should not be there at all, the community may ignore both its existence and its destruction.[87] Kant has to admit that there are cases in which the punishment cannot be exactly equivalent to the crime, as in bestiality, for instance. It should then be equivalent according to the spirit of law: the man whose offence has reduced him to the level of an animal should be expelled from civil society and deprived of human rights, as he is unworthy to be treated as a human being. Rape and pederasty, again, should be punished with castration.[88] Here we have a revival of the savage custom of punishing the offending member; for the principle that the sole object of punishment is retribution excludes the idea of using it as a means for preventing the possibility of a repetition of the crime.

[86] *Ibid.,* § 49 (vi. 334).
[87] *Ibid.,* § 49 (vi. 335 *sq.*).
[88] *Ibid.,* Anhang (vi. 363).

When Kant says that punishment can never be administered merely as a means for promoting another good, either with regard to the criminal himself or to the civil society, he evidently bases his doctrine of retribution on one of his formulas of the categorical imperative, although it is difficult to see that the retributive theory itself treats the criminal as an "end in himself"; on the contrary, even though his punishment is not used as a means either of reforming him or of deterring anybody else, it is nevertheless actually a means of gratifying the resentful feelings of the community. But Kant has not made any attempt to show why practical reason requires punitive justice at all, and least of all why it requires the rule of tit for tat. His theory of punishment is simply an expression of the emotion of moral resentment of a more primitive type than that which is embodied in the criminal legislation of our own time. Amongst other things, he has in view only the external resemblance between the injury done by the offender and the nature of the punishment inflicted on him, without trying to correlate the pain with the real inward guilt.[89]

Kant's ethics is the most gigantic attempt ever made to found a theory of morals on reason alone. He has not resorted to the convenient method adopted by many other moralists of simply appealing to intuitions in order to establish the objective validity of their propositions. He has endeavoured to derive the rules of duty by a mere logical process from a supreme moral law the essence of which is formal self-consistency. He says himself that he has not thought of introducing "a new principle of morality," just as if all the world before him were ignorant what duty

[89] *Cf.* A. C. Ewing, *The Morality of Punishment* (London, 1929), p. 15.

was or had been in thorough-going error;[90] the knowledge of what every man is bound to do, and therefore also to know, is within the reach of every man, even the commonest.[91] He has only wanted to set forth a "new formula." But with the deepest regard for the tremendous earnestness of his purpose, I cannot but think that his struggle to harmonize the moral experience of mankind with his own rational deductions has been a colossal failure. I have tried to show that in his alleged dictates of reason the emotional background is transparent throughout. And if I have succeeded in such an attempt in the case of the greatest of all moral rationalists, I flatter myself with the belief that I have, in no small measure, given additional strength to the main contentions in this book: that the moral consciousness is ultimately based on emotions, that the moral judgment lacks objective validity, that the moral values are not absolute but relative to the emotions they express.

[90] *Kritik der praktischen Vernunft,* Vorrede (v. 8 n.*; Abbott, p. 93 n. 1).
[91] *Grundlegung,* sec. i. (iv. 404; Abbott, p. 20).

INDEX